ArtScroll Mesorah Series®

Rabbi Nosson Scherman / Rabbi Meir Zlotowitz
General Editors

SHABBOS

A collection of enlightening
and stimulating comments
on the parashah

Published by
Mesorah Publications, ltd

DELIGHTS

RABBI ARYEH LEIB LOPIANSKY

FIRST EDITION
First Impression ... November 2001

Published and Distributed by
MESORAH PUBLICATIONS, LTD.
4401 Second Avenue / Brooklyn, N.Y 11232

Distributed in Europe by
LEHMANNS
Unit E, Viking Industrial Park
Rolling Mill Road
Jarow, Tyne & Wear, NE32 3DP
England

Distributed in Australia and New Zealand by
GOLDS WORLDS OF JUDAICA
3-13 William Street
Balaclava, Melbourne 3183
Victoria, Australia

Distributed in Israel by
SIFRIATI / A. GITLER — BOOKS
6 Hayarkon Street
Bnei Brak 51127

Distributed in South Africa by
KOLLEL BOOKSHOP
Shop 8A Norwood Hypermarket
Norwood 2196, Johannesburg, South Africa

ARTSCROLL SERIES®
SHABBOS DELIGHTS
© Copyright 2001, by MESORAH PUBLICATIONS, Ltd.
4401 Second Avenue / Brooklyn, N.Y. 11232 / (718) 921-9000 / www.artscroll.com

---

ALL RIGHTS RESERVED
The text, prefatory and associated textual contents and introductions
— including the typographic layout, cover artwork and ornamental graphics —
have been designed, edited and revised as to content, form and style.

**No part of this book may be reproduced
IN ANY FORM, PHOTOCOPYING, OR COMPUTER RETRIEVAL SYSTEMS
— even for personal use without written permission from
the copyright holder, Mesorah Publications Ltd.**
except by a reviewer who wishes to quote brief passages
in connection with a review written for inclusion in magazines or newspapers.

THE RIGHTS OF THE COPYRIGHT HOLDER WILL BE STRICTLY ENFORCED.

ISBN:
1-57819-788-0 (hard cover)
1-57819-789-9 (paperback)

Typography by CompuScribe at ArtScroll Studios, Ltd.
Printed in the United States of America by Noble Book Press Corp.
Bound by Sefercraft, Quality Bookbinders, Ltd., Brooklyn N.Y. 11232

*This lovely sefer of Shabbos vertlach
is dedicated L'iluy Nishmas*
Naomi (Tzirel Nehamah) Bulka,
of blessed memory.

*In the years that the world was blessed with Naomi,
she touched many lives, and in so many ways.*

*Her shining personality came through in such radiance at the
Shabbos table. The quiet dignity with which she prepared the
table, the warm but delicate way in which she served the guests,
her respectful manner of conversation, all came together
to make the Shabbos table a place of holiness.*

*This was the place that her gracefulness and righteousness made
an indelible imprint on her children. This was the place that everyone from family to strangers felt at home.
This was the place where many people received their first real taste
of Yiddishkeit in all its beauty.*

*Her entire life reflected her grace and dignity at the Shabbos Table.
Our mother never spoke ill of others, and never spoke
of all the kindnesses she proffered on others.*

*She was always available, and always ready with an
encouraging word to those fighting serious illness,
or a helping hand to those who needed it.
Her greatness in life was only exceeded by her humility.*

*Her's was a life that was "kulo Shabbos" -
full of the gentleness, harmony, contentedness and
completeness that Shabbos embodies.*

*We hope the words of Torah in this volume,
which are so superbly put together by Rav Leibel Lopiansky,
will enliven and inspire your Shabbos table,
and stand as a testimony to the sacred memory
of an unforgettable lady.*

Dedicated by her loving children

RABBI MOISHE STERNBUCH

Vice President "Eda Hacharedit"
And Dayan Jerusalem Beth-Din
Head Torah Centre Community
Johannesburg S.A.

ב"ה

משה שטרנבוך

סגן נשיא העדה החרדית בעיה"ק
מח"ס "מועדים וזמנים", "תשובות והנהגות" ועוד
ראב"ד דק"ק חרדים ביוהנסבורג

חכתובת בירושלים:
רח' משקלוב, 13, הר-נוף, ירושלים
טל: 6519610 :Tel

בעזהי"ת, יום ___ סיון תשס"ח

[handwritten Hebrew letter]

Table of Contents

Introduction   I
Acknowledgments   IV
Prologue   VIII

✆ Bereishis

Parashas Bereishis	11
Parashas Noach	18
Parashas Lech Lecha	24
Parashas Vayeira	30
Parashas Chayei Sarah	36
Parashas Toldos	43
Parashas Vayeitzei	49
Parashas Vayishlach	55
Parashas Vayeishev	61
Parashas Mikeitz	67
Parashas Vayigash	73
Parashas Vayechi	79

✆ Shemos

Parashas Shemos	87
Parashas Va'eira	93
Parashas Bo	98
Parashas Beshalach	103
Parashas Yisro	109
Parashas Mishpatim	114
Parashas Terumah	121
Parashas Tetzaveh	127
Parashas Ki Sisa	133
Parashas Vayakhel	139
Parashas Pikudei	143

ಹಿVAYIKRA

Parashas Vayikra	149
Parashas Tzav	156
Parashas Shemini	161
Parashas Tazria	166
Parashas Metzora	170
Parashas Acharei Mos	175
Parashas Kedoshim	180
Parashas Emor	185
Parashas Behar	190
Parashas Bechukosai	195

ಹಿBAMIDBAR

Parashas Bamidbar	199
Parashas Naso	205
Parashas Behaalos'cha	212
Parashas Shelach	218
Parashas Korach	224
Parashas Chukas	229
Parashas Balak	235
Parashas Pinchas	241
Parashas Mattos	248
Parashas Masei	258

ಹಿDEVARIM

Parashas Devarim	267
Parashas Va'eschanan	272
Parashas Eikev	277
Parashas Re'eh	282
Parashas Shoftim	287
Parashas Ki Seitzei	293
Parashas Ki Savo	299
Parashas Nitzavim	304
Parashas Vayelech	309
Parashas Haazinu	314
Parashas Vezos Haberachah	318

INTRODUCTION

THE CUSTOM OF DISCUSSING THE WEEKLY PORTION OF THE TORAH at the Shabbos table has ancient roots. The Gemara (*Megillah* 12b) mentions that on Shabbos "the Jews eat and drink, and begin their meal with words of Torah, and words of praise." In fact, the Mishnah (*Avos* 3:4) proclaims that – even on a weekday – if three people are sitting together at a table and have spoken words of Torah it is as if "they ate from Hashem's table."

For a period of time, I was privileged to teach Chumash to American students studying Torah in Eretz Yisrael for one year. They often spent Shabbos at the homes of other Americans residing in Eretz Yisrael. I realized that many hosts would appreciate hearing *divrei Torah* from their young guests. However, many of the students found it tedious and time consuming to sift through the multitude of available *sefarim,* and prepare a brief and enjoyable *dvar Torah,* and so every week I prepared my students for the Shabbos table. I soon began receiving favorable comments from both students and hosts. One host – a grandfather of a student – could not wait to hear "two per meal," and on Friday night would instruct his grandson to recite all of his prepared *divrei Torah* then and there! Many people urged me to publish these *divrei Torah* for the sake of the general English-speaking public. Expecting it to be a quick and easy job, I agreed.

However, desiring to do a quality work, the project became both lengthy and laborious. I set myself a goal of six *divrei Torah* – two for each Shabbos meal — per *parashah*. I searched for the six that were most enjoyable with a uniform style for all of them. The style I chose is the one prevalent today in the yeshivah world — explanations based upon halachah. Even with those, there are disparities among the styles used. A *dvar Torah* that my heart felt was too far fetched was rejected. I sifted through many *sefarim*, until I found those that fit my guidelines. But that was not all. Every source mentioned in the *dvar Torah* was researched and checked for its veracity. And to my amazement, I discovered that several well-known *divrei Torah* are based upon non existent "Midrashim"! Of course, I omitted those and included others. Occasionally there seemed to be a difficulty with some aspect of the *vort*. When this happened I painstakingly sought the first edition of the *sefer* where the *vort* originally appeared. Several times the matter was clarified because of it. As a result this project took much longer than originally envisioned. In addition, I took the liberty to slightly revise any *vort* that would confuse the reader, to facilitate the understanding of it. Where a major revision was made, I duly noted it. The reader should also be aware that I mention the earliest source found. If there is more than one source mentioned, the basic idea is found in both *sefarim*, but details were gleaned from both of them.

A few pointers are in place. Since this is an anthology to *divrei Torah* from different authors, one can expect variant premises and cannot pose contradictions from one source to another. Also, some authors employed the *pilpul* method in their explanation. The beauty of these *divrei Torah* lies in their superficial brilliance, despite their inability to withstand close scrutiny, and should be appreciated as such. Lastly, it is obvious that all that is written is not meant to be applied in practical halachah.

This *sefer* is intended for the full spectrum of contemporary Jewry: from the beginner student of Torah who is not yet proficient enough in Hebrew to prepare on his own a *vort* to the Kollel-member who is immersed in the study of Gemara and Rishonim, and does not have the time to find that enjoyable *vort*. Educators stress the importance of utilizing the Shabbos meal as a means of transmitting a deep-seated love and appreciation for Judaism. An integral part of the Shabbos table are the *divrei Torah* discussed. This *sefer* is an excellent tool and it is my hope that it will be used for this purpose.

Acknowledgments

My first and foremost thanks are to my parents, Reverend Bentzion Lopiansky זצ"ל, and Mrs. Esther Lopiansky שתחי'. They have always given selflessly of themselves, and devoted their lives to my brother and me. My father's *vertlach* at the Shabbos table left an indelible impression on me, and sowed the first seeds of this work. May my mother experience only good health, and *nachas* from all her children, grandchildren, and great-grandchildren.

I am also deeply grateful to my in-laws, Rav Shlomo and Rebbetzin Basha Ribner שיחיו who have done all in their power to enable me to remain within the confines of the *Beis Hamidrash*. They have encouraged and assisted all my Torah projects, including this one. May they merit long and happy years filled with much *nachas* from all their descendants.

The *divrei Torah* presented here were first taught to the students of Yeshivat Ohr Yerushalayim, in Eretz Yisrael. The Rosh Yeshivah, Rav Moshe Chaim Sosevsky *shlit"a*, and the Menahel, Rav Shmuel Wagner *shlit"a*, gave me free rein in structuring the style of my Chumash *shiur* and thus laid the foundation for this *sefer*. It has been an immensely enjoyable and satisfying experience working with them in imparting Torah knowledge and attitudes. May they continue to see much success in their holy work.

The students themselves must also be commended. Their questions and comments helped refine the *divrei Torah*. A special thanks must be awarded to the students of the past year who, despite knowing that these *divrei Torah* were shortly to be printed, they listened diligently and wrote them down. Outstanding among them are Tzvi Aronin, Levi Mark, and Craig Smulevitz, who rarely missed writing down a *shiur*. I owe a *yasher koach* to Rav Mordechai Malek, a former student, who today is a fine *talmid chacham*. It was at his instigation that I started on the writing of this *sefer*.

My introduction to "Brisk"-style *divrei Torah* on Chumash was during a summer at Yeshiva Zichron Moshe of South Fallsburg, New York. Rav Yeruchem Gorelick *zt"l*, would repeat *divrei Torah* from his *rebbi*, the Brisker Rav *zt"l*, with such a look of rapture on his face, that although I did not always understand them, I felt that there was a treasure lying there. Many years later, I witnessed how vast and deep *divrei Torah* on Chumash could be when I attended the *shiurim* of my close friend Rav Yehudah Levenberg *shlit"a* of Lakewood, N.J. They were subsequently published in a series of *sefarim* titled *Imrei Chein*. His love for every *vort* of the Brisker Rav is contagious, and inspiring. May he continue writing *sefarim* on all areas of the Torah.

There are several individuals who graciously sponsored this project, and I owe them a great debt. They are:

Mr. and Mrs. Yehudah and Rinah Levy. Yehudah's extensive interest, encouragement, and assistance at the publication stage was invaluable, and is immensely appreciated. Furthermore, Mrs. Levy's mother passed away shortly before the pubication of the *sefer* so Yehudah and Rinah are dedicating the *sefer* in her memory. May Hashem grant them their greatest desire: to be involved in other worthy projects.

Mr. and Mrs. Tzvi and Sharonne Rudman. The tattered notebook of *divrei Torah* that Tzvi transcribed testifies to his great appreciation for them. A Shabbos never goes by that he does not retell them! His generous help is greatly appreciated.

The Gold family. Mr. and Mrs. Joel and Miriam Gold and Mr. and Mrs. Chanoch and Aliza Gold truly appreciate the hard-working *ba'al-habayis* who exerts himself to also learn Torah. It is only natural for them to welcome this *sefer*, which is intended for their use. Mr. and Mrs. Evan and Chaya Sara Genack, of this family, also participated in this endeavor.

The Zuckerman family. My friend Mr. Howard Zuckerman, was instrumental in forging my connection with ArtScroll, and having my work speedily evaluated for publication. His son Ezra, with whom I enjoy a close relationship since his years in Eretz Yisrael, and daughter-in-law Lauren helped sponsor this *sefer* in memory of her father, Mr. Allan Rozner.

The Hirth family. The Lopiansky and Hirth families enjoy a friendship that spans half a century and includes four generations. The Hirth family as a whole, and Yechiel Hirth, who was my student, in particular, enthusiastically joined the list of sponsors.

Mr. and Mrs. Efraim and Gila Gerszberg. Every Pesach *seder* without fail Efraim pulls out his red notebook containing the *divrei Torah* he heard for the *seder*. He has long awaited the publication of this work, and warmly assisted in its sponsorship.

Mr. and Mrs. Lee and Marcia Weinblatt. Their son Kenny heard these *divrei Torah* and repeated them to his parents. To show their appreciation, this work was added to the list of other projects they have helped sponsor.

Mr. and Mrs. Avrum and Elana Weissman. Avrum's enthusiasm for this project was heart-warming and inspiring. The pleasant memory of the year I studied *Ramban* with Avrum has not faded.

Mr. and Mrs. Shloimy and Risha Schwartz. A descendant of one of the greatest Rabbonim of Hungary, Shloimy has a true appreciation of Torah learning, and especially of this style of *divrei Torah*. He never fails to inquire about the progress of this *sefer*.

Mr. and Mrs. David and Esther Wiener. David faithfully recorded the Chumash *shiurim* he heard, and was overjoyed at the news of their imminent publication. Together with the **Wiener** family, the **Gindoff, Davidson, Samuelson,** and **Weinreb** families sponsored this work in memory of **"Nana" – Ethel Wolinsky**, a loving grandmother, great-grandmother, and great-great-grandmother.

Mr. and Mrs. Yehudah and Linda Isaacs. Both their son and son-in-law are admirers of these *divrei Torah*. The Isaacs joined them in sponsoring this work, in memory of Linda's mother Rivkah Matil *bas* R' Yaakov of blessed memory.

There were others who assisted in various forms, whether financial or otherwise, and also deserve a thank-you. Those who contacted me to offer their help without being asked deserve an even greater thanks. They are: Mr. Martin Goldberg, Mr. And Mrs. Akiva and Devorah Grossman, the Gottlieb family, Phil Richter Esq., Mr. Menashe Rudnick, Mr. Josh Goldberg, Mr. Yonah Wolf, Dr. Reuben Koolyk and Dr. Fran Flug, Mr. Aryeh Mezzei, Neil Shevlin Esq., Rabbi and Mrs. Yona and Leah Katz, Mr. William Ahdout, Mr. Yoel Bertram, Mr. Yehonoson Teitelbaum, Mr. and Mrs. Jeffrey and Sharona Weinberg, Mr. and Mrs. Howard and Susan Freundlich, Mr. and Mrs. Mendy and Chanie Horowicz, Mr. and Mrs. Daniel and Rivkah Gleich, Mr. and Mrs. Martin and Alison Zelmanovitch, Rabbi and Mrs. Mordechai and Sarah Malek, Mr. and Mrs. Tzvi and Karen Kahn, Mr. and Mrs. Dan and Susan Wisotsky, and Mr. Ezra Adler. My blessing to them is:

"ימלא ה' משאלות לבכם לטובה"

And my final thanks, which is an ongoing never-ending thank-you, goes to my wife Temmy. The proverbial *aishes chayil*, she took it upon herself to manage the daily needs of our family, and enable me to devote myself to Torah. Without her, this project would never have come to fruition. May Hashem grant us both health and happiness, and together may we be privileged to see much *nachas* from our children.

PROLOGUE

"But is it true?" Every year this question was inevitably raised. Admiring an ingenious explanation, someone would question whether the explanation was only intellectually stimulating, or was it a possible true explanation of the pasuk. To answer this question properly, I write this prologue.

THE CHIDA, WHO LIVED IN THE BEGINNING OF THE 18TH CENTURY, in his monumental *Shem HaGedolim* (under *Darashos HaRan*) traces the history of the various schools of commentaries on Chumash. He concludes that the most recent method is one where the Torah is explained according to halachah. This method originated with R' Eliyahu ibn Chaim (*Raanach*), and R' Yosef Trani (*Maharit*), who resided in Turkey in the 17th century. The various *sefarim* quoted here prove that this method remains in vogue until today. In recent times, this has become the predominant method of study in the "yeshivah world." The Brisker style of study of Chumash, which is one form of this method, has gained much popularity. In the past decade many prominent scholars have printed novellae on Chumash using this format.

Rashi (*Bereishis* 33:20) states that just as "a hammer shatters a stone into many pieces, likewise there are many explanations for the Torah." This can be better understood in light of the words of the *Zohar* (*Acharei* 73a) which states that "the Torah and Hashem are one." Thus, just as Hashem is infinite, so is His Torah. If so, it is logical that there are a never-ending number of explanations on the Torah. Every person, according to the nature of his soul, sees and understands the Torah differently. Every explanation, which is based upon traditional methods of study, is valid. The method presented is immensely intellectually satisfying and was chosen to imbue my students with a deep love for Torah. Although I am aware of the dictum of *Chazal* (*Tanchuma, Pinchas,* 10) "Just as people look different, so too they think differently." I did not include several *divrei Torah* that are oft quoted since my heart felt they were too far fetched. I only chose those that I felt were plausible.

The Mishnah states that with the death of Rabbi Akiva there ceased to exist "honor for Torah" (*Sotah* 49a). Rashi states that Rabbi Akiva could explain the message derived from every seemingly superfluous word, or even letter. More so, R' Akiva explained even the purpose of every "crown" on every letter! When people see how every letter in the Torah has a purpose it adds to the glory of the Torah. This is another reason for choosing this style. When one hears these *divrei Torah*, and realizes the intricate connection between the Written Law (Chumash) and the Oral Law (Gemara), one cannot help but be overwhelmed by the depth of the Torah. One recognizes at that moment that only Hashem could have authored such a work! In a similar vein, Rav Chaim Soloveitchik *zt"l* made the following observation. In all disciplines, every level requires a separate textbook. The math book used in second grade is not the one used in first grade. A college student does not use a high-school textbook. All this notwithstanding, the Chumash that the young child finds satisfaction in, is the very same one in which the preeminent scholar finds the greatest satisfaction! This is the best proof of the Divine origin of the Torah!

The Klausenberger Rav *z"tl* (*Shefa Chaim* 3:174) discusses the method of study of *pilpul*. He writes that although the bulk of one's study should be to know the basic *Gemara* with commentaries nevertheless many great scholars — when in need of respite — engaged in *pilpul* as an occasional valid alternate to the main studies. Furthermore, through this brilliant facet of Torah they attracted thousands to devote themselves to the study of Torah.

Additionally, I believe there is an even greater and deeper significance to hearing and studying these *divrei Torah*. Rav Chaim ibn Attar, in his classic commentary *Ohr HaChaim* (*Tazria* 13:37), claims that Hashem revealed all of the Oral Law to Moshe Rabbeinu, but He did not disclose where it is alluded to in the Written Law. Therefore, states the *Ohr HaChaim*, based upon *kabbalah*, it is incumbent upon and of utmost importance for Torah scholars to discover and reveal that connection. That has been the task of scholars throughout the generations, as evident by the various halachic Midrashim on Chumash. It appears that the Gra was also of this opinion. It is recorded that in his old age the Gra would study only Chumash, and would recite all of the Oral Law and show its connection to the Chumash (*Maalos HaSulam,* para. 11). These *divrei Torah* indicate a connection between the Oral and Written Laws and that in itself legitimizes its study.

Rebbi Meir Yechiel of Ostrovtza, in his *sefer Ohr Torah* (*parashas Chayei Sarah*), combines several statements in the Gemara to explain a phrase uttered by Ephron. He then concludes that although Ephron was not aware of it nevertheless "everything is alluded to in the Torah, and everything is led by Divine Providence." Ephron was unwittingly guided to utter that phrase which based upon the Oral Law had so much meaning and that is why it was written in the Torah. Similarly, it says in the *Zohar* (*Shelach*, para. 29) that Hashem guided Lavan to unintentionally describe a situation accurately, and then be quoted in the Torah. It is clear from this that every statement quoted in the Torah, even if uttered by a non-Jew, has to be true and conform to the dictates of the Oral Law. Therefore one can show the halachic background for everything written in the Torah, even if uttered by one unaware of its halachic significance!

Thus, my answer is: "The *dvar Torah* is most probably a true and viable explanation. And even if one finds it difficult to accept, then at the very least it is a means of showing a link between the Oral and Written Laws."

BEREISHIS

In the beginning... (1:1)   בְּרֵאשִׁית ... (א:א)

R ASHI QUOTES A MIDRASH (*OSIYOS D'RABBI AKIVA*, 2) WHICH states that the word *bereishis* can be interpreted exegetically to teach us that everything in this physical world was created for the sake of the Jewish people, and for the sake of the Torah. This exegesis can clarify a seemingly hard-to-understand Gemara.

The following *aggadah* is found in the Gemara.

In the future Hashem will place a *sefer Torah* on His lap, and announce that all those who engaged in the study of Torah in this world should come to receive their reward. The Romans will arrive first and say, "Master of the universe! We set up many marketplaces, we built many bathhouses, and it was all done in order that the Jews should be able to study Torah! [Therefore we deserve to get rewarded.]" Hashem will respond, "Fools! Whatever you built was for your own selfish needs — not to help the Jews." The other nations will then engage in similar dialogues with Hashem (*Avodah Zarah* 2b).

On a superficial level, this *aggadah* is difficult to comprehend. How will the nations have the audacity to lie to Hashem and claim that all their projects were intended to benefit the Jews?! It's a blatant falsehood! Furthermore, the nations will say that their **sole** motive was the Jews' benefit. This seems even more preposterous. More so, Hashem will call them fools and not liars, which seems to indicate that they are actually telling the truth.

The explanation for this is based on a profound concept. In the initial creation of the world everything was created to assist the Jews in their study of Torah, likewise everything that is subsequently built or anything which occurs in this world is for this very same purpose. Rambam (*Intro. to the Mishnah*) addresses this point, and writes that an individual may build a beautiful palace and its Divine purpose is that one day many years later a pious man will find refuge in the shade of the walls and thereby save his life. Therefore it is true that everything the Gentiles built — marketplaces, bridges and bathhouses – were built for the sake of the Jews — to facilitate their study of the Torah.

Today, one cannot discern how everything serves the Jews. It is only with the arrival of Mashiach that this will become obvious to everyone, Jew and non-Jew alike. The nations will then ask to be rewarded since they will see how everything they did was indeed for the benefit of the Jews. Hashem's response will be that although that was the true Divine purpose behind all their activities, since at the time that was not their intention they do not deserve to be rewarded.

(*Chidushei Maran Riz HaLevi*)

This explanation of the Gemara was told to the preeminent Rosh Yeshivah Rav Boruch Ber Leibowitz. He allegedly commented, "The explanation is correct, but it's still a chutzpah on the Gentiles' part to say what they did..."

It is recorded that when the Brisker Rav said the above *dvar Torah* he added that the Divine purpose of the new train route between St. Petersburg and Berlin was to facilitate students traveling to the renowned Volozhin Yeshivah. Likewise, the construction of the Trans-Siberian train route was extremely costly and took its toll of human lives. It was perceived as being of no value. The Brisker Rav commented that its Divine purpose was to transport the yeshivah students from Eastern Europe to Shanghai in relative comfort during World War II.

(*Chidushei HaGriz*—stencil)

וַיַּעַשׂ אֱלֹקִים אֶת שְׁנֵי הַמְּאֹרֹת הַגְּדֹלִים אֶת הַמָּאוֹר הַגָּדֹל לְמֶמְשֶׁלֶת הַיּוֹם וְאֶת הַמָּאוֹר הַקָּטֹן לְמֶמְשֶׁלֶת הַלַּיְלָה וְאֵת הַכּוֹכָבִים. (א:ט״ז)

*And G-d made the **two great luminaries**, the greater luminary to dominate the day, and the **lesser luminary** to dominate the night; and the stars (1:16)*

The Gemara finds an obvious contradiction in this *pasuk*. At first both the sun and moon are referred to as great luminaries, which implies that the moon is also a great luminary. Further in the *pasuk* the moon is designated a lesser luminary. To resolve this problem the Gemara quotes a Midrash which states that originally the moon was as large as the sun but was subsequently reduced in size, thereby qualifying to be referred to both as large and as small (*Chullin* 60b).

Another explanation can be offered as well. The Gemara elsewhere states that although the term *kattan* usually refers to a minor, an adult who is not self-sufficient and must rely upon others for support is also called a *kattan* (*Bava Metzia* 12b)! This explains why the moon is refered to as both *gadol* [large] and *kattan* [small]. In physical size the moon is large and warrants the title *gadol*. The moon, however, does not produce its own light, but reflects the light of the sun. In this respect it is not "self-sufficient" and may justifiably be called *kattan*!

(*Bris Shalom*, quoted by *Pardes Yosef*. See also *Har Tzvi*.)

Bereishis / 13

> וַיֹּאמֶר אֱלֹקִים נַעֲשֶׂה אָדָם בְּצַלְמֵנוּ כִּדְמוּתֵנוּ ... (א:כ"ו)

> *And G-d said, "Let us make man in Our image,*
> *after Our likeness ... (1:26)*

The Gemara states that if one is haughty it is as if he had worshiped an idol (*Sotah* 4b). This comparison between haughtiness and idolatry seems difficult to understand and begs an explanation.

The *pasuk* says: Hashem said, "Let **us** make man." This implies that Hashem created man in conjunction with another deity. We know that this is not the case. Why then does it say "us"? The Midrash (*Bereishis Rabbah* 8:8) explains that Hashem asked the angels' opinions whether He should create Man. The Torah alludes to this by the word "us." This fact is recorded to teach us that even a great person should be humble and confer with those of lesser stature.

Anyone who is haughty will refute any explanation implying that one should be humble! That person would explain "us" to denote that Hashem created man together with another deity. This in effect is akin to idol-worship!

(Chanukas HaTorah)

> וַיֹּאמֶר אֱלֹקִים הִנֵּה נָתַתִּי לָכֶם אֶת כָּל עֵשֶׂב זֹרֵעַ זֶרַע אֲשֶׁר עַל פְּנֵי כָל הָאָרֶץ וְאֶת כָּל הָעֵץ אֲשֶׁר בּוֹ פְרִי עֵץ זֹרֵעַ זָרַע לָכֶם יִהְיֶה לְאָכְלָה. (א:כ"ט)

> *G-d said, "Behold, I have given to you all herbage yielding*
> *seed that is on the surface of the entire earth, and every tree*
> *that has seed-yielding fruit; it shall be yours for food." (1:29)*

Earlier (*pasuk* 11), Hashem refers to the trees which he was creating as *eitz pri* ["fruity" tree]. Here, when Hashem permits Adam to eat from the trees, they are called *asher bo pri eitz* [trees which contain fruits]. Why the change in language?

The Gemara explains that an *eitz pri* is a tree whose bark tastes similar to its fruit, and adds that an *esrog* tree is such a type of tree (*Succah* 35a). According to one opinion in the Midrash (*Bereishis Rabbah* 15:7) the *eitz hada'as* [Tree of Knowledge of Good and Evil] was an *esrog* tree. If so, the discrepancy in language can now be explained. Hashem did not want to say that Adam could eat an *eitz pri* since that would mean that he would be allowed to eat from all *esrog* trees. This was not the case, since Adam was prohibited to eat from the *eitz hada'as*! Therefore Hashem said that he could eat only from those trees *asher bo pri eitz*, which are the usual fruit-bearing trees.

(Meshech Chochmah)

וּמִפְּרִי הָעֵץ אֲשֶׁר בְּתוֹךְ הַגָּן אָמַר אֱלֹקִים לֹא תֹאכְלוּ מִמֶּנּוּ וְלֹא תִגְּעוּ בּוֹ פֶּן תְּמֻתוּן. (ג:ג)

Of the fruit of the tree which is in the center of the garden G-d has said: "You shall neither eat of it nor touch it, lest you die." (3:3)

The Gemara states that there are times when adding is actually detracting! It then quotes this *pasuk* as an example (*Sanhedrin* 29a). Hashem only prohibited Adam and Chavah to eat from the *eitz hada'as* [Tree of Knowledge]. The *Minchas Chinuch* understands that Adam heard the prohibition from Hashem, but as an added measure of precaution, told Chavah that it was prohibited even to merely touch the tree under penalty of death. When Chavah told this to the serpent, he pushed her against the tree. The serpent then persuaded Chavah that just as she did not die as a result of touching the tree, she likewise would not die if she would eat from the tree. Chavah's adding to the prohibition was actually detrimental and in the end led to the sin.

This Gemara seems to imply that Adam erred in adding a protective prohibition of his own. However, the Gemara states explicitly that one fulfills a mitzvah of *ushmartem es mishmarti* [you should guard My precepts] (*Vayikra* 18:30) if one adds a protective prohibition (*Yevamos*, 21a)! In fact, many Rabbinical prohibitions are of this nature: prohibitions to prevent us from transgressing the laws of the Torah. How can these two statements be reconciled?

The Rambam remarks (*Mamrim* 2:9) that if the Rabbis enact a protective prohibition, and explicitly inform the people that the prohibition is only of Rabbinical nature, it is permitted. However, if the Rabbis lead the people to believe that the Torah prohibits an enactment they instituted, then they have transgressed the commandment of *bal tosif*.

The Rambam's words are the key towards understanding the two seemingly conflicting Gemaras. One Gemara states that it is laudable and required of the Rabbis to enact new prohibitions. That is only true if the Rabbis clearly state that they are the initiators of the prohibitions. Adam, on the other hand, did not inform Chavah that he was the one who was instructing her not to even touch the tree. She was led to believe that Hashem had prohibited it. For such an action, the other Gemara criticized Adam.

(*Minchas Chinuch, mitzvah* 454)

וַיִּהְיוּ כָּל יְמֵי אָדָם אֲשֶׁר חַי תְּשַׁע מֵאוֹת שָׁנָה וּשְׁלֹשִׁים שָׁנָה וַיָּמֹת.

*All the days **that Adam lived** were nine hundred and thirty years; and he died. (5:5)*

An obvious difficulty in this *pasuk* is the phrase "that ... lived." This phrase is seemingly superfluous, and is not mentioned in conjunction with any other person listed here. Two interesting solutions to this problem are:

The Midrash (*Bamidbar Rabbah* 14:12) reveals that, after the sin, Adam was originally destined to live for one thousand years.

However, he granted seventy years of his life to King David, and therefore only lived for nine hundred and thirty years. It is possible that the Torah is alluding to this fact. Adam's intended life span was actually longer than that recorded in the Torah. The years mentioned here are the actual years **that Adam lived** in this world.

This phrase is also mentioned with regard to Avraham's demise (*Bereishis* 25:7). There too this phrase needs an explanation. The Midrash (*Bereishis Rabbah*, 63:12) states that Avraham was to have lived for one hundred and eighty years; Hashem shortened his life by five years in order that he should not suffer anguish upon seeing his grandson Eisav stray from the proper path. Thus Avraham actually lived for only 175 years.

(Gra, quoted by Beis Yitzchak)

The Midrash (*Bereishis Rabbah*, 14:7) states that Adam and Chavah were created mature: They had the physical and mental composition of twenty-year-olds. Therefore, it can be suggested that the Torah is pointing out that although Adam was as developed as a person twenty years older, the years that he lived were only nine hundred and thirty.

The Gemara states that halachically when a Gentile converts it is considered as though he was just born (*Yevamos* 97b). According to this, one should count the years of the life of Avraham from when he accepted Hashem as the Creator of the world. The Torah, nonetheless, counts the years of his physical life. To emphasize this fact, the Torah adds the words "that he lived."

(Aleh Yonah)

NOACH

...*perfect* in *his generations (6:9)*   ... תָּמִים הָיָה בְּדֹרֹתָיו (ו:ט)

Rashi, quoting the Gemara (Sanhedrin 108a), mentions two conflicting explanations of the Torah's intention in mentioning "his generations." One explanation is that the Torah is praising Noach: If in his degraded generation he rose to such spiritual heights, all the more so if he would have lived in an elevated generation. The other explanation is that Noach was called a *tzaddik* only relative to his generation. Had he lived in the generation of Avraham he would not have merited such a title. Two different Amoraim offer these two explanations. One wonders why one Amora presented a derogatory explanation if he could just as well have been complimentary as his colleague was.

Rashi, later in the *parashah* (7:7), quotes a Midrash (*Bereishis Rabbah* 32:6) which comments that Noach did not fully believe that the Flood would actually arrive. He only entered the ark after the torrents of rain became unbearable. In the Midrash, this comment is attributed to Rabbi Yochanan. In the aforementioned Gemara one will find that the Amora who interpreted this *pasuk* belittlingly is Rabbi Yochanan! This reinforces his negative explanation. Rabbi Yochanan was of the opinion that Noach lacked perfect faith in Hashem; he therefore felt that the Torah could not intend to praise Noach, but rather to downplay his greatness.

At the end of the *Zichronos* section of Rosh Hashanah Mussaf there is a sentence which begins, "**Therefore** you remembered Noach [and saved him]...." The commentaries are unsure to what this "therefore" is referring. The previous sentence concludes with the mention of the iniquities of the generation of Noach. One can suggest that the author of this prayer agreed with Rabbi Yochanan's explanation that Noach was only a *tzaddik* relative to his generation. The "therefore" is explaining that Noach was only saved because all the other people of his generation were so evil.

The Yerushalmi (*Avodah Zarah*, 1:2) states that the author of the aforementioned prayer is Rav. The Gemara states that Rabbi Yochanan was a student of Rav (*Chullin*, 95b)! It is appropriate that Rabbi Yochanan holds with the opinion of his teacher.[1]

(*Torah Temimah*)

צֹהַר תַּעֲשֶׂה לַתֵּבָה ...

A tzohar shall you make for the ark... (6:16)

Rashi mentions that there is a dispute in the Midrash (*Bereishis Rabbah*, 31:11) what this *tzohar* was. One opinion is that it was a window. The other opinion is that it was a jewel that gave off light.

In the beginning of our parsha, (6:9) Rashi cited a dispute among the Amoraim regarding whether Noach was objectively a *tzaddik*, righteous, or whether he was righteous only when compared to the others in his generation. Superficially, this dispute and the dispute regarding the *tzohar* seem unrelated.

The Torah relates (19:17) that when Lot was fleeing Sodom he was instructed by the rescuing angel not to turn around and witness Sodom being destroyed. Rashi explains that since Lot

---

1. [EDITOR'S NOTE: See the note at the end of the next *dvar Torah* for an addition to this *dvar Torah*.]

participated in the sins of the Sodomites, and was saved only in the merit of Avraham, it was inappropriate that he witness Sodom being punished as he was being rescued.

We can now link the question of the *tzohar* to our discussion of Noach's merits at the beginning of the *parashah*. The opinion which states that the *tzohar* was a window also holds that Noach was truly a *tzaddik* and deserved to be saved on his own merit. Therefore he was allowed to build a window in the ark and witness the destruction of his generation. The opinion that states that the *tzohar* was a jewel follows the view that Noach was great only relative to the others and therefore did not deserve to see his fellows perish.[2]

(Toras Moshe)

וַיִּבֶן נֹחַ מִזְבֵּחַ לַה׳ ... וַיַּעַל עֹלֹת בַּמִּזְבֵּחַ. (ח:כ)

Then Noach built an altar to Hashem ... and offered burnt-offerings on the altar. (8:20)

The first time Noach brought a sacrifice was after the Flood. An obvious question is why he waited that long. He should have brought one earlier in order to beseech Hashem not to bring the Flood.

The Midrash (*Tanchuma*, par. 12) states that the generation of the Flood was so corrupt that even animals mated with different species. Such animals are disqualified for use as offerings. Furthermore, says the Mishnah, if such animals are mixed in with purebred animals, even at a ratio of one to ten thousand, they are all disqualified from being brought as offerings (*Zevachim* 70b).

This answers our question. Since all the animals were invalid for use as a sacrifice he could not bring any sacrifices! The situa-

---

2. [EDITOR'S NOTE: The *Torah Temimah* offers a similar explanation. In fact, the *Torah Temimah* states that Rebbi Yochanan is of the opinion that the *tzohar* was a jewel (*Sanhedrin* 108b) and that he was the author of the statement that Noach was not of such a high stature (*Sanhedrin* 108a)! See also the previous *dvar Torah* that concurs with this one.]

tion changed after the Flood. The ark contained animals that had not been defiled. As a result, Noach knew that he could offer the animals that had been in the ark as a sacrifice, and proceeded to offer them. *(Midrash Yehonasan)*

וְאַתָּה קַח לְךָ מִכָּל מַאֲכָל אֲשֶׁר יֵאָכֵל וְאָסַפְתָּ אֵלֶיךָ
וְהָיָה לְךָ וְלָהֶם לְאָכְלָה. (ו:כ"א)

And as for you, take yourself of every food that is eaten and gather it in to yourself, that it shall be as food for you and for them. (6:21)

Rav Yitzchak Yeruchem Diskin zt"l (quoted in *Chidushei Maharil Diskin*) points out that the *pasuk* first mentions that the food which Noach will amass shall be **as food for you** [Noach] to eat and afterwards says that it will be also **for them** [the animals] to eat. This would imply that Noach was allowed to eat before feeding the animals. Yet the Gemara states that one is required to feed one's animals before himself (*Berachos* 40a). Obviously, the Gemara's prohibition did not apply to Noach. Why not?

The Gemara says that Noach and his children were overburdened with work, since some animals had to be fed by day and other animals at night (*Sanhedrin* 108b). The Midrash (*Tanchuma*, para. 9) adds that due to this rigorous feeding schedule Noach and his family did not sleep the entire time they spent in the ark!

This clarifies the matter. There were animals eating around the clock. If Noach would have to wait and not eat before he fed the animals he would never be able to eat! Therefore Hashem made an exception for Noach and permitted him to eat anytime he wished, despite the fact that there some animal was always waiting to be fed. *(Darchei Shalom* [extract])

וְהִנֵּה עֲלֵה זַיִת טָרָף בְּפִיהָ

and behold! an olive leaf it had plucked with its bill (8:11)

The Gemara (*Sanhedrin* 108b) comments that the dove brought a leaf from an olive tree saying that she prefers bitter food directly from Hashem to sweet food from the hand of man (*Sanhedrin* 108b). The commentaries point out that this message could have been accomplished with a leaf from any bitter fruit tree; why did the dove specifically pick an olive tree?

The Gemara (ibid. 108a) states that the people of the generation of the Flood crossbred different species of animals on a grand scale. It is most likely that they also crossbred different types of trees. This is prohibited even for gentiles to do (*Rambam, Melachim* 10:6). If so, just as Hashem destroyed all the animals because they had been corrupted, likewise all trees were swept away (See *Bereishis Rabbah*, 30:8; 31:7).

The Yerushalmi (*Kelayim* 1:7) writes that there exists one type of tree that does not accept grafted material — the olive tree. Therefore, that was the only type of tree that was not corrupted in the Flood era, and consequently was not destroyed! Since the olive tree was the only existing type of tree, the dove was forced to take a leaf from that tree.

(*Milin Yakirin,* quoted by *Gan Raveh*)

כָּל הַחַיָּה כָּל הָרֶמֶשׂ וְכָל הָעוֹף כֹּל רוֹמֵשׂ עַל הָאָרֶץ לְמִשְׁפְּחֹתֵיהֶם יָצְאוּ מִן הַתֵּבָה.

Every living being, every creeping thing, and every bird, everything that moves on earth came out of the ark by their families. (8: 19)

The Gemara states that only the offspring of the insects left the ark and not the original insects (*Sanhedrin* 108b). The commentaries wonder what is the source of the Gemara's statement.

The Gemara mentions that a creature which does not have vertebrae can not live longer than twelve months (*Chullin*, 58a). The Mishnah (*Eduyos* 2:10) states that the Flood lasted twelve months. If so, all insects [since they did not have vertebrae] which entered the ark had died by the time the Flood was over! Only their young were alive and these left the ark.

(*Chelkei Avanim*, quoted by *Gan Raveh*. See *Gan Raveh* and *Pardes Yosef* for an extensive discussion of this explanation.)

Lech Lecha

וַיַּעְתֵּק מִשָּׁם הָהָרָה מִקֶּדֶם לְבֵית אֵל וַיֵּט אָהֳלֹה בֵּית אֵל
מִיָּם וְהָעַי מִקֶּדֶם ... (י״ב:ח)

From there he relocated to the mountain east of Beth-el and pitched his tent, with Beth-el on the west and Ai on the east... (12:8)

THE TORAH AT FIRST DESCRIBES THE MOUNTAIN WHERE AVRAHAM pitched his tent in reference to the city of Beth-el (e.g. "east of Beth-el"). This is understandable, since Beth-el is a known place and the mountain is an undistinguished area. However, the end of the *pasuk* describes Beth-el and Ai in relation to the mountain. This is surprising, since it is odd to place greater importance to the mountain than to the known cities.

While traveling by train I overheard a Jew ask another where the city of Lida is situated. The reply was that it's near Radin. This surprised me, since Lida is a city with a large population, whereas Radin is a small village. Why describe Lida in reference to Radin? The answer is simple. The world-famous Chafetz Chaim lived in Radin! Due to him, Radin overshadowed Lida in importance.

The same idea can be applied here. Before Avraham moved to the mountain it was insignificant and was described in relation to Beth-el. However, once Avraham pitched his tent there, the mountain became the most important place in that area! Therefore, after the Torah mentions that Avraham pitched his tent it describes Beth-el as being west of Avraham's residence.

(*MiShulchan Govoha*, in the name of R' Yehudah Leib Fein *zt"l*)

וַיֹּאמֶר אֶל שָׂרַי אִשְׁתּוֹ הִנֵּה נָא יָדַעְתִּי כִּי אִשָּׁה ...
יְפַת מַרְאֶה אָתְּ. (י"ב:י"א)

...he said to his wife Sarai, "See now, I have known that you are a woman of beautiful appearance (12: 11)"

Why does Avraham say that he has known that she is beautiful? What is important is that he is *now* aware of her beauty; why then did he speak in the past tense?

The Gemara states that every husband is charmed by his wife (*Sotah* 47a). It is the norm for a husband to think that his wife is beautiful although others may not agree. This being the case, although Avraham thought she was beautiful he need not have been concerned for Sarah's safety. However, Avraham knew that she was beautiful even before he married her, when he was not biased. The Gemara writes that Sarah was called Yiscah because everyone would gaze at her unusual beauty (*Megillah* 14a). Avraham was aware of this and therefore was sure that Sarah was truly objectively beautiful; and that in all probability the Egyptians would try to kidnap her. That is why Avraham emphasized that he has known — from before their marriage — that she is beautiful.

(*Panim Yafos*)

And he trusted in Hashem... (15:6)   וְהֶאֱמִן בַּה' ... (ט"ו:ו')

Rashi points out that Avraham had full faith in Hashem concerning the promise of children, and did not ask for any sign that it would be fulfilled. This is in contradistinction to the promise of receiving Eretz Yisrael, concerning which Avraham requested a sign. Rashi, however, offers no explanation why Avraham discriminated between the two promises.

We would like to suggest that the purpose of asking for a sign was to make sure the promise would be fulfilled under all circumstances! Avraham feared that he might not merit receiving Eretz Yisrael, and Hashem would therefore not feel obligated to fulfill His promise. Hashem's making a sign would guarantee that no matter what would transpire Hashem would fulfill His promise. (See *Rashi, Bereishis* 9:9.)

This anxiety was only valid concerning the promise of Eretz Yisrael. The Gemara (*Moed Kattan* 28a) states that being granted children from Hashem is not based on the merits of a person at all. Therefore, Avraham was confident that Hashem would grant the promised children since nothing Avraham would do would cause Hashem to retract from His words. There was no need for Avraham to request a sign vis-a-vis the promise of children. (*Arvei Nachal*)

... אוּלַי אִבָּנֶה מִמֶּנָּה ... (ט״ז:ב)

> ...perhaps I will build up through her... (16:2)

We find in the Torah that the Matriarchs gave their handmaidens to their husbands as a means of themselves raising children. It is difficult to understand how this was meant to be a help for them.

We can suggest as follows. The Matriarchs suspected that for some reason they deserved to be punished by death from Hashem, and that Hashem had substituted childlessness for death, since the Talmud states that a childless person is considered as dead (see *Nedarim* 64b). They therefore looked to inflict upon themselves a different punishment that is considered like death, so that Hashem would release them from their childlessness.

The Midrash (*Devarim Rabbah* 9:9) writes that jealousy is worse than one hundred deaths. Furthermore, the Gemara states that a woman is most jealous of her *tzarah*, i.e. her husband's other wife (*Megillah* 13a). Therefore the Matriarchs gave their handmaidens to their husbands as wives, and thus created jealousy in the hearts of the Matriarchs. Since jealousy is worse than death they would no longer warrant to be punished and as a result Hashem would nullify the decree of barrenness!   *(Tiferes Yehonasan)*

וַיִּפֹּל אַבְרָם עַל פָּנָיו ... (י"ז:ג)

Abram threw himself on his face... (17:3)

The Midrash (*Pirkei D'Rebbi Eliezer* Ch. 29), quoted by Rashi, explains that Avram threw himself on his face because the awe of Hashem's presence was too overwhelming at a time when he was not yet circumcised. Only after he circumcised himself was he able to remain standing when communicating with Hashem. This explanation appears to be contradicted by an earlier *pasuk* (12:7), which states that Hashem appeared to Avram, without adding that Avram threw himself on his face, implying that he did not do so.

The Gemara states that a Kohen who is not circumcised, and still has an *orlah* (foreskin), is prohibited to eat *terumah* and can not use *terumah* oil as an ointment (*Yevamos* 70a). This is true even if the Kohen could not be circumcised due to medical reasons (e.g. two of his brothers who had been circumcised had hemorrhaged and as a result had died of the procedure). However, a Kohen may use *terumah* as a salve until he is eight days old despite the fact that he is not yet circumcised (*Yerushalmi, Yevamos* 8:1). The difference between the two cases

Lech Lecha / 27

is that since the mitzvah of circumcision does not go into effect until the eighth day then the foreskin is not legally considered an *orlah* – something that can intercede [i.e. between man and Hashem] – until then.

The same principle can be applied here. Until Avram was commanded to circumcise himself, there was nothing offensive about the foreskin and it did not prevent him from standing while communicating with Hashem. It was only now, that Avram was being told to circumcise himself (*Rashi*, 17:1), that the foreskin became an *orloh* and hence objectionable, and because of it he fell on his face.

(*Meshech Chochmah*)

וַיֹּאמֶר אֱלֹקִים אֶל אַבְרָהָם שָׂרַי אִשְׁתְּךָ לֹא תִקְרָא
אֶת שְׁמָהּ שָׂרָי כִּי שָׂרָה שְׁמָהּ. (י"ז:ט"ו)

And G-d said to Avraham, "As for Sarai your wife – do not call her name Sarai, for Sarah is her name. (17:15)

Earlier in the *parashah* (17:5), when Hashem changed Avram's name, Hashem said, "Your name shall [from now on] be Avraham." In this *pasuk*, Hashem says "for Sarah is [already] her name." The future tense is used regarding Avraham's name change, while in discussing the change of Sarai's name the present tense is used. This discrepancy needs an explanation. Furthermore, it would seem more appropriate to use the future tense with regard to Sarai since her name had not yet been changed.

The Gemara explains that the implication of the changing of Sarah's name is that "Sarai" means she is the leader of her nation, while "Sarah" connotes that she is the leader of all nations (*Berachos* 13a). Earlier when Hashem told Avraham that his name was changed, he was told that from now on he would be the leader, or king, of all nations. If so, Sarah, at that time, by virtue of the fact that she was his wife, was also elevated to being the queen of all nations. This explains the past tense being used now when discussing Sarah. Hashem was telling Avraham that Sarah's name is already Sarah from when his name had been changed to Avraham!

(Yalkut HaUrim, in the name of *Geulas Yisrael)*

VAYEIRA

וְהוּא יֹשֵׁב פֶּתַח הָאֹהֶל כְּחֹם הַיּוֹם...
וַיִּשָּׂא עֵינָיו וַיַּרְא וְהִנֵּה שְׁלֹשָׁה אֲנָשִׁים נִצָּבִים עָלָיו
וַיַּרְא וַיָּרָץ לִקְרָאתָם מִפֶּתַח הָאֹהֶל וַיִּשְׁתַּחוּ אָרְצָה. (י״ח:א,ב)

> ...while he was sitting at the entrance of the tent in the heat of the day. He lifted his eyes and saw: and behold! three men were standing over him. He perceived, so he ran toward them from the entrance of the tent, and bowed toward the ground. (18: 1,2)

THE TORAH MENTIONS THAT AVRAHAM WAS SITTING AT THE ENTRANCE of his tent when he noticed the three guests. It therefore follows that when he ran toward them he was running from his tent. If so, it is superfluous for the Torah to mention that Avraham ran from his tent. Yet the Torah does write it. Why?

The Gemara states that when one leaves a synagogue one is prohibited to run, since it appears as though it was burdensome for him to have been there and he is overjoyed to leave. Conversely, if someone is headed towards a synagogue he should run, since it shows that he is enthusiastic to be there. This rule applies to all mitzvos (*Berachos* 6b).

We may query what should one do if he is going from fulfilling a mitzvah to a different place to perform another mitzvah. On the one hand, he is required to run toward the place of the new mitzvah. But on the other hand, he is prohibited from running away from the vicinity of the old mitzvos!

The solution appears to be as follows. If the second mitzvah is greater than the first one, then one should run to the second mitzvah. If the first mitzvah that he performed is greater, then he should walk away from it slowly. If both mitzvos are equal, then the first half of his walk he should go slowly, and the second half he should run!

The Gemara indicates from Avraham's action that to receive guests is greater even than to greet the Divine Presence. Avraham interrupted Hashem's communication with him to invite the three visitors (*Shabbos* 127a). Since according to Rav receiving guests is greater than greeting Hashem, Avraham was required to run the entire way toward the guests. This is why the Torah notes that he ran immediately upon leaving the entrance of his home!

(Kehillas Yitzchak, in name of R' Shalum of Prizina)

...and sustain your hearts... (18:5)   ... וְסַעֲדוּ לִבְּכֶם ... (י"ח:ה)

A Gerer *chassid*, Rav Bentzion Ostrover, was privileged to live to a ripe old age. During his long lifetime, he was the disciple of three Gerer Rebbes — the *Chidushei Harim*, *Sfas Emes*, and *Imrei Emes*. He knew the *Imrei Emes* [Rav Avraham Mordechai Alter] from when the Rebbe was a child. One of the stories that he related about the childhood years of the *Imrei Emes* was as follows:

"One day I met him in the courtyard of Ger and asked what he had learned with his father [the *Sfas Emes*] that day. He replied: 'The Chumash and Rashi of the weekly *parashah*,' which was *Vayeira*. I then queried if he had asked his father any questions. He told me the following : 'Rashi writes in the name of the Midrash that Avraham said "*libchem*" and not "*levavchem*" because angels have no evil inclination so it is as though they have only one heart. But Avraham did not know that they were angels; why did he say "*libchem*"?!'

" 'My father explained that Hashem guards and directs *tzaddikim* that they should not state any falsehood. Even if they are not fully apprised of all necessary information Hashem will not allow them to inaccurately describe it. Therefore, Hashem caused Avraham to inadvertently use the term *"libchem"* since that was true of the angels.'

" 'Were you satisfied with that answer?' I asked the child. 'No,' he replied. 'I asked my father that if it is so, why didn't Avraham now realize that they were angels since he had been Divinely guided to say *libchem*?'

"I tried to elicit from the child what his father had responded to that, but by now he was tired of my badgering and ran away..."³

(*Rosh Golas Ariel*, p. 27)

וּכְמוֹ הַשַּׁחַר עָלָה וַיָּאִיצוּ הַמַּלְאָכִים בְּלוֹט ...

*And just as dawn was breaking,
the angels urged Lot on... (19:15)*

The Midrash (*Bereshis Rabbah* 50:1) states that the angels who were appointed to destroy Sodom were "angels of mercy," and therefore did not hasten and destroy Sodom immediately after Avraham's failed attempt to save the city. If so, it is difficult to understand why at the crack of dawn Lot was rushed out of Sodom.

Lot was guilty for not reproaching his fellow townspeople of Sodom. There is a positive commandment in the Torah of *hocheiach tochiach* and Lot had not fulfilled it. However, the Gemara (*Menachos* 41a) writes that Hashem punishes for failing to fulfill a positive command only when He is "angry." One

---
3. EDITOR'S NOTE: The Melo HaOmer writes that it is appropriate to say to evil people "libchem" since they too have only "one heart" — for doing evil. If so, we can suggest as an answer to the question of the Imrei Emes, that Avraham thought that he had been inspired to say "libchem" because his guests were evil idol worshipers (see Rashi, 18:4), and not because they were angels.

time of Divine anger exists when the sun comes up and many kings bow to the sun (*Berachos* 7a).

These facts explain the *pasuk* mentioned here. Since Hashem was punishing the people of Sodom, Lot would have been punished with them had he been there at the moment of Hashem's anger, which is sunrise. This was especially true regarding Sodom, since the people of Sodom worshiped the sun (*Bereishis Rabbah* 50:12) Therefore the *pasuk* points out that at sunrise Lot was already in a different city and out of harm's way!

(*Pnei Yehoshua, Shabbos* 55a)

וְעַתָּה הָשֵׁב אֵשֶׁת הָאִישׁ כִּי נָבִיא הוּא ... (כ:ז)

But now return the man's wife for he is a prophet... (20:7)

The Gemara (*Bava Kamma* 92a) comments that the *pasuk* seems to be implying that only because Avraham was a prophet did Avimelech have to return Avraham's wife. Although the Gemara ultimately rejects this understanding of the *pasuk*, it is possible to explain it in accordance with this interpretation.

It can be inferred from the Mishnah that if a person marries a woman and then discovers that she is an *aylonis*, a woman who never matured physically and is incapable of having children, then legally they were never married (*Yevamos* 2b). Implicit in every act of marriage is the understanding that he married her on the presumption that she *can* bear children.

There is a different Gemara which states that Sarah was an *aylonis* (*Yevamos* 64b). This presents a difficulty. When Hashem commanded Avimelech to return Sarah to Avraham since she was his wife, Avimelech could have responded that Sarah was not Avraham's wife since she was an *aylonis*!

However, the Mishnah also writes that if a person knew before his marriage that his future wife is an *aylonis* and mar-

Vayeira / 33

ried her anyway, then his marriage is valid, and she has all the rights of a regular wife (*Kesubos* 100b). This explains Hashem's answer to Avimelech. Hashem forestalled the aforementioned possible response of Avimelech. Hashem told Avimelech to return Sarah to Avraham because he was a prophet and knew beforehand that Sarah was an *aylonis*! Since when Avraham married Sarah he knew of her imperfection, their marriage was valid.

(*Chanukas HaTorah*)

... כָּל הַשֹּׁמֵעַ יִצְחַק לִי (כ"א:ו)

... *whoever hears will mock me. (21:6)*

The Midrash (*Tanchuma, Toldos*, para. 1 and 6), as quoted by Rashi, relates that when Yitzchak was born people did not believe that Avraham had fathered him. Since Yitzchak was born shortly after the encounter with Avimelech, people mockingly claimed that Avimelech was the true father. To refute this rumor, Hashem created Yitzchak's face identical to that of Avraham. Anyone who saw Yitzchak knew instantly that Avraham was his father.

This only silenced those people who actually saw Yitzchak and observed the striking resemblance. Those who only heard of Yitzchak's birth and didn't actually see Yitzchak continued scoffing at Avraham and Sarah. This explains why Sarah said, "... whoever **hears** about this will mock me." Only someone who merely hears will mock; not someone who will see Yitzchak!

(*Peninim Yekarim*, in name of *Nachalas Yaakov*)

וַתֹּאמֶר מִי מִלֵּל לְאַבְרָהָם הֵינִיקָה בָנִים שָׂרָה... (כ"א:ז)

And she said, "Who is the One Who said to Avraham, 'Sarah would nurse children?'" (21: 7)

An obvious question is: Why did Sarah say that she nursed **children**, implying more than one child? Yitzchak was the only child she bore. The Gemara explains that on the day Yitzchak was weaned, Avraham and Sarah made a grand feast to which they invited all the great people of their generation along with their wives. These people had been murmuring that Yitzchak was not Sarah's biological child, but was rather an orphan bought in the market. This invitation was intended to lay that rumor to rest. They came with their babies, but without their nursemaids. A miracle occurred and Sarah was able to nurse all the babies present, proving that Sarah was indeed capable of having given birth to Yitzchak. This is what Sarah meant: that she nursed many children (*Bava Metzia* 87a).

This story, however, presents us with a new question. Why did Sarah wait this long to refute the slander being said against her? Why didn't she nurse other children earlier?

Rambam (*Ishus* 21:12) posits that a husband is permitted to prevent his wife from nursing someone else's child as long as she is still nursing his child. Apparently, as long as a woman has milk to offer, if she does not feed it to her own child, then he is being deprived. As long as Yitzchak was able and willing to nurse, Sarah did not want to deprive him of something that was rightfully his. Only after Yitzchak was weaned did Sarah attempt to stop the slander by nursing other children.

(*R' Chaim Soloveitchik*, quoted in *Chidushei HaGriz*)

Chayei Sarah

וַתָּמָת שָׂרָה בְּקִרְיַת אַרְבַּע הִוא חֶבְרוֹן בְּאֶרֶץ
כְּנָעַן וַיָּבֹא אַבְרָהָם לִסְפֹּד לְשָׂרָה וְלִבְכֹּתָהּ. (כ״ג:ב)

*Sarah died in Kiriath-arba that is Chevron in the land
of Canaan; and Avraham came to eulogize
Sarah and to bewail her. (23: 2)*

SEVERAL QUESTIONS CAN BE ASKED REGARDING THIS PASUK: 1) The Torah first mentions that Avraham came to eulogize and then mentions that he also came to cry. The Gemara instructs us that a mourner should limit his expressions of grief to three days of crying which are the first three of the seven days of mourning (Moed Kattan 27b). Since the period of mourning continues after the crying has ceased, it would seem more appropriate for the Torah to write first that Avraham came to cry and then to mention that he came also to eulogize.

2) In the word וְלִבְכֹּתָהּ the כ is written in the Torah smaller than usual. The Baal HaTurim suggests that the reason for this anomaly is to inform us that Avraham cried only a little bit. But an explanation is still warranted as to why Avraham behaved in this fashion.

3) *Rashi* quotes the explanation of the Midrash (*Bereishis Rabbah* 58:5) that the Torah juxtaposed the story of Sarah's

demise with the story of *akeidas Yitzchak* [binding of Yitzchak] because it was the event of the *akeidah* that led to her death. *Rashi* writes this explanation regarding the words "to eulogize Sarah and to bewail her." This seems odd, since it would seem more appropriate regarding the words "and Sarah died."

It is recorded (*Asarah Ma'amaros*) that the *akeidah* took place on the afternoon of Yom Kippur. It is written in the Torah (*Bereishis* 22:4) that it took Avraham three days to travel from his house in Be'er Sheva to Har Hamoriah, where the *akeidah* took place. It follows then that it took three days to travel home, arriving on the thirteenth day of Tishrei. Upon arriving home, he discovered that Sarah had died and began mourning for her. However, the next night began the fifteenth day of Tishrei — the Yom Tov of Succos. According to halachah (*Moed Kattan* 19a), the arrival of a Yom Tov discontinues the period of mourning. If so, Avraham, who observed *halachah* (*Yoma* 28b), did not cry and eulogize the usual seven days, but rather only slightly more than one day.

All the earlier questions can now be answered. Generally the period of eulogy extends beyond the period of crying. In this instance they both ended simultaneously with the arrival of Succos. To point this out, the Torah first mentions the eulogizing of Avraham and then the crying. This also explains why Avraham cried very little. He only had one day to cry, not the usual three days.

The last question we raised is also resolved. Rashi was troubled by our two questions. To answer these, he cited the Midrash that told the story of Sarah's death. It is therefore most appropriate for Rashi to quote the Midrash here, rather than at the beginning of this *pasuk*.

(*Maaseh Roke'ach*)

וַיָּקָם שְׂדֵה עֶפְרוֹן אֲשֶׁר בַּמַּכְפֵּלָה... לְאַבְרָהָם לְמִקְנָה לְעֵינֵי בְנֵי חֵת ... וְאַחֲרֵי כֵן קָבַר אַבְרָהָם אֶת שָׂרָה אִשְׁתּוֹ... וַיָּקָם הַשָּׂדֶה וְהַמְּעָרָה אֲשֶׁר בּוֹ לְאַבְרָהָם לַאֲחֻזַּת קָבֶר מֵאֵת בְּנֵי חֵת. (כ"ג:י"ז-כ)

> And Ephron's field which was in Machpelah, ... was confirmed as Avraham's as a purchase in the view of the children of Heth... And afterwards Avraham buried Sarah his wife... Thus, the field with its cave was confirmed as Avraham's as an estate for a burial site, from the children of Heth. (23: 17 – 20)

Reading these *pesukim* one is immediately struck by a glaring redundancy. The Torah twice states that Ephron's field was confirmed as Avraham's property!

The Rambam (*Zechiyah U'matanah* 1:14), following the opinion of Rav Hai Gaon, writes that a Jew can legally acquire land from a Gentile only by digging or making a change to the property. If a Jew pays money to a Gentile for his land, the land is no longer the Gentile's but does not yet belong to the Jew. Only when the Jew subsequently works the land does it become his.

According to the Torah, when Avraham paid Ephron for his land it did not belong to Avraham at that point. However, the people of Heth, who assumed that Avraham was a Gentile, thought that upon payment it became Avraham's property. The Torah therefore first writes that "Ephron's field confirmed ... as Avraham's as a purchase **in the view of the children of Heth.**" Only in **their** eyes it was a valid transaction; not according to the Torah! It was only after Avraham buried Sarah, and thereby worked on the land, that the land actually became his. The Torah points this out by writing "and afterwards Avraham buried Sarah his wife" and then writing that the field was in reality only now confirmed as Avraham's.

(Meshech Chochmah)

וְאַבְרָהָם זָקֵן בָּא בַּיָּמִים ... (כ״ד:א)

Now Avraham was old, well on in years... (24:1)

The Torah mentions Avraham as being old before it relates the story of Avraham sending Eliezer to find a wife for his son Yitzchak. This would seem to imply that only when Avraham was old was he able to marry off Yitzchak. Why was that so?

There is a tradition mentioned in the Gemara that until the era of Avraham people did not show any effects of old age! Since Avraham and Yitzchak had identical facial features, and Avraham's face showed no signs of old age, people would confuse the two! The Gemara then states that Avraham prayed to Hashem that people should age, and his prayer was answered, as it says in the Torah, "And Avraham was old..." (*Bava Metzia* 87a). One may wonder why Avraham requested the phenomenon of the aging of the human body. It might seem that the reason for Avraham's praying was to put an end to the confusion of identities. This idea is difficult to accept. For such a trivial reason one does not ask to bring on the debilitating effects of old age!

Every person's voice is unique and can be used as a means of identification. The Gemara states that this method of identification is valid even according to the Torah. Otherwise, how would a blind man be allowed to live with his wife! The only way he identifies her is by her voice (*Gittin* 23a). In fact, we are all in a similar predicament in the dark of night. Why did people mistake Avraham for Yitzchak and vice versa; couldn't they be discerned by their voices? One must conclude that even their voices were identical!

Our questions can now be answered. As long as Avraham was physically young, and Yitzchak looked and sounded exactly like him, Yitzchak could not marry! Yitzchak's wife would not be certain that it was not Avraham who stood in front of her! That is the reason why Avraham prayed for old age. When Avraham looked and sounded older than Yitzchak, he began to seek a wife for Yitzchak.

(*Kehillas Yitzchak, in the name of R' Yaakov Yosef zt"l*)

וַה׳ בֵּרַךְ אֶת אַבְרָהָם בַּכֹּל. (כ"ד:א)

...and Hashem had blessed Abraham with everything. (24:1)

The Torah prefaces the story of Avraham seeking a wife for Yitzchak with the mention of Hashem having blessed Avraham by giving him "everything." There is an opinion [Rebbi Yehudah], that this means that Avraham had a daughter (*Bava Basra* 16b). There is no clue to this interpretation in the *pasuk*. What then prompted Rebbi Yehudah to explain the word "everything" as meaning a daughter?

If a father and a son each need a wife, then the father should first find a wife for himself and afterwards for his son (*Tosefta, Bechoros* 6:3). This would seem to contradict Avraham's actions in first seeking a wife for Yitzchak and then marrying Keturah. This can be resolved by limiting the halachah of a father's precedence to a situation where the father has still not fulfilled his obligation of *pru u'revu* [procreation]. Only if a man has not fathered a boy and a girl is he required to marry before his son marries. We can thus suggest that Avraham had a daughter also, and therefore first married off Yitzchak. This is the basis for Rebbi Yehudahh's opinion. The Torah points out that Avraham had "everything" — a daughter — and therefore was allowed to seek a *shidduch* for Yitzchak before himself.

(*Tiferes Yehonasan*)

וַיִּקַּח הָעֶבֶד עֲשָׂרָה גְמַלִּים מִגְּמַלֵּי ... (כ"ד:י)

Then the servant took ten camels of his master's camels... (24:10)

The Midrash (*Bereishis Rabbah* 59:11), quoted by Rashi, writes that Avraham's camels were unique in that they were muzzled so that they should not graze from other people's property.

A different Midrash (ibid. 60:8) relates that the donkey belonging to Rabbi Pinchas ben Yair was on a lofty spiritual level, and would not eat any food that was prohibited to a Jew! If so, asks the Midrash, why was it necessary for Avraham to muzzle his camels? Surely they were as spiritual as the donkey of Rabbi Pinchas ben Yair and would not eat stolen food.

Earlier in the *parashah* (23:4), when Avraham spoke to the people of Heth, he prefaced his words by declaring that he was a *toshav* [permanent resident] of Eretz Yisrael. The Midrash (58:6) explains that legally Avraham could have taken their land without asking since Hashem promised him that land; it was only out of the kindness of his heart that he compensated them.

The question of the Midrash can now be answered. Avraham's camels would surely not consume anything that was prohibited. But all the land in Eretz Yisrael actually belonged to Avraham, and therefore they had a right to graze from every field! Avraham who wished to be stringent and did not want his animals to graze without paying had to muzzle his camels.

This can also explain why Eliezer took Avraham's camels when traveling from Eretz Yisrael to find a wife for Yitzchak. Eliezer was instructed not to take a wife from Eretz Yisrael for Yitzchak. The camels were his indicator of whether he was in Eretz Yisrael or not. If they began to eat from someone else's field, he would be sure that they were still in Eretz Yisrael.

(*Tiferes Yehonasan*)

וַיֹּאמֶר לֹא אֹכַל עַד אִם דִּבַּרְתִּי דְּבָרָי וַיֹּאמֶר דַּבֵּר. (כ"ד:ל"ג)

...but he said, "I will not eat until I have spoken my piece."
And he said, "Speak." (24:33)

An obvious question is: Why did Eliezer refuse to eat the food Rivkah's parents offered before explaining the purpose of his trip?

There is a custom among Jews for a man to send gifts to his betrothed. If subsequently they do not marry, the presents are returned. However, she does not have to return the gifts if the man ate in her house (*Rama, Even HaEzer* 50:3).

Upon meeting Rivkah, Eliezer was so confident that she was the one destined to be Yitzchak's wife that in his role as Yitzchak's agent he gave her the betrothal gifts immediately (see earlier 24:22). However, he now had second thoughts, and was concerned that Rivkah's parents might not agree to the match. Should that happen, and he had eaten in their home, then he would not be able to retrieve the gifts. Therefore, he declined to eat until he first informed them of the purpose of his journey and was assured by Rivkah and her parents that she would marry Yitzchak.

(*Pardes Yosef,* in the name of *Mishnas Rebbi Eliezer*)

TOLDOS

וַיֵּעָתֶר לוֹ ה׳ ... (כ״ה:כ״א)

...Hashem allowed himself to be entreated by him... (25:21)

THE WORD THE TORAH USES TO STATE THAT HASHEM LISTENED to the prayer of Yitzchak is וַיֵּעָתֶר. Rashi explains that the precise meaning of the word is that Hashem was "moved by entreaties, appeased, and convinced." The implication is that Hashem was very reluctant to grant Yitzchak's request that Rivkah conceive. Why?

There is a story told that may help us understand Hashem's actions. The Chasam Sofer was approached to pray for a certain woman who was in the throes of a long drawn-out childbirth. To their great surprise he refused, but justified himself. The Gemara writes that a *tzaddik* will not die unless another *tzaddik* has been born to take his place (*Kiddushin,* 72b). The Chasam Sofer knew that the child who would be born would fill the void which would arise as the result of the demise of a different *tzaddik*. How could he pray for a quick birth if it resulted in the demise of another *tzaddik*!

The Midrash (*Bereishis Rabbah* 63:12) states that originally Avraham was destined to have lived one hundred and eighty years. Hashem shortened his life span by five years so that he should not suffer the aggravation of seeing his grandson Eisav commit serious transgressions. If so, it follows that the earlier Eisav would be born, the sooner Avraham would die. Therefore, Hashem wished to delay Rivkah's pregnancy as much as possible. Only after much pleading by Yitzchak did Hashem relent.

There is a proof of sorts to this explanation. The *gematria* [numerical equivalence] of וַיֵּעָתֶר לוֹ י-ה-ו-ה and חמש שנים (five years) are the same (748), indicating that it was because of five years that Yitzchak had to pray so hard.

(R' Yosef Chaim Sonnenfeld, quoted by Shai LeTorah)

אִם כֵּן לָמָּה זֶּה אָנֹכִי... (כ"ה:כ"ב)   ...If so, why am I thus... (25:22)

Rivkah prayed long and hard to conceive. However, there was something so unusual about her pregnancy that she had regrets. What could have happened that, had she been aware of it earlier, she would not have desired to conceive?

The Gemara narrates that King Chizkiyahu did not marry by choice. He had perceived through *ruach hakodesh* [Divine inspiration] that although some of his descendants would be extremely righteous, others would be evildoers. The prophet Yeshayahu brought him a message from Hashem that he was sinning by not fulfilling the mitzvah of *pru u'revu* [procreation]. Although logically he was correct in not wanting to bring sinners into the world, that consideration did not override the obligation of having offspring (*Berachos* 10a).

The Midrash (*Bereishis Rabbah* 63:6) states that when Rivkah would pass by a yeshivah, Yaakov would react and try to push his way out of the womb. Whenever she would pass a place of idol worship, Eisav would in turn begin pushing. Rivkah thus realized that she was carrying one son who was a *tzaddik* and one son who was a *rasha*. Had she known the nature of the child beforehand, she would not have prayed to conceive, since it would mean bringing a *rasha* into this world. Since women are exempt from the commandment of *pru u'revu*, that would have been the proper thing to do.

Rivkah said, "Why did I exert so much effort?" Yitzchak, who was required to have children, would have been obligated to have them even if he would have had prior knowledge of Eisav's nature. However, Rivkah, who was exempt, need not have prayed so diligently. (*Chidushei Maran Riz HaLevi*)

...If so, why am I thus... (25:22) (כ"ה:כ"ב) ...אִם כֵּן לָמָּה זֶּה אָנֹכִי

Rivkah was amazed that she was undergoing such a troubling pregnancy. It is not unusual for women to have difficulties at the time of pregnancy; why was Rivkah surprised?

The Gemara states that righteous women are privileged not to have to suffer the pains of pregnancy (*Sotah* 12a). Elsewhere, we find that Hashem created the Matriarchs barren because Hashem desires the prayers of righteous people (*Yevamos* 64a). Being childless, the Matriarchs would perforce pray to Hashem.

Rivkah was barren for many years. She therefore assumed that Hashem considered her a righteous woman and made her childless in order that she should pray. She was confident that being a righteous woman she would not have any suffering during her pregnancy! She was thus greatly shocked at the onset of her pain. What she meant by exclaiming, "Why am I thus?" was: "If I am really righteous, why am I experiencing pain; if not, why was I barren!"[4] (*Chanukas HaTorah*)

---

4. [EDITOR'S NOTE: The Torah states that Rivkah posed this question to Hashem and received a response that the progenitors of two antagonistic nations are in her womb. One could suggest that according to the *Chanukas HaTorah's* explanation of Rivkah's question, Hashem answered that in actuality Rivkah is a righteous woman. However, what she was experiencing was not pain due to pregnancy, but rather a conflict between two warring nations!]

... וַיֹּאמֶר הַקֹּל קוֹל יַעֲקֹב וְהַיָּדַיִם יְדֵי עֵשָׂו. ... וַיְבָרְכֵהוּ. (כ"ז:כ"ב, כ"ג)

> ... and said, "The voice is Yaakov's voice, but the hands are Eisav hands." ... so he blessed him (27: 22, 23)

Yitzchak had conflicting evidence as to who was in his presence. The manner of speech was one that Yaakov generally used; but the hands were hairy, as were Eisav's. Despite the evidence to the contrary, Yitzchak assumed Eisav was standing in front of him, and blessed him. Why? Why did he come to that conclusion?

One can suggest the following. Eisav suspected that Yaakov would try to receive the blessings for himself. He assumed that Yaakov would change his manner of speaking to sound like Eisav. To prevent that, Eisav informed Yitzchak that he [Eisav] would instead mimic Yaakov's mannerism, and that would be the sign that it's really Eisav! Yaakov outsmarted Eisav and spoke in his usual style, causing Yitzchak to conclude that Eisav was standing in front of him! When Yitzchak said, "The voice is similar to that of Yaakov and the hands are similar to those of Eisav," he was not pointing out a contradiction. He was saying that there are two proofs that it is Eisav! Therefore he blessed him.

Later (pasuk 35), Yitzchak tells Eisav that Yaakov received the blessings for himself using מִרְמָה. The usual translation of מִרְמָה is "deceit." *Targum Onkeles* translates it here as meaning "wisdom." Yaakov did not have to use trickery to receive the blessings. Rather, by being wise, and acting his usual self, he obtained Yitzchak's blessing. (*Beis HaLevi*)

... so he blessed him. (27: 22) ... וַיְבָרְכֵהוּ (כ"ז:כ"ג)

The Torah states that Yaakov disguised himself and was able to pass himself off to Yitzchak as Eisav. Yitzchak then proceeded to bless him. Later (*pesukim* 27-29) Yitzchak again blesses Yaakov, but this time in greater detail. It would seem that the second blessing was the real blessing that Yitzchak had always intended to give. If so, what was the purpose of the first blessing?

Yaakov came to Yitzchak and claimed that he was Eisav. Yitzchak was not sure if it was indeed Eisav. The hands did feel like the hands of Eisav; but the tone and manner of speaking was that of Yaakov. Yitzchak therefore implemented the following ruse. He first blessed the person in front of him, but not with the actual originally intended blessing. He then said to him, "Are you my son Eisav? (*pasuk* 24); i.e. you have already received my blessing, so now tell me the truth!" Yitzchak assumed that if it were Yaakov then he would now admit it. Yaakov realized this and did not confess. This convinced Yitzchak that it was indeed Eisav standing before him, and he gave him the real blessings.

(Kehillas Yitzchak, in the name of R' N. Rabinowitz)

וַיַּעַן יִצְחָק אָבִיו וַיֹּאמֶר אֵלָיו הִנֵּה מִשְׁמַנֵּי הָאָרֶץ יִהְיֶה מוֹשָׁבֶךָ ... (כ״ז:ל״ט)

So Yitzchak his father answered, and said to him, "Behold, of the fatness of the earth shall be your dwelling..." (27: 39)

When Eisav realized that Yaakov had deceived Yitzchak and had received the blessings, he begged Yitzchak also to be blessed. Yitzchak replied that he had already promised everything to Yaakov, and nothing remained with which to bless Eisav. After further pleading, Yitzchak blessed Eisav that he should dwell in "the fatness of the earth." The Midrash (*Bereishis Rabbah* 67:6), quoted by Rashi, writes that this refers to Rome. Why does the Midrash assume that Yitzchak is referring to Rome?

The Gemara relates that when Shlomo *HaMelech* married the daughter of Pharaoh, the angel Gavriel descended to this world and stuck a reed into the ocean, around which a sandbank was formed. Eventually Rome was built upon this land (*Shabbos* 56b).

Yitzchak had granted Yaakov all that existed. He could only present Eisav with something that did not exist at that time! That was Rome. The Midrash therefore knew that Yitzchak could only have been referring to Rome.

(Chanukas HaTorah)

VAYEITZEI

וַיֵּצֵא יַעֲקֹב מִבְּאֵר שָׁבַע וַיֵּלֶךְ חָרָנָה. (כ"ח:י)

*Yaakov departed from Be'er-Sheva
and went toward Haran. (28: 10)*

RASHI EXPLAINS THE PHRASE וַיֵּלֶךְ חָרָנָה TO MEAN THAT WHEN Yaakov left Be'er-Sheva he intended to go directly to Haran. This would seem to contradict the Gemara, which was quoted earlier by Rashi (28:9), which relates that after leaving Be'er-Sheva, Yaakov went directly to the yeshivah of Eiver, where he remained for fourteen years studying the Torah diligently (Megillah 17a).

The Gemara raises the issue as to which should come first: to marry or devote oneself to the intense study of Torah. It concludes, if one is wealthy and does not have to work for a livelihood then he should first marry, and afterwards devote himself to the study of Torah. If marriage will place a financial burden upon him, then he should first study Torah and only later get married (*Kiddushin* 29b).

Yaakov left his parents' home a wealthy man, and therefore planned on traveling directly to Haran to find a wife for himself. On the way, Eliphaz the son of Eisav pursued him and stole all his money (see *Rashi* 29:11). Now that he was penniless, his first obligation was to study Torah. He therefore changed direction and went to study Torah at Eiver's yeshivah! (*Asifas Kohen*)

וַיַּחֲלֹם וְהִנֵּה סֻלָּם מֻצָּב אַרְצָה וְרֹאשׁוֹ מַגִּיעַ הַשָּׁמָיְמָה וְהִנֵּה מַלְאֲכֵי אֱלֹקִים עֹלִים וְיֹרְדִים בּוֹ. (כ"ח:י"ב)

> And he dreamt, and behold! A ladder was set earthward and its top reached heavenward; and behold! angels of G-d were ascending and descending on it. (28: 12)

When the first Rebbe of Rizhin, Reb Yisrael, was a young boy in *cheder* [elementary school], he was so bright that he would raise the very questions that Rashi does. When the class reached *parashas Vayeitzei*, the teacher assumed that Yisrael would point out the obvious problem that Rashi addresses. The *pasuk* first mentions that the angels were going up; being that angels reside "up in heaven," it should first have said that the angels were descending and only afterwards returning to heaven. The teacher paused but no question was forthcoming. Even after mentioning that there was a problem here, Yisrael did not venture a guess. Finally, the teacher presented Rashi's question to the young boy, and asked why he did not think of it. Replied Yisrael, "That's not a question! The Torah is recording the contents of Yaakov's dream. One doesn't ask questions on a dream!" (*Hearsay*)

וַיִּיקַץ יַעֲקֹב מִשְּׁנָתוֹ וַיֹּאמֶר אָכֵן יֵשׁ ה' בַּמָּקוֹם הַזֶּה וְאָנֹכִי לֹא יָדָעְתִּי. (כ"ח:ט"ז)

> Yaakov awoke from his sleep and said, "Surely Hashem is present in this place and I did not know!" (28:16)

Yaakov dreamt that the ground he was sleeping on was holy and upon awakening declared it as such, and added, "and I did not know!" What was the intent of this last comment?

Yaakov was trying to prove that he had a prophetic vision and not merely a dream. The Gemara states that a person only dreams of what he thought about by day (*Berachos* 55b). Thus Yaakov was saying that he did not at all know beforehand that this spot was holy and had not given it a thought! It must therefore have been a communication with Hashem and not a dream.

(*Chanukas HaTorah*, in the name of *R' Yaakov of Lublin*)

וַיִּדַּר יַעֲקֹב נֶדֶר לֵאמֹר אִם יִהְיֶה אֱלֹקִים עִמָּדִי וּשְׁמָרַנִי בַּדֶּרֶךְ הַזֶּה אֲשֶׁר אָנֹכִי הוֹלֵךְ וְנָתַן לִי לֶחֶם לֶאֱכֹל וּבֶגֶד לִלְבּשׁ. וְשַׁבְתִּי בְשָׁלוֹם אֶל בֵּית אָבִי ... (כ"ח:כ,כ"א)

> Then Yaakov took a vow, saying, "If G-d will be with me, and will guard me on this way that I am going; and will give me bread to eat and a garment to wear; and I will return safely to my father's house...' (28: 20, 21)

The renowned *Gaon*, Rav Yosef Dov Soloveitchik, author of *Beis HaLevi*, once spent the night in a hotel in Minsk. While there, many townspeople came to visit him, including a former student of his who resided in Minsk and owned a business there. Rav Yosef Dov was overjoyed to see him and asked, "How are you doing?" The student responded, "*Baruch Hashem*, I am successful in my business. A year ago, I and my brother-in-law established a wholesale sugar store and the business is growing every day."

After conversing with several other guests, Rav Yosef Dov again turned to his former pupil and repeated his original question, to which he received the same reply. A while later this question was repeated yet a third time! Puzzled by this, the student respectfully asked Rav Yosef Dov to explain his strange conduct. He replied:

"It was evident from your initial answer that you didn't comprehend my question. I therefore repeated it. Even after hearing the same response, I had hoped that you would understand from my second repetition that I had something else in mind when asking my question. Now that I see that you still haven't grasped what my intention is, I'll explain it to you. The Gemara states that "everything is in the hands of Hashem except for the fear of Hashem (*Berachos* 33b)." This means that Hashem predestines man's physical lot in this world — his social standing, financial means, health, etc. Man's success or lack of it regarding material pursuits is wholly in Hashem's hands. Only spiritual matters were given over to humans. If a person succeeds spiritually, that is truly his own accomplishment. I asked you how **you** are doing. My intention was to know how are you succeeding in activities that are up to you — studying Torah, giving charity, etc. Instead, you told me about success that Hashem is granting you!"

This point is evident from Yaakov's words. When Yaakov mentions physical comforts, he attributes it to Hashem: "If **G-d** will be with me ... will give me bread to eat, and a garment to wear ... " When mentioning spiritual success, he personally takes the credit: "And **I** will return "safely" to my father's home..." [Rashi explains that "safely" means unblemished by sin.]

(Mekor Baruch)

וַיִּדַּר יַעֲקֹב נֶדֶר לֵאמֹר אִם יִהְיֶה אֱלֹקִים עִמָּדִי וּשְׁמָרַנִי בַּדֶּרֶךְ הַזֶּה אֲשֶׁר אָנֹכִי הוֹלֵךְ ... וְשַׁבְתִּי בְשָׁלוֹם אֶל בֵּית אָבִי ... (כ"ח:כ,כ"א)

Then Yaakov took a vow, saying, "If G-d will be with me, and will guard me on this way that I am going ... and I return unblemished to my father's house..." (28: 20, 21)

Yaakov vowed that if he returns home spiritually unblemished after residing with the evil Lavan, then he would build a "house of G-d." The word Yaakov used was בְשָׁלוֹם which is translated "unblemished" The Gemara states that when a person takes leave of a living person then he should say, "לֵךְ לְשָׁלוֹם," and to a dead person, "לֵךְ בְּשָׁלוֹם" (*Berachos* 64a). It is difficult to understand why Yaakov expressed his wish concerning himself using the term בְשָׁלוֹם.

The commentaries explain that there is a difference in meaning between לְשָׁלוֹם and בְּשָׁלוֹם. The former indicates that one should continue to grow spiritually and in the future achieve perfection. That is the reason it is used when addressing a person who can still advance. The word בְּשָׁלוֹם indicates that one will remain at his present level. Consequently, it is used when departing from a dead person, since he can no longer progress.

Yaakov did not delude himself into thinking that he would advance spiritually in Lavan's company. He only hoped and prayed that at least he would not regress there! Therefore he used the word בְּשָׁלוֹם concerning himself.

(*Kehillas Yaakov*, in the name of *Yad Yosef*)

וַיֹּאמֶר הֵן עוֹד הַיּוֹם גָּדוֹל לֹא עֵת הֵאָסֵף הַמִּקְנֶה ... (כ"ט:ז)

He said, "Look, the day is still long; it is not yet time to bring the livestock in..." (29:7)

Rashi explains that Yaakov discerned from the actions of the shepherds that they intended returning home early with their sheep. He chided them to remain at their jobs, and not depart as yet. In his words of rebuke, he mentioned that "there still is a long day ahead of us." These words seem unnecessary, since the shepherds were well aware of what time it was, and how much daylight remained.

The Midrash (*Bereishis Rabbah* 68:10), quoted by Rashi earlier, writes that on the preceding day Hashem caused the sun to set prematurely. It was possible that the shepherds were concerned that the phenomenon might reoccur that day, and were rushing home. Yaakov therefore informed them that they need not worry, and that the day would be of normal duration.

(Tiferes Yehonasan)

VAYISHLACH

וַיִּירָא יַעֲקֹב מְאֹד וַיֵּצֶר לוֹ...(ל״ב:ח)

*Yaakov became very frightened,
and it distressed him ... (32: 8)*

THE MIDRASH (BEREISHIS RABBAH 76:2), QUOTED BY RASHI, explains that Yaakov was **very frightened** because of the possibility that he might be killed, and he was **distressed** because he might kill Eisav. The commentaries wonder why Yaakov should be concerned about killing Eisav; Eisav was attacking Yaakov and it is permissible to kill in self-defense.

In the episode of Eisav's selling of his birthright, Yaakov requested the sale of Eisav's birthright and also asked him to swear to attest to this. What was the purpose of this oath? The answer is as follows. According to Jewish law (*Choshen Mishpat* 209:4), something that is not yet in your possession cannot be sold. Thus, Eisav's birthright, the future double portion of inheritance, could not be transferred to Yaakov. However, if one swears that he will give over that item, then he is obligated to abide by his words (ibid.). Therefore, to assure that Eisav would not retract from the sale, Yaakov made him swear.

There was one unresolved problem with Eisav's sale. Only Eisav was obligated to abide by his oath. Were Eisav to die before

Yitzchak, then Eisav's heirs would not be obligated to fulfill the promise of their father (see ibid.). This explains the distress of Yaakov. If Yaakov would kill Eisav, the much-desired birthright would not be transferred to Yaakov! (*Imrei Shefer*)

... וַיַּחַץ אֶת הָעָם אֲשֶׁר אִתּוֹ וְאֶת הַצֹּאן וְאֶת הַבָּקָר וְהַגְּמַלִּים לִשְׁנֵי מַחֲנוֹת. וַיֹּאמֶר אִם יָבוֹא עֵשָׂו אֶל הַמַּחֲנֶה הָאַחַת וְהִכָּהוּ וְהָיָה הַמַּחֲנֶה הַנִּשְׁאָר לִפְלֵיטָה. (ל״ב:ח,ט)

> *...So he divided the people with him, and the flocks, cattle, and camels, into two camps. For he said, "If Eisav comes to the one camp and strikes it down, then the remaining camp shall survive." (32: 8,9)*

Rashi explains that when Yaakov said that "the remaining camp shall survive" it was said with a tone of certainty, not merely of hope. From where did Yaakov draw this self-confidence? Just as Yaakov was afraid that Eisav would be able to kill him, likewise Eisav could destroy the other camp.

Rivkah had said to Yaakov, "…why should I be bereaved of you both on the same day!" (27:45). Yaakov sensed that this was a burst of prophecy and therefore knew that Eisav would die on the same day as Yaakov (see *Rashi* ibid.). He therefore devised the following strategy. He placed a day's distance between the two camps. Then he proceeded to the first camp ready to face Eisav in battle (see 33:3). He knew that even if he would be killed in battle, Eisav would never reach the second camp alive, since it would take longer than one day to reach it! Thus he was certain they would survive.

[Yaakov's actual words were: "If Eisav comes to "הַמַּחֲנֶה הָאַחַת," which can be translated as meaning "to the distinguished camp," i.e. the camp where Yaakov is found. Only if Eisav would come there first would the other camp be definitely saved.]

(*Chanukas HaTorah, Nachal Kedumim, Maharil Diskin*)

וַיָּקָם בַּלַּיְלָה הוּא וַיִּקַּח אֶת שְׁתֵּי נָשָׁיו וְאֶת שְׁתֵּי שִׁפְחֹתָיו
וְאֶת אַחַד עָשָׂר יְלָדָיו ... (ל"ב:כ"א)

*But he got up that night, and took his two wives,
two handmaids, and his eleven children ... (32:23)*

Rashi, quoting a Midrash (*Bereishis Rabbah* 76:9), asks, "Where was Dinah?" Yaakov had twelve children and the Torah writes that he only took eleven children. How does Rashi [or rather the Midrash] know that Dinah was the missing child? There is no indication in the *pasuk*.

Many reasons are offered why Binyamin was privileged to have the Beis HaMikdash built on his portion of land. One of the reasons given is that Binyamin did not bow to Eisav when Yaakov met with him, since he had not yet been born at the time (see *Megillas Esther, Targum Sheni* 3:3). If so, it can be logically proven that Dinah was the one hidden. If any of her brothers would have not been there and thus not have bowed to Eisav, then he too should have merited to have the Beis HaMikdash on his property! Dinah did not inherit land in Eretz Yisrael; therefore Binyamin was the only tribe which had land and did not bow. (*Gan Raveh*, in name of *Adnei Paz*)

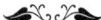

וַיְהִי בַיּוֹם הַשְּׁלִישִׁי בִּהְיוֹתָם כֹּאֲבִים וַיִּקְחוּ שְׁנֵי בְנֵי יַעֲקֹב
שִׁמְעוֹן וְלֵוִי אֲחֵי דִינָה אִישׁ חַרְבּוֹ וַיָּבֹאוּ עַל הָעִיר בֶּטַח וַיַּהַרְגוּ
כָּל זָכָר. וְאֶת חֲמוֹר וְאֶת שְׁכֶם בְּנוֹ הָרְגוּ לְפִי חָרֶב וַיִּקְחוּ
אֶת דִּינָה מִבֵּית שְׁכֶם וַיֵּצֵאוּ. (ל"ד:כ"ה,כ"ו)

*And it came to pass on the third day, when they were in pain,
that two of Yaakov's sons, Shimon and Levi, Dinah's brothers,
each took his sword and they came upon the city confidently,
and killed every male. And Chamor and Shechem his son
they killed at the point of sword. Then they took Dinah
from Shechem's house and left. (34: 25,26)*

After mentioning that the residents of Shechem were killed, the Torah singles out Chamor and his son Shechem as having been killed. This seems superfluous since they too lived in Shechem.

Chamor had proposed to the children of Yaakov that they and the people of Shechem intermarry. He was told that this would only be acceptable if the people of Shechem were circumcised. Chamor and his son Shechem immediately agreed to this and circumcised themselves (34:18-9). They then conveyed the message of the children of Yaakov to their fellow townspeople. The people of Shechem likewise agreed and circumcised themselves. On the third day following **their** circumcision, when the Shechemites were at their weakest, Shimon and Levi attacked them and easily wiped them out without much, if any, resistance. The only exceptions were Chamor and his son who had by then recovered from their own surgery! They put up a strong fight and resisted fiercely until they were killed. That is why the Torah accords them a special mention.

When the Torah mentions the death of Chamor and his son, the Torah uses the phrase "they killed them at the point of **sword**." This is a phrase reserved for indicating killed during battle (see *Devarim* 20:13). This phrase is written only by the death of Chamor and not by the death of the other townspeople, since only Chamor and his son waged a battle against the sons of Yaakov. Furthermore, the Torah mentions the release of Dinah after Chamor and his son were killed. This is most appropriate, since they were the chief, if not only, obstacles to her freedom. (*Maharil Diskin*)

וַיְהִי בְהַקְשֹׁתָהּ בְּלִדְתָּהּ וַתֹּאמֶר לָהּ הַמְיַלֶּדֶת אַל תִּירְאִי כִּי גַם זֶה לָךְ בֵּן. (ל"ה:י"ז)

And it was when she had difficulty in her labor that the midwife said to her, "Have no fear for this one too is a son for you." (35:17)

Rachel was having a difficult and life-threatening labor. The midwife tried to relieve her by telling her that the child was a boy. Under the circumstances, why was that news so comforting?

The Gemara notes that a woman who is not careful in observing the laws of family purity will be punished by dying during childbirth (*Shabbos* 31b). Rachel, realizing her serious condition, feared the worst and was distressed that if she would die in childbirth then people would suspect that it was due to laxity in the observance of the laws of family purity. However, the Midrash (*Pesikta d'Rav Kahana* Chap. 30, Buber ed.) writes that in the merit of observing the laws of family purity properly a woman will be blessed with a boy. Therefore, the news that her child was a boy was heartening since people would not think badly of her! Having a boy was a clear indication that she was righteous.

(*Peninim Yekarim*, in the name of *Kosnos Ohr*)

וַיְהִי בְהַקְשֹׁתָהּ בְּלִדְתָּהּ וַתֹּאמֶר לָהּ הַמְיַלֶּדֶת אַל תִּירְאִי כִּי גַם זֶה לָךְ בֵּן. (ל"ה:י"ז)

And it was when she had difficulty in her labor that the midwife said to her, "Have no fear for this one too is a son for you." (35:17)

From the midwife's words it is apparent that having a girl would have greatly disappointed Rachel. Why? Also, it would seem that there was a reason to suspect that the child was a girl. What prompted Rachel to assume that?

The Midrash (*Bereishis Rabbah* 72:6) writes that the Matriarchs were prophets and knew that Yaakov would father twelve sons from whom the Twelve Tribes would descend. Therefore, Rachel was now anxious that she should have a boy and not a girl, since a girl would not be one of the sacred tribes.

The Gemara states that righteous women are not included in the "curse of Chavah" and do not experience difficulty in giving birth (*Sotah* 12a). It can be assumed that Rachel, being a righteous person, had an easy birth with Yosef. Only now, when she was destined to die in childbirth because of Yaakov's curse (see *Rashi* 31:32), was she undergoing such difficulty. The Gemara writes that giving birth to a girl is a more painful experience than giving birth to a boy (*Niddah* 31a). Since this childbirth was so much more difficult than her first one, Rachel naturally assumed that this time she was giving birth to a girl!

(Vayitzbor Yosef, in the name of *Orach Chaim;* based on *Sforno*)

VAYEISHEV

אֵלֶּה תֹּלְדוֹת יַעֲקֹב יוֹסֵף בֶּן שְׁבַע עֶשְׂרֵה שָׁנָה הָיָה רֹעֶה אֶת אֶחָיו בַּצֹּאן וְהוּא נַעַר אֶת בְּנֵי בִלְהָה וְאֶת בְּנֵי זִלְפָּה נְשֵׁי אָבִיו וַיָּבֵא יוֹסֵף אֶת דִּבָּתָם רָעָה אֶל אֲבִיהֶם. (ל"ז:ב)

> *These are the chronicles of Yaakov: Yosef, at the age of seventeen, was a shepherd with his brothers by the flock, but he was a youth with sons of Bilhah and the sons of Zilpah, his father's wives; and Yosef **would bring** evil reports about them to **their** father (37: 2)*

THREE DIFFICULTIES COME TO MIND WHEN READING THIS PASUK: 1) Of what relevance is it to mention that Yosef would associate with the children of Bilhah and Zilpah, and not with the other brothers?

2) Why does the Torah write that Yosef "**would bring** evil reports" concerning his brothers to his father? The word וַיָּבֵא "told," וַיְסַפֵּר would seem more appropriate than "would bring."

3) Why is it written "to **their** father"? It should say "to **his** father" since they shared a common father.

If one witnesses a person transgressing, he is prohibited from revealing this to another person. Doing so would constitute the sin of *lashon hora*. However, the one who witnessed the act should reproach the sinner. If he wishes to reveal this matter to the parent or teacher of the sinner in order that they should reproach him, there are three conditions that must be met beforehand: a) He must first attempt to rebuke, or be certain that if he rebukes it will be disregarded. b) He should relate the event exactly as it occurred without any exaggeration. c) His intention should be solely for the benefit of the sinner without any expectation of personal gain.

Based upon this, we can explain that the Torah wants to point out that Yosef did not transgress the prohibition of *lashon hora* when he spoke disparagingly about his brothers to his father, and fulfilled all the necessary conditions. First, he would associate with the children of the handmaidens whom the other brothers despised; therefore he was convinced that the children of Leah would not accept his rebuke. Second, he "brought" evil reports about his brothers — implying that he "brought the news as is" without adding anything at all to the story. Third, he brought the news to "their" father; it was as though Yaakov was not his father — he did not intend to become his father's "favorite" by putting down his fellow brothers. (*Afikei Yam*, end of vol. 1)

וַיִּקָּחֻהוּ וַיַּשְׁלִכוּ אֹתוֹ הַבֹּרָה וְהַבּוֹר רֵק אֵין בּוֹ מָיִם. (ל"ז:כ"ד)

Then they took him, and cast him into the pit; the pit was empty, no water was in it. (37: 24)

The Gemara comments that the end of the *pasuk* is superfluous. If the Torah states that the brothers threw him into a pit which was empty, that means that nothing was inside it — not even water. Why does the Torah then mention it explicitly? Therefore, the *pasuk* must be teaching us that water was not inside it — but snakes and scorpions were (*Shabbos* 22a)!

This seems very puzzling. The brothers threw Yosef into a pit because they agreed not to kill him (see *pasuk* 22). If there were snakes and scorpions in the pit he would surely be bitten by them and die! [Ed.- see *Yevamos* 121a]

The *Tosefos Yom Tov* (*Tamid* 1:4) posits that whenever the verb וַיַּשְׁלִכוּ, "thrown," is written in the Torah it means that something was thrown a minimum of twenty *amos* (forty feet). Therefore, since it is written here that they threw him into a pit, it implies that the pit was at least twenty *amos* deep.

The Gemara writes that anything which is twenty *amos* high is not within the sphere of vision of a person; therefore a Chanukah candle which is lit twenty *amos* above the ground is disqualified (*Shabbos* 22a). We can suggest that since the pit was twenty *amos* deep the brothers did not notice the poisonous creatures inside it!

This also explains why these two statements mentioned here are juxtaposed in the aforementioned Gemara; there is a common logic between them.

(*Pardes Yosef*)

וַיֹּאמֶר יְהוּדָה אֶל אֶחָיו מַה בֶּצַע כִּי נַהֲרֹג אֶת אָחִינוּ וְכִסִּינוּ אֶת דָּמוֹ. (ל"ז:כ"ו)

Yehudah said to his brothers, "What gain will there be if we kill our brother and cover up his blood?" (37: 26)

A novel explanation can be offered as to what Yehudah meant with his words of protest. Yehudah reasoned that, if they killed Yosef, their father would eventually through *ruach hakodesh* [Divine inspiration] know that they were the murderers. Although when the initial report would reach Yaakov he would be saddened, and thus unable to receive *ruach hakodesh*, eventually he would forget about Yosef, since those who have passed away are eventually forgotten (*Pesachim*, 54b). When his peace of mind would return, he would regain his *ruach hakodesh* and know that they killed him! It was better that Yosef be sold into slavery, and therefore the sorrow would never leave Yaakov, and thus his *ruach hakodesh* would not return.

Yehudah said to his brothers, "What do we gain if we kill our brother? Will we have covered his blood? I.e. our father will eventually know we did it."

(Nachal Kedumim)

וַיָּקֻמוּ כָל בָּנָיו וְכָל בְּנֹתָיו לְנַחֲמוֹ ... (ל"ז:ל"ה)

All his sons and all his daughters arose to comfort him... (37:35)

One can be sure that many people attempted to console Yaakov. Why does the Torah make special mention of Yaakov's children's attempt to comfort?

The Gemara states that if a person mourns his relative beyond a reasonable amount then he will be punished by having to mourn yet another relative (*Moed Kattan* 27b). This fact caused great concern to Yaakov's children. Due to Yaakov's excessive mourning, one of them will die! Therefore, they, more than anyone else, tried their utmost to console Yaakov. Thus, special mention is made of their efforts.

(*Yalkut HaUrim*, in the name of *She'aris Yaakov*)

וַיֹּאמֶר יְהוּדָה לְתָמָר כַּלָּתוֹ שְׁבִי אַלְמָנָה בֵית אָבִיךְ עַד יִגְדַּל שֵׁלָה בְנִי כִּי אָמַר פֶּן יָמוּת גַּם הוּא כְּאֶחָיו...(ל"ח:י"א)

Then Yehudah said to Tamar, his daughter-in-law, "Remain a widow in your father's house until my son Sheilah grows up" – for he thought, "Lest he also die like his brothers." (38: 11)

Yehudah was concerned that if his son Sheilah would marry Tamar then he too would die. He therefore asked Tamar to wait until Sheilah grew up. What would Yehudah gain by this delay? Why was he not afraid for Sheilah's life were he to marry Tamar once he was an adult?

A woman who was married and widowed twice is legally considered a *katlanis* — someone who "kills" husbands — and one should not marry her (*Kesubos* 43b). However, someone who wishes to perform the mitzvah of *yibum* is permitted to do so since "no evil shall befall one who performs a mitzvah" (*Koheles* 8:5). This permission only applies to an adult who definitely fulfills a mitzvah through this marriage. A child, on the other hand, could eventually be a *soris* — someone who does not physically mature and cannot beget children — and would thus not have fulfilled the mitzvah. He would therefore not be immune from harm. Although it is a minute possibility, in matters of danger we are concerned even with such remote possibilities (see *Chullin* 9b).

This clarifies Yehudah's response. He said that Sheilah should wait until he matures physically and becomes an adult and is definitely not a *soris*. Only then would he surely be eligible to take Tamar in *yibum* and no harm would befall him.

(*Noda BiYehudah, Kamma, E.H*, 10)

וַיְהִי כְּמִשְׁלֹשׁ חֳדָשִׁים וַיֻּגַּד לִיהוּדָה לֵאמֹר זָנְתָה תָּמָר כַּלָּתֶךָ וְגַם הִנֵּה הָרָה לִזְנוּנִים וַיֹּאמֶר יְהוּדָה הוֹצִיאוּהָ וְתִשָּׂרֵף.

And it was when about three months had passed, that Yehudah was told, "Your daughter-in-law has committed harlotry, and moreover, she has conceived by harlotry." (38: 24)

The person who informed Yehudah of Tamar's presumed wrongdoing intended to motivate Yehudah to have Tamar killed. If so, of what importance was it to mention that Tamar was pregnant. She deserved to die for the illicit relations that she had, not for the resulting pregnancy.

Vayeishev / 65

Tamar was a widow; not a married woman If so, why did she deserve to die for what she did? One of the answers given is that she was a *yevamah*. She was bound to the brother of her deceased husbands, and until she was released from this commitment was considered somewhat "married."

If one marries a woman and subsequently discovers that she is an *aylonis* — a woman who never matured physically and who therefore cannot bear children — the marriage is considered as never having taken effect (*Sanhedrin* 69b). Such a woman is not a *yevamah* if her husband dies childless, since he was never legally her husband (see *Yevamos* 2b).

Tamar was married twice and did not have children. It was therefore very possible that Tamar was an *aylonis*. As such, she had never been married and was not now a *yevamah* and did not deserve to die for her sin. Therefore, the informant added that Tamar was pregnant which proves that she was not an *aylonis!*

(*Yalkut HaUrim*, in the name of *Poras Yosef*)

MIKEITZ

וְעַל הִשָּׁנוֹת הַחֲלוֹם אֶל פַּרְעֹה פַּעֲמָיִם כִּי נָכוֹן הַדָּבָר
מֵעִם הָאֱלֹקִים וּמְמַהֵר הָאֱלֹקִים לַעֲשֹׂתוֹ. (מ״א:ל״ב)

*As for the repetition of the dream to Pharaoh – two times –
it is because the matter stands ready before G-d,
and G-d is hastening to accomplish it. (41: 32)*

PHARAOH MENTIONED TO YOSEF THAT THE SAME DREAM APPEARED to him twice in one night. Yosef interpreted that to signify that whatever was being foretold in the dream would occur shortly. How did Yosef know that this was the meaning of the repetition? What's the connection between the two?

The Gemara states that a solar eclipse is a bad omen for idol worshipers. Furthermore, if it occurs in the morning it is an indication that the calamities will soon occur; in the evening, then the disasters will be delayed in coming (*Succah* 29a). Rashi explains that this indication of when it will happen is based on logic. If the sign came early then the event will occur early; if the sign is late then the event is late.

This logic can be applied also to dreams. If a person dreams in the beginning of the night, Hashem is indicating to him that the events portrayed in the dream will soon occur. If he dreams at the end of the night, those events will be slow in coming.

The Gemara lists those dreams which are of a prophetic nature and will be fulfilled. One of those is a dream that occurs in the morning just before the individual wakes up (*Berachos* 55b). The reason for this is that when one goes to sleep his digestive system is hard at work and all those chemicals in his body cause him to dream. In the morning when his body is at rest and nevertheless he has a dream, it is of a prophetic nature.

Yosef's response to Pharaoh can now be understood. Hashem wanted to convey to Pharaoh that the dreams are of a prophetic nature and are **true,** and also that they will **soon** be fulfilled. Therefore, one dream appeared at the beginning of the night to signal that it would occur in the near future. And the very same theme was repeated a second time early in the morning to prove that the dream was an actual communication from Hashem. Yosef said: כִּי נָכוֹן הַדָּבָר, which can be translated as meaning "for the matter is **true and correct.**" And: וּמְמַהֵר הָאֱלֹקִים לַעֲשׂתוֹ — "and Hashem will cause it to happen **soon.**" (*Beis HaLevi*)

וַיַּכֵּר יוֹסֵף אֶת אֶחָיו וְהֵם לֹא הִכִּרֻהוּ. (מ"ב:ח)

*Yosef recognized his brothers,
but they did not recognize him (42:8)*

The Midrash (*Bereishis Rabbah* 91:7) explains that the brothers did not recognize Yosef because when they last saw him he had been a beardless youth and now he had a beard. Nevertheless, it is still difficult to understand why they could not discern it was Yosef from the sound of the voice. The Gemara states that a blind person is permitted to lead a normal life with his wife despite the fact that he cannot see her and ascertain that this actually is his wife (*Gittin* 23a). The basis for this statement is that since the blind person recognizes the voice it is valid identification. If so, why did this method of identification not serve for Yosef's brothers?

This can be answered by suggesting that voice identification is only effective if one is talking in his usual language. If one is speaking in a different language, the listener will not necessarily recognize the voice. The Torah writes (42:23) that Yosef did not speak Hebrew to his brothers but rather spoke Egyptian to a translator who repeated it to them in Hebrew. They were accustomed to Yosef's tone in Hebrew and therefore did not recognize it.

When Yosef subsequently revealed himself to his brothers and wanted to prove to them that he was their brother, he told them that they "see the mouth which is speaking to them" (45:12). The Midrash (*Bereishis Rabbah* 93:10) explains that he was indicating that he was speaking Hebrew. In light of the above, this can be interpreted to mean that he was prodding them to recognize his voice, since now he was speaking Hebrew and therefore his voice should be familiar.

(*Gerer Rebbe* — *R' Avraham Mordechai Alter*,
quoted by *Likutei Yehudah*)

וְאֶת אֲחִיכֶם הַקָּטֹן תָּבִיאוּ אֵלַי וְיֵאָמְנוּ דִבְרֵיכֶם ... (מ׳ב:כ)

*Then bring your youngest brother to me so
your words will be verified...(42:20)*

Yosef instructed his brothers to bring to him Binyamin in order to verify their story. One can ask: How would Yosef know if the person they brought was indeed Binyamin? He did not know him personally, and they could have brought anyone and claim that he is Binyamin.

The answer is simple. Shimon was left behind. Yosef could bring a lineup consisting of the person they would bring along with some strangers and ask Shimon to identify his brother. If it would not be Binyamin, Shimon would not recognize him.

(*R' Yitzchak Zev Soloveitchik*)

... וְאֶת הַכֶּסֶף הַמּוּשָׁב בְּפִי אַמְתְּחֹתֵיכֶם תָּשִׁיבוּ בְיֶדְכֶם ... (מ"ג:י"ב)

...and the money that was returned in the mouth of your sacks return in your hands... (43: 12)

The Rambam writes (*Gezeilah VaAveidah*, 11:3) that an object lost by a Gentile should generally not be returned. If so, how were the brothers permitted to return the found money to Yosef who was assumed at the time to be a Gentile?

The Rambam, after writing the above, adds (ibid.) that if the intention in returning the lost object is to sanctify Hashem's Name, that people should say that Jews are trustworthy people, then it is permitted.

It can be suggested that this was the intention of Yaakov when he commanded his children to return the found money. This also explains why Yaakov instructed them to "return [the money] **in your hands**." Since the purpose of returning it was in order to sanctify Hashem's Name, then if they would carry the money openly in their hands, and would make many people aware of their act, it would be all the more laudable!

(*Chidushei HaGriz*)

... וַיִּשְׁתּוּ וַיִּשְׁכְּרוּ עִמּוֹ.

...they drank and became intoxicated with him. (43:34)

The Gemara states that from the time the brothers sold Yosef the brothers had forsworn drinking wine. This was the first time they allowed themselves to partake of wine (*Shabbos* 139a). The Maharsha (ibid.) explains that what had originally influenced them to make their decision to sell Yosef had been excessive eating and drinking (see Rashi, earlier 37:12); to avoid a recurrence they opted to abstain from wine. Only now, out of fear of Yosef, did they change their custom.

This explanation needs clarification. Nowhere is it mentioned that Yosef ordered them to drink wine! Why should Yosef be upset if they would abstain from wine at his meal?

Rav Moshe Alshich, in his commentary, suggests that Yosef instructed the brothers to bring their younger brother in order to interrogate him and see if the brothers were telling the truth. It is much easier to obtain true information from a youngster than from adults. For this reason they were all invited to a meal by Yosef.

It is well known that under the influence of wine one reveals matters unwittingly. As the Gemara (*Eruvin* 65a) states, "When wine enters the body, the secrets come out!" If so, if the brothers were to refrain from drinking wine in Yosef's presence it would prove that there was information that they wished to prevent from accidentally spilling out. This would prove Yosef right in his accusation against them and would thus endanger their lives. Therefore, they had to drink wine together with Yosef.

(Kehillas Yitzchak, in the name of R' Elyakim Getzel of Dvinsk)

הֵם יָצְאוּ אֶת הָעִיר לֹא הִרְחִיקוּ וְיוֹסֵף אָמַר לַאֲשֶׁר עַל בֵּיתוֹ
קוּם רְדֹף אַחֲרֵי הָאֲנָשִׁים ... (מ׳ד:ד)

They had left the city, had not gone far, when Yosef said to the one in charge of his house, "Get up, chase after the men..." (44: 4)

A person who embarks on a journey between two cities is required to say *tefillas haderech* – a special prayer asking Hashem for Divine protection against the unique hazards of the road. This prayer is to be said after one has already slightly distanced himself from the city (see Orach Chaim 110:7; and commentaries there).

Yosef knew that his brothers would surely recite *tefillas haderech* and would thus be protected from his harassment and libel. He therefore made sure to tell his servants to chase after the brothers before they had gone far ["and had not gone far"], thus being assured that they had not yet recited *tefillas haderech*.

This can explain why Yosef instructed his servants to fill up the sacks of the brothers to overflow capacity (44:1). He wanted the animals of the brothers to be weighed down and thus have to move slowly, so that his servants could catch up to them before they had the legal opportunity to say *tefillas haderech*.

(R' Chaim Vital; last paragraph added by R' Avraham Mordechai Alter – Gerer Rebbe; quoted by Likutei Yehudah)

Vayigash

לְכֻלָּם נָתַן לָאִישׁ חֲלִפוֹת שְׂמָלֹת וּלְבִנְיָמִן נָתַן
שְׁלֹשׁ מֵאוֹת כֶּסֶף וְחָמֵשׁ חֲלִפֹת שְׂמָלֹת. (מ"ה:כ"ב)

> *To each of them he gave changes of clothing; but to Binyamin he gave three hundred pieces of silver and five changes of clothing (45: 22)*

THE WORDS THE TORAH USES FOR "CHANGES OF CLOTHING" ARE חֲלִפוֹת שְׂמָלֹת. When the Torah mentions that Yosef gave the brothers suits, the Torah spells חֲלִפוֹת with a ו — which is the usual spelling of that word. But at the end of the *pasuk*, when mention is made of Binyamin's five suits, the same word is spelled without a ו. What is the reason for this?

The Midrash (*Shemos Rabbah*, 41:6), referring to a different instance, explains that if a word which refers to something plural is spelled without a ו, it comes to teach that all the items are equal and the same.

This idea can be applied here too. The beginning of the *pasuk* refers to the various suits presented to the brothers. In all probability, they wore different sizes of clothing. Therefore, the word חֲלִפוֹת is spelled in the usual fashion. The end of the *pasuk* is referring to the five suits that were all given to Binyamin. They were all the same size! The word חֲלִפֹת is therefore spelled without a "ו" to indicate that. *(R' Chaim Berlin, quoted by Gan Raveh)*

> ... וּלְבִנְיָמִן נָתַן שְׁלֹשׁ מֵאוֹת כֶּסֶף ... (מ"ה:כ"ב)

> ...but to Binyamin he gave
> three hundred pieces of silver...(45: 22)

The Torah relates that Yosef presented only to Binyamin, from all the brothers, three hundred pieces of silver. Upon reading this, two questions immediately come to mind: Why specifically three hundred, and why only to Binyamin.

The Gemara states that whoever sells his slave to a Gentile is fined and must pay ten times the value of the slave (*Gittin* 44a). In the Torah (*Shemos* 21:32) it is written that if one's animal kills another person's slave the owner of the animal pays thirty pieces of silver to the owner of the slave. This indicates that the value of a slave is thirty pieces of silver. Thus, Yosef's brothers, who sold him into slavery, deserved to be fined three hundred pieces of silver.

Yosef intended to hint to his brothers that they were liable to pay three hundred silver coins as a fine for selling him. Giving three hundred silver coins only to Binyamin was a message to his brothers: You, who were involved in selling me, are in effect being fined by not receiving this present.

(Tosefos HaShalem, Chizkuni)

> וְאֶת יְהוּדָה שָׁלַח לְפָנָיו... (מ"ו:כ"ח)

> He sent Yehudah ahead of him... (46: 28)

Rashi quotes a Midrash (*Tanchuma* par.11) which explains that Yaakov sent Yehudah ahead of everyone to establish a yeshivah before their arrival. Why was this necessary? Why couldn't Yehudah go to Egypt together with everyone and upon arrival found a yeshivah?

The Gemara states that it is prohibited to emigrate from Bavel. The reason for this is that Bavel was unique in its abundance of yeshivos and widespread Torah study (*Kesubos* 111a). This implies that one is prohibited from moving from an area with an existing yeshivah to a place that does not have any yeshivah at all.

The Gemara states that wherever the Patriarchs settled they established a yeshivah and studied Torah there (*Yoma,* 28b). It follows then that a yeshivah existed at Yaakov's place of residence. When Yosef sent the message to his father urging him to move to Egypt, Yaakov was unable to fulfill this request. Therefore, he first sent Yehudah there to establish a yeshivah. Once a yeshivah existed in Egypt, Yaakov was permitted to move to Egypt.

(*Darchei Shalom* [extract])

... וַיֵּרָא אֵלָיו... (מ״ו:כ״ט)

...he appeared before him... (46:29)

Rashi quotes a Midrash (*Derech Eretz Zuta* 1:10) which points out that Yaakov did not "fall on Yosef's neck," and did not kiss him. The reason for Yaakov's conduct was that he was reciting *Krias Shema* and did not want to interrupt. This begs an explanation. Why did Yaakov choose to recite *Shema* at that moment?

Furthermore, upon meeting Yosef, Yaakov's first statement was: "After seeing you, I'm prepared to die." Why did Yaakov mar the happiness of the moment by mentioning his own demise?

The Gemara offers advice how one can withstand temptations of sin. First, one should be involved in the study of Torah. If that does not suffice, then one should recite *Krias Shema*. If even that is not adequate, then a person should think about his eventual death (*Berachos* 5a).

Before entering Egypt, the land of vice and temptations, Yaakov was frightened of possible spiritual harm. Therefore, he decided to employ the above methods for protection from sinning. First, he sent Yehudah to establish a yeshivah there. This would assure that he would have the "weapon" of the study of Torah readily available. Then, immediately upon entering Egypt, he recited *Krias Shema*, and mentioned his own eventual death — the other two methods indicated in the Gemara! Yaakov hoped that by doing all this he would remain immune to the immorality and evil of Egypt.

(*Chortkover Rebbe*, cited by in *Ner LeYisrael*)

... וַיֵּרָא אֵלָיו...(מ"ו:כ"ט)

...he appeared before him... (46:29)

Rashi quotes a Midrash (*Derech Eretz Zuta* 1:10) which explains that Yaakov did not kiss Yosef because Yaakov was saying *Krias Shema*. The commentaries express their surprise at this. Why did Yaakov pick this moment to say *Krias Shema*? And if this was the proper time, then why didn't Yosef likewise say *Shema*?

Up until his arrival in Egypt, Yaakov was involved in the performance of a mitzvah. As it says in the [Pesach] Haggadah, Hashem instructed Yaakov to descend into Egypt. Thus Yaakov's journey to Egypt constituted a mitzvah. The Gemara states that whoever is engaged in doing a mitzvah is exempt from performing other mitzvos at that time (*Succah* 25a). Therefore, until this time Yaakov was exempt from reciting *Krias Shema*. Upon entering Egypt, Yaakov had fulfilled this mitzvah and thereupon became obligated to recite the *Shema*, which he promptly did! Yosef, on the other hand, had already recited the *Shema* at its proper time.

(*R' Chaim Soloveitchik*)

וַיֹּאמֶר פַּרְעֹה אֶל יַעֲקֹב כַּמָּה יְמֵי שְׁנֵי חַיֶּיךָ. וַיֹּאמֶר יַעֲקֹב אֶל פַּרְעֹה יְמֵי שְׁנֵי מְגוּרַי שְׁלֹשִׁים וּמְאַת שָׁנָה מְעַט וְרָעִים הָיוּ יְמֵי שְׁנֵי חַיַּי... (מ"ז:ח,ט)

> *Pharaoh said to Yaakov, "How many are the days of the years of your life?" Yaakov answered Pharaoh, "The days of the years of my sojourns have been a hundred and thirty years. Few and bad have been the days of the years of my life..." (47: 8,9)*

Upon meeting Yaakov for the first time, Pharaoh asked his age. This question seems out of place. Yaakov was a distinguished foreign personage, and surely it is inappropriate to immediately ask his age. Also Yaakov's response was puzzling. After stating his age, Yaakov lamented that he had a life filled with hardships. Pharaoh never asked Yaakov about his quality of life. Why then did Yaakov feel it necessary to unburden his woes to a total stranger?

The Gemara writes that as Yaakov stepped foot into Egypt the famine ceased (*Tosefta, Sotah* 10:1-3). This overjoyed Pharaoh. However, when Pharaoh met Yaakov, Pharaoh was stunned and frightened: Yaakov looked old enough to die any day! Perhaps the famine would recur after Yaakov's demise! Unthinking, Pharaoh blurted out what came to his mind: "How old are you?!" Yaakov understood that Pharaoh was not asking his age out of curiosity, but rather out of concern for his own welfare. Therefore, to calm Pharaoh, Yaakov explained that he was not that old; it was the suffering that he had gone through in life that had aged him.

This explanation was given by Rav Aryeh Leib, author of the classic work *Shaagas Aryeh*. When he was 70 years old, he was elected to become the Rav of the Metz community in France. There were murmurs in the community that the new Rav looked very old, and it did not seem that he would last long. Traces of these comments reached Rav Aryeh Leib. In his inauguration speech, the above explanation of the dialogue between Pharaoh and Yaakov was offered. Rav Aryeh Leib then concluded, "The above applies to myself. I have had a difficult life and therefore appear old. I promise you that I shall be with you for many more years!" Rav Aryeh Leib lived for another twenty years, and died at the old age of 90!

(Zichron Yitzchak, MiShulchan Govoha)

VAYECHI

וַיִּקְרְבוּ יְמֵי יִשְׂרָאֵל לָמוּת וַיִּקְרָא לִבְנוֹ לְיוֹסֵף וַיֹּאמֶר
לוֹ אִם נָא מָצָאתִי חֵן בְּעֵינֶיךָ שִׂים נָא יָדְךָ תַּחַת יְרֵכִי
וְעָשִׂיתָ עִמָּדִי חֶסֶד וֶאֱמֶת ... (מ"ז:כ"ט)

The time approached for Yisrael to die, so he called for his son, for Yosef, and said to him, "Please – if I have found favor in your eyes, please place your hand under my thigh and do kindness and truth with me… (47: 29)

Yaakov beseeched Yosef to swear to bury him in Eretz Yisrael. Why did Yaakov request this favor from Yosef? Yaakov, being his father, could have commanded Yosef to bury him in Eretz Yisrael, and Yosef would have been required to obey his father because of the precept of honoring one's parents.

The Gemara states that if one swears and obligates himself to perform a specific mitzvah, then his oath does not take effect (*Shevuos* 27a). Yaakov wanted Yosef to be under oath to take him out of Mitzrayim. Yaakov therefore took care not to command Yosef to perform that act, because this command would have made this a *mitzvah* for Yosef. Instead, he requested it of him. Had it been a mitzvah for Yosef to take Yaakov's remains from Egypt, the oath would not have been valid!

This sheds new light on Yaakov's words. Yaakov said, "Do **kindness** and **truth** with me." Yosef's consent to swear is a **kindness** since Yaakov did not command him to do anything. Once Yosef swore, however, then **truth** dictates that he fulfill his oath.

(*Chidushei Maharil Diskin*)

וַיִּשְׁתַּחוּ יִשְׂרָאֵל עַל רֹאשׁ הַמִּטָּה (מ״ז:ל״א)

...*then Yisrael prostrated himself toward the head of the bed. (47: 31)*

Rashi explains that Yaakov prostrated himself as a gesture of thanks to Hashem that all of his children were righteous — including Yosef who was a king and who had been lost among the Gentiles for so long. It seems that Yaakov was confident that Yosef would always remain virtuous. Why was Yaakov so sure?

Yosef was 30 years old when he met Pharaoh (*Mikeitz* 41:46). Nine years elapsed [seven years of plenty and two years of hunger] until Yaakov arrived in Mitzrayim. Yaakov lived seventeen years in Mitzrayim until his demise. Yosef was then 56 years old. Since Yosef was destined to live one hundred and ten years (see 50:26), at this point Yosef had already passed the midpoint of his life. The Gemara statesm that a person who is righteous most of his life will be protected by Hashem for the rest of his life against sinning (*Yoma* 38b). Therefore, Yaakov was confident that Yosef would continue to lead a sin-free life.

(*Meshech Chochmah*)

> וַאֲנִי בְּבֹאִי מִפַּדָּן מֵתָה עָלַי רָחֵל בְּאֶרֶץ כְּנַעַן בַּדֶּרֶךְ ...
> וָאֶקְבְּרֶהָ שָּׁם ... (מ"ח:ז)

But as for me – when I came from Paddan, Rachel died on me in the land of Canaan on the road ... and I buried her there... (48: 7)

Jewish law dictates (*Yoreh Deah* 363:2) that a person must be buried in the city where he died, and should not be transferred to another location for burial. An exception to this is that a corpse may be taken from *chutz laAretz* to Eretz Yisrael.

Yaakov wanted to subtly explain why he did not bury Rachel in Chevron although he himself was requesting that of Yosef. He therefore mentioned that Rachel died in Eretz Yisrael, and thus had to be buried in the closest city and could not be taken to Chevron. Yaakov, on the other hand, was going to die in Mitzrayim and would be allowed to be transferred to Eretz Yisrael.

(Peh Kadosh)

> וַיֹּאמֶר יוֹסֵף אֶל אָבִיו בָּנַי הֵם אֲשֶׁר נָתַן לִי אֱלֹקִים בָּזֶה ... (מ"ח:ט)

And Yosef said to his father, "They are my sons whom G-d has given me here..." (48: 9)

Rashi, based upon a Midrash (see *Targum Yehonasan*), explains that Yosef showed his marriage contract to his father. What prompted Yosef to do that?

The commentaries point out two seemingly contradictory concepts in the Torah. The Torah writes (*Devarim* 21:21) that a *ben sorer umoreh*, a rebellious and gluttonous son, is given the death penalty. The Gemara explains that although at this point the youth is not deserving of death, the Torah advises to kill him now, since otherwise he will someday become a mortal threat to society (*Sanhedrin* 71b). On the other hand, the Torah relates (*Bereishis* 21:17) that when Yishmael was near death, Hashem spared his life — despite the fact that one day his descendants would murder Jews. The Gemara explains that Hashem only took into account Yishmael's present actions, whereupon he was deserving of life (*Rosh Hashanah* 16b). Why did Hashem only look at the present when judging Yishmael, and yet look to the future when deciding the fate of the *ben sorer umoreh*?

One of the answers offered is that there is a crucial difference between the origin of the *ben sorer umoreh* and that of Yishmael. The Gemara notes that the Torah juxtaposes the law of a Jewish soldier marrying a Gentile prisoner of war with that of a *ben sorer umoreh* to teach that such a son is the natural product of this type of disdainful union (*Sanhedrin* 107a). Although the Torah permits this marriage, it is permitted reluctantly — were it not permitted they would anyway live in sin (*Kiddushin* 21b). Therefore, he is dealt with harshly, and even for a future crime is sentenced to death. Yishmael, on the other hand, was born from a qualified union, and was not held responsible for his future actions.

Rashi (48:8), based on the Midrash, explains that Yaakov refused to bless the children of Yosef since Yaakov perceived that evil people would descend from them. If Yaakov acted towards Yosef's children based on the future, it indicated that Yaakov must have felt that they were born from an unlawful marriage. Therefore, Yosef showed his marriage document to his father to prove that his marriage was legal, and that consequently Yaakov should not take the future into account in dealing with Yosef's children!

(Peninim Yekarim)

וַיֹּאמֶר יִשְׂרָאֵל אֶל יוֹסֵף רְאֹה פָנֶיךָ לֹא פִלָּלְתִּי
וְהִנֵּה הֶרְאָה אֹתִי אֱלֹקִים גַּם אֶת זַרְעֶךָ. (מ"ח:י"א)

Yisrael said to Yosef, "I dared not accept the thought that I would see your face, and here G-d has shown me even your offspring!" (48:11)

The Gemara notes that the spiritual sickness of licentiousness is manifested physically by the onset of the disease *hydroken* which causes the face to turn sallow and have a greenish color (*Yevamos* 60b). This engenders a novel interpretation of Yaakov's words: "I never expected to see your face — your original clear face. I was sure that being lost for so long among the immoral Egyptians would have swayed you to sin and that consequently your face would be green. I am overjoyed now to see your very same face, which is proof that you are unmarred by sin!"

However, one can question Yaakov's assumption of Yosef's righteousness. The Gemara informs us that there is a potion which clears a person's face if it is greenish (*Shabbos* 110a). If so, it is possible that Yosef had sinned, turned green, and immediately prior to Yaakov's arrival restored his skin color with this potion!

The answer to this lies in the aforementioned Gemara. This potion, which removes facial discoloration, also causes sterility. The color change in a person that it produces is only a secondary effect. Yosef, explain the commentaries, had additional children after Yaakov immigrated to Egypt (see *Ramban* 48:15). Therefore, Yaakov was confident that Yosef had not drunk the potion, but, rather, had never sinned at all!

This enhances the explanation offered above. The Torah quotes Yaakov as saying: "I never expected to see your face, yet Hashem showed me also your children." What Yaakov intended with this statement is as follows: "I never expected to see **both together** — your original clear face and your new children! I thought that you would either have a greenish face because of sin, or that you would have drunk that potion to restore your original complexion, but I would not see you produce any more children."

(Chanukas HaTorah, Pnei David)

וַיֹּאמֶר פַּרְעֹה עֲלֵה וּקְבֹר אֶת אָבִיךָ כַּאֲשֶׁר הִשְׁבִּיעֶךָ. (נ:ו)

> And Pharaoh said, "Go up and bury your father as he adjured you." (50: 6)

The Gemara (*Sotah* 36b) reveals details of the dialogue between Yosef and Pharaoh which are not written in the Torah. Yosef informed Pharaoh of his wish to fulfill his promise to his father to bury him in Eretz Yisrael. Pharaoh refused Yosef's request and instructed him to renege on his promise. Yosef responded by saying that if he is coerced into relinquishing the promise made to his father, then he will likewise forgo the promise made to Pharaoh! What was that promise? Although both Pharaoh and Yosef were proficient in many languages, Yosef knew one additional language — Hebrew. When Yosef attempted to teach this to Pharaoh, Pharaoh could not grasp it. Were this to become public knowledge, it would be catastrophic for Pharaoh. Therefore, Pharaoh had forced Yosef to swear to him that he would never reveal this piece of information.

It would seem from a superficial understanding of this Gemara that Yosef was blackmailing Pharaoh. Yet anyone with some knowledge of ancient history would find this inconceivable! Pharaoh was the absolute ruler of Egypt. If someone would threaten him in any manner whatsoever, Pharaoh would surely have him eliminated with a mere flick of the finger!

There is a deeper understanding of what Yosef actually intended to say. There is an inborn feeling that one should honor one's promise at all costs. A person's word is sacred to himself. And if a person ever does break his promise, then this aura of sacredness is broken. Yosef did not threaten Pharaoh; he would not dare.

Rather, he was pointing out an inevitable consequence of not keeping his word to his father. Should he even once not stand by his word, then subconsciously he would not be careful about any of his promises and could inadvertently reveal the secret about which Pharaoh was so concerned. Pharaoh realized that Yosef had a valid argument and therefore allowed Yosef to leave Egypt to bury Yaakov.

(Birkas Peretz)

SHEMOS

וַיִּקְרָא מֶלֶךְ מִצְרַיִם לַמְיַלְּדֹת וַיֹּאמֶר לָהֶן מַדּוּעַ עֲשִׂיתֶן
הַדָּבָר הַזֶּה וַתְּחַיֶּיןָ אֶת הַיְלָדִים. וַתֹּאמַרְןָ הַמְיַלְּדֹת אֶל פַּרְעֹה
כִּי לֹא כַנָּשִׁים הַמִּצְרִיֹּת הָעִבְרִיֹּת... (א:י״ח-י״ט)

> The king of Egypt summoned the midwives and said to them, "Why have you done this thing, that you have kept the boys alive? The midwives said to Pharaoh, "Because the Jewish women are unlike the Egyptian women ..." (1:18-19)

THE GEMARA STATES THAT ONE IS REQUIRED TO OBEY THE LAWS OF the country in which one lives (*Nedarim* 28a). However, if the government discriminates against the Jews and legislates oppressive laws only against Jews, then the Jews are not required to obey (*Rabbeinu Tam*, quoted by *Beis Yosef*, Choshen Mishpat, Chap. 369).

This engenders a new explanation of the dialogue between Pharaoh and the Jewish midwives. Pharaoh asked the midwives why were they disobeying the laws of the land and not killing the newborn Jewish boys. The midwives responded that "the Jewish women are not similar to the Egyptian women" in this decree, i.e. only the Jewish women were being oppressed, and therefore they were not required to obey. Thereupon, Pharaoh passed a decree that all newborn males — Jewish and Egyptian — should be given equal treatment and killed (1:22).

(Shev Shmaatsa, quoted by Peninim Yekarim)

וַיְהִי כִּי יָרְאוּ הַמְיַלְּדֹת אֶת הָאֱלֹהִים וַיַּעַשׂ לָהֶם בָּתִּים.

And it was because the midwives feared Hashem that He made for them houses (1: 21)

The Gemara explains that the houses, which Miriam and Yocheved received as a reward from Hashem, refer to "houses of priesthood and royalty" (Sotah 11b). Aharon, who was a Kohen, and Moshe, who was a Levite, were children of Yocheved, and David Hamelech was a descendant of Miriam.

It is axiomatic that Hashem rewards in a manner of *middah keneged middah*. There is a logical correlation between one's action and one's eventual reward. One therefore wonders: Why did the action of saving the Jewish babies merit specifically that their descendants should be the Kohanim, Levites, and royal family?

Pharaoh decreed that all Jewish male babies should be killed — the females were allowed to live. Even if his decree had been carried out, the Jewish nation would have continued to exist. A child born of a Jewish mother is Jewish even if the father is not (*Yevamos* 45a). Had the lack of Jewish males forced the Jewish girls to marry Egyptian husbands their offspring would nevertheless have been Jewish.

However, had Pharaoh accomplished his goal, the institutions of *Kehunah* and monarchy would have ceased to exist. In order to serve as a Kohen one must be a paternal descendant of the tribe of Levi. In order to be a monarch one must have a distinguished lineage – i.e. both parents must be born Jewish (see *Tosefos, Sotah* 41b). If all Jewish male babies had been killed, there would no longer be paternal descendants of Levi nor, indeed, of any Jewish father.

Yocheved and Miriam disobeyed Pharaoh and did not kill the infant boys. As a restult of their courage there are Kohanim and kings. It is therefore most appropriate, and *middah keneged middah,* that these Kohanim, Levites, and kings descend from their saviors — Yocheved and Miriam.

(R' Yosef Dov Soloveitchik, zt"l [Rosh Yeshivas Brisk])

וַיְצַו פַּרְעֹה לְכָל עַמּוֹ לֵאמֹר כָּל הַבֵּן הַיִּלּוֹד הַיְאֹרָה תַּשְׁלִיכֻהוּ... (א:כ"ב)

Pharaoh commanded his whole nation saying: Every boy who is born should be thrown into the river... (1:22)

Pharaoh commanded every person in his country, including the Egyptians, to throw their newborn boys into the river. The Gemara explains, that on the day of Moshe's birth, Pharaoh's astrologers informed him that on this day the savior of the Jews has been born, but it is not clear whether he is a Jew or an Egyptian. They also added that his downfall would be through water. Therefore, Pharaoh commanded that on that particular day all male newborns should be drowned, Jew and Egyptian alike (*Sotah* 12a).

Reading this interpretation, one wonders why the astrologers could not decipher that Moshe was of Jewish origin.

The Gemara states, "If someone raises an orphan in his home it is as though that person gave birth to that child." The Gemara proves this from Moshe: The Torah (*Divrei Hayamim I* 4:18) once calls him the "son of Basya" [Pharaoh's daughter, who raised him] despite the fact that Yocheved was his biological mother (*Megillah* 13a). Based upon this Gemara, one can say that in a sense Moshe had two mothers –one Jewish and one Egyptian. The astrologers saw these two mothers and were confused.

Therefore, they told Pharaoh that they were not sure whether the child was of Egyptian origin or of Jewish origin.

(*Gur Aryeh*)

... בָּל־הַבֵּן הַיִּלּוֹד הַיְאֹרָה תַּשְׁלִיכֻהוּ... (א:כ״ב)
*...every boy who is born should be thrown **into the river**... (1:22)*

Why did Pharaoh specify that the babies be thrown into a river? Any method of murder would have been as effective.

Egypt was the land of magic. Pharaoh was concerned that the Jews would create "babies" using magic and have these babies "murdered," instead of handing over their actual infants to be killed. There was only one method to prevent this. The Gemara relates that anything created by magic has an inherent fault: It will dissolve in water and return to its original state (*Sanhedrin* 67b). By throwing the infants in water, the Egyptians would be able to discern whether the real babies were being killed. If the infant would dissolve, then it was not the real child; if it would drown, it was the actual infant.

Later in the *parashah* (Chap. 4), Hashem tells Moshe to perform three miracles to prove that he was the true emissary of Hashem: (a) to change his staff into a snake, (b) to cause leprosy on his hand, and (c) to turn water into blood. Hashem added that even if the first two miracles would not be convincing, surely the last one would suffice. Why was the last miracle special? The Egyptians could claim that the first two were created by magic. But the third miracle, which involved water, could not have been done through magic but must have been Hashem's work.

(*Kehillas Yitzchak*, in the name of *R' Bentzion of Shkod*)

וַיִּפֶן כֹּה וָכֹה **וַיַּרְא כִּי אֵין אִישׁ** וַיַּךְ אֶת הַמִּצְרִי וַיִּטְמְנֵהוּ בַּחוֹל. (ב:י"ב)

> *He turned this way and that, **and saw that there was no man**, so he struck down the Egyptian and hid him in the sand (2:12)*

The Midrash (*Yalkut Shimoni, remez* 167), quoted by Rashi, interprets the words "and saw that there was no man" to mean that Moshe saw [with Divine inspiration] that no descendant of this Egyptian would ever convert to Judaism. This Midrash seems puzzling. This Egyptian deserved to die. Of what significance was it if he would have a righteous descendant.

The Midrash (*Shemos Rabbah* 1:30), quoted by Rashi later on, points out that Moshe killed the Egyptian by uttering Hashem's Name. This too needs an explanation. Why did Moshe kill the Egyptian through this unorthodox method?

The Rambam (*Melachim* 10:6) posits that a Gentile who hits a Jew and wounds him deserves to die. However only Hashem can kill him; a *beis din* does not have that legal right. This law answers all our questions. The Egyptian who beat the Jew deserved to die. But Moshe was not permitted to kill him. Only by invoking Hashem's Name — by means of which Hashem is doing the killing — could Moshe eliminate the Egyptian. However, since it was considered a death by the Hand of Hashem, Moshe had to take many factors in consideration, just as Hashem does before punishing. One of those factors was whether among his descendants there would be a proselyte.

(*Chidushei HaGriz*, stencil)

... שַׁל נְעָלֶיךָ מֵעַל רַגְלֶיךָ כִּי הַמָּקוֹם אֲשֶׁר אַתָּה עוֹמֵד עָלָיו אַדְמַת קֹדֶשׁ הוּא. (ג:ה)

> ... *"Remove your shoes from your feet, since the place upon which you are standing is holy ground." (3:5)*

It is dangerous to walk barefoot in the desert, since there are poisonous snakes crawling around (see *Devarim* 8:15). Therefore, Moshe might have been apprehensive about removing his shoes. However, the Mishnah records (*Avos* 5:5) no one was ever bitten by a snake in Yerushalayim. Rav Ovadiah MiBartenura explains that this was due to the great holiness of the place.

This explains what Hashem said to Moshe. "Remove your shoes from your feet, [and don't be concerned about snakes] since the place upon which you are standing is holy ground [and therefore snakes will not harm you]."

(*Gan Raveh*, in name of *Eidus BiHosef*)

VA'EIRA

וַיֵּהָפְכוּ כָל הַמַּיִם אֲשֶׁר בַּיְאֹר לְדָם...
וַיַּעֲשׂוּ כֵן חַרְטֻמֵּי מִצְרַיִם בְּלָטֵיהֶם... (ז:כ,כ"ב)

...and all the river's water was transformed into blood ... And the Egyptian sorcerers did likewise with their magic... (7: 20, 22)

IBN EZRA WONDERS WHERE THE EGYPTIAN SORCERERS OBTAINED water to perform their magic: All of their water had been transformed to blood. Furthermore, it is incomprehensible how they were able to affect the water. The Gemara explains that anything created by magic will revert back to its original state upon coming in contact with water (*Sanhedrin* 67b). Surely then it is impossible to change water into something else.

The following suggestion can answer the questions. Moshe actually turned all the water into blood. The Egyptian sorcerers took some blood and made it appear as water through their magic. They then presented that liquid, claiming it was water, and reverted it back to its state of blood!

(*Shir Maon*)

... וּמָלְאוּ בָּתֵּי מִצְרַיִם אֶת הֶעָרֹב וְגַם הָאֲדָמָה אֲשֶׁר הֵם עָלֶיהָ (ח:י״ז)

> ... the homes of the Egyptians will be filled with the mixture of animals, **and also the earth upon which they are.** (8:17)

The end of this *pasuk* — "and also the earth upon which they are" — is obscure and needs an explanation.

The Mishnah (*Klayim* 8:5) refers to an animal called *adnei hasadeh*. According to some commentaries (see *Rashi* ibid.), this is the *yidoa* who is part animal and part plant. It has humanlike features and is connected to the ground with an "umbilical cord." If the umbilical cord is severed, the animal dies.

The Torah writes that the plague of *arov* comprised all the wild animals. But how could Hashem have sent the *yidoa* if sending him to Egypt would cause him to die? Therefore, Hashem sent the *yidoa* still attached to the ground, together with that clump of earth! This is the explanation of the phrase "and also the earth upon which they are"! (*R' Shimshon* of *Ostropoli*, quoted by *Kehillas Moshe*)

... וּמָלְאוּ בָּתֵּי מִצְרַיִם אֶת הֶעָרֹב וְגַם הָאֲדָמָה אֲשֶׁר הֵם עָלֶיהָ (ח:י״ז)

> ... the homes of the Egyptians will be filled with the mixture of animals, **and also the earth upon which they are.** (8:17)

The end of this pasuk — "and also the earth upon which they are" — is obscure and needs an explanation.

The Gemara explains a psychological fact regarding animals. If an animal is not in its natural habitat, it will not be as bold and aggressive as usual (*Eruvin* 61a). Thus the wild animals which Hashem sent from other countries would not be as dangerous as usual. Therefore, Hashem sent the animals along with earth from their places of origin. The animals smelled their familiar earth and had the courage to be ferocious. This is what is meant by "and also the earth upon which they are." (*Nachalas Yaakov*)

הִנֵּה יַד ה' הוֹיָה בְּמִקְנְךָ אֲשֶׁר בַּשָּׂדֶה בַּסּוּסִים בַּחֲמֹרִים
בַּגְּמַלִּים בַּבָּקָר וּבַצֹּאן דֶּבֶר כָּבֵד מְאֹד. (ט:ג)

*The hand of Hashem will be in your livestock in the field;
in the horses, in the donkeys, in the camels, in the cattle,
in the sheep; a very harsh plague. (9:3)*

The Mishnah (*Bechoros* 28b) mentions that Egypt bred expensive hogs that were of superior quality. The Torah does not mention that these pigs will be affected by the plague. Why were the pigs spared?

The Gemara explains that when there is a plague among pigs then a public fast is declared. The reason for this is since the intestines of pigs are similar to those of humans, it is easy for the plague to spread to humans *(Taanis* 10a*)*.

Hashem did not wish to cause a plague among the Egyptians themselves; only their animals. If the plague had affected the pigs it would most likely have spread to the people. Therefore, the pigs were not affected by the plague.

(*Chamudei Yitzchak*, quoted by *Talelei Oros*)

וַיַּעַשׂ ה' אֶת הַדָּבָר הַזֶּה מִמָּחֳרָת וַיָּמָת כֹּל מִקְנֵה מִצְרָיִם
וּמִמִּקְנֵה בְנֵי יִשְׂרָאֵל לֹא־מֵת אֶחָד. וַיִּשְׁלַח פַּרְעֹה וְהִנֵּה
לֹא מֵת מִמִּקְנֵה יִשְׂרָאֵל עַד אֶחָד... (ט:ו,ז)

*On the next day, Hashem did this, and all the livestock in
Egypt died. Of the Jews' livestock not a single one died.
Pharaoh sent word and discovered that among the Jews'
livestock not a single one had died. ... (9:6,7)*

In *pasuk* 6, the Torah states that none of the cattle owned by Jews died in the plague. In the following *pasuk* (7), the Torah mentions that Pharaoh's investigators confirmed this. There are however discrepancies between them. When mentioning the actual fact the Torah writes: And when mentioning what Pharaoh's informants determined, the Torah writes: וּמִמִּקְנֵה בְנֵי יִשְׂרָאֵל לֹא מֵת אֶחָד

These two discrepancies [בְנֵי־יִשְׂרָאֵל vs. יִשְׂרָאֵל, and אֶחָד vs. עַד אֶחָד] need an explanation.

When the Jews were in Egypt, an individual [the son of the Egyptian killed by Moshe] whose father was an Egyptian and whose mother was a Jewess resided among them. Some scholars are of the opinion that this person was legally considered a Gentile (see *Ramban, Vayikra* 24:10). To an observer, he seemed to be a Jew since he was raised among the Jews, and dressed and behaved like them.

Hashem declared that the livestock of the Jews would not die during the plague. Pharaoh sent inspectors to check if Hashem's prediction was upheld. They found that all the livestock of the Jews had been saved — except for the ones belonging to the son of that Egyptian. Assuming that he was Jewish, they reported to Pharaoh that one Jew's cattle had indeed died. That is why they said *ad echad*, which translates "until one," i.e. one's cattle had died.

This also explains the other discrepancy. "*Bnei Yisrael*" refers to those who are actually Jews. The Torah mentions that from the *bnei Yisrael* no one's cattle perished. Only from *Yisrael*, those who appear to be Jews, did one person lose his livestock.

(*Pardes Yosef*, in name of *Shemen HaMor*)

וַיֹּאמֶר אֵלָיו מֹשֶׁה כְּצֵאתִי אֶת הָעִיר אֶפְרֹשׂ אֶת כַּפַּי אֶל ה'... (ט:כ"ט)

Moshe said to him, "When I leave the city I will spread out my hands [in prayer] to Hashem... (9:29)

The Midrash (*Mechilta, Bo,* par.1), quoted by Rashi, explains that Moshe did not want to pray within the city since it contained many idols. Therefore, Moshe told Pharaoh that he would pray for him after leaving the city. Since the Torah only mentions this here, it implies that Moshe left the city before praying only at this plague. The obvious question is: Why didn't Moshe leave the city by the other plagues? Wasn't the city filled with idols even then?

What were the idols of Egypt? Rashi points out that the Egyptians worshiped their sheep (*Bereishis* 46:34). This clarifies the matter. At the time of the other plagues, the sheep grazed in the fields outside of the city. Therefore, Moshe had to pray in the city. However, before the plague of *barad* all those who heeded Moshe's advice and feared Hashem brought their sheep into their houses, which were in the city (9:20). Therefore, Moshe could no longer pray in the city. Any sheep that had remained out of doors were killed in the plague (9:25). Thus Moshe could freely pray outside the city.

(Chanukas HaTorah)

Bo

... הִנְנִי מֵבִיא מָחָר אַרְבֶּה בִּגְבֻלֶךָ וְכִסָּה אֶת עֵין הָאָרֶץ וְלֹא יוּכַל לִרְאֹת אֶת־הָאָרֶץ ... (י:ד-ה)

*...tomorrow I will bring a plague of locust to your territories. It will cover the ground, **and will not be able to see the ground** ... (10:4-5)*

RASHI EXPLAINS THAT THE PHRASE "AND WILL NOT BE ABLE TO SEE the ground" refers to the people. This is awkward since the subject of the sentence is the locust; the Torah should have written "and the people will not be able...". Furthermore, this is a trivial effect of the plague, and should have been placed at the end of the list of damages caused by the locusts. Finally, later on (*pasuk* 15) it is written "and the earth became dark and it ate all the grass." This implies that because it was dark the locust ate everything. What is the connection between the two?

The Gemara explains that a person only becomes satiated from food if he can see the food he is eating. Therefore, blind people are always hungry (*Yoma* 74b). This explains everything. The Torah is saying that there will be so many locusts that they will block out the sun and will not be able to see the food which they are eating from the ground. If so, they will never feel full, and will eat all the existing vegetation! The darkening of the sun is an important aspect of the plague and is therefore mentioned first. Also, it is because of the darkness that the locusts consumed everything.

(*Kli Yakar, Maharil Diskin*)

וַיִּשָּׂא הָעָם אֶת בְּצֵקוֹ טֶרֶם יֶחְמָץ מִשְׁאֲרֹתָם צְרֻרֹת בְּשִׂמְלֹתָם עַל שִׁכְמָם. (י״ב:ל״ד)

The people took their dough before it could rise. Their leftover dough was wrapped in their robes and placed on their shoulders. (12:34)

The Midrash (*Mechilta*) points out that the Jews had many animals, and therefore questions why their food was not carried by their animals.

One is permitted to carry on Yom Tov only something which is useful on Yom Tov (*Tosefos*, Beitzah 12a). In case of monetary loss, one may prior to Yom Tov place baggage on his animal to be carried on Yom Tov, even if it is prohibited for a Jew to carry it (*Shabbos* 153a).

The Jews departed from Egypt on the Yom Tov of Pesach. They were prohibited to carry their silver and gold, for which they had no use on Yom Tov, but were permitted to carry their food. Therefore, they carried their food themselves, and had the animals carry the silver and gold which they themselves were prohibited to carry.

(*Panim Yafos*)

וּבְנֵי יִשְׂרָאֵל עָשׂוּ כִּדְבַר מֹשֶׁה וַיִּשְׁאֲלוּ מִמִּצְרַיִם כְּלֵי כֶסֶף
וּכְלֵי זָהָב וּשְׂמָלֹת (י"ב:ל"ה)

The Jews did as Moshe had said. They borrowed from the Egyptians silver and gold vessels, and garments. (12:35)

The Gemara states that the Egyptian valuables were granted to the Jews in payment for the debt which the Egyptians owed to the Jews for all the work which they had performed for them (*Sanhedrin* 91a).

According to Jewish law (*Choshen Mishpat* 91:28), a creditor is prohibited from collecting the belongings of a debtor's wife. Why did Hashem grant the Jews the garments of the Egyptian women (see here, and earlier 3:22)?

The *poskim* point out (ibid. *Sma*) that a creditor may collect very expensive clothing from a debtor's spouse — especially those bedecked with jewels.

The word שִׂמְלָה refers to an expensive garment (see *Yeshayahu*, 3:6). In fact, Rashi notes that since the Torah lists the שִׂמְלֹת after the silver and gold vessels it indicates that the garments were the most precious of the group. This answers our question. Since the dresses were expensive, Hashem granted them to the creditors of the Egyptians — the Jews.   (*Maharil Diskin*)

וּמוֹשַׁב בְּנֵי יִשְׂרָאֵל אֲשֶׁר יָשְׁבוּ בְּמִצְרַיִם שְׁלֹשִׁים שָׁנָה
וְאַרְבַּע מֵאוֹת שָׁנָה. (י"ב:מ)

The Jews resided in Egypt four hundred and thirty years. (12:40)

All the commentaries strive to explain how Hashem's prophecy to Avraham that the Jews would be in Egypt for four hundred and thirty years was fulfilled, considering that the Jews were in Egypt for only two hundred and ten years.

The Midrash (*Shemos Rabbah* 18:7) records that the Egyptians coerced the Jews into working days and nights. Generally slaves work only by day (*Kiddushin* 15a). If one takes into account all the nights that the Jews worked in addition to the days, Hashem calculated that this equaled the full term of work. (*Chanukas HaTorah* [extract])

בְּבַיִת אֶחָד יֵאָכֵל לֹא תוֹצִיא מִן הַבַּיִת מִן הַבָּשָׂר חוּצָה וְעֶצֶם לֹא תִשְׁבְּרוּ בוֹ. (י"ב:מ"ו)

In one house shall it be eaten, you should not take any meat outside, and you should not break any of its bones. (12:46)

The prohibition of removing the meat of a *korban pesach* from a house is written in singular form [לֹא תוֹצִיא]. However, the prohibition of breaking any of its bones is written in plural form [לֹא תִשְׁבְּרוּ]. Why did the Torah differentiate between the two?

Rambam (*Korban Pesach* 9:1) posits that the prohibition of *lo sotzi* cannot be performed twice on the same piece of meat. Once the meat leaves the house it is disqualified and no further act effects its unfitness. But if a person repeatedly breaks a bone of the *korban pesach* he is committing an additional transgression with every break (ibid. 10:4).

Since, pertaining to a specific piece of meat, only one person can transgress the prohibition of the removal of meat, the Torah expressed the prohibition in singular form. However, if many individuals break a bone, one after the other, they are all transgressing. Therefore, the Torah wrote that prohibition in plural form.

(*Toldos Adam*)

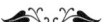

בְּבַיִת אֶחָד יֵאָכֵל לֹא תוֹצִיא מִן הַבַּיִת מִן הַבָּשָׂר חוּצָה וְעֶצֶם לֹא תִשְׁבְּרוּ בוֹ. (י"ב:מ"ו)

> *In one house shall it be eaten, you should not take any meat outside, and you should not break any of its bones. (12:46)*

The prohibition of removing the meat of a *korbon pesach* from a house is written in singular form [לֹא תוֹצִיא]. However, the prohibition of breaking any of its bones is written in plural form [לֹא תִשְׁבְּרוּ]. Why did the Torah differentiate between the two?

The Gemara states that if on Shabbos two people together perform a prohibited act which can easily be done by only one person, then they are exempt from punishment according to Torah law (*Shabbos* 92b). This applies solely to the laws of Shabbos; in all other areas of Jewish law they would still be liable as transgressors.

The Gemara derives from the laws of Shabbos certain aspects of the laws of removing the meat of a *korban pesach* from a house (*Pesachim* 85b). It can therefore be suggested that also in this respect they are similar: If two people together remove the meat, they are exempt from punishment.

This explains the discrepancy in the *pasuk*. The prohibition of the removal of the meat was written in singular form since if two people do it together they are exempt. However, if two people break the bone they would both be punished; therefore, that prohibition was written in plural form.

(*Pardes Yosef,* in the name of *Ben Poras*)

BESHALACH

וַיְהִי בְּשַׁלַּח פַּרְעֹה אֶת הָעָם... (י"ג:י"ז)

It was when Pharaoh sent the nation... (13:17)

THE MIDRASH (SHOCHAR TOV, 113) RELATES THAT MOSHE TOLD Pharaoh that the Jews would not leave Egypt until Pharaoh legally released them from their servitude. This seems strange. There was nothing preventing the Jews from leaving Egypt. Why did Moshe choose to wait for Pharaoh's permission?

The Torah (*Devarim* 15:14) instructs a slaveowner to provide generously for his slave upon granting him his freedom. This was to be severance pay for his work. The Midrash (*Sifri, parashas Re'eh*) explains that this principle was the basis whereby the Jews took money from the Egyptians when they left Egypt: It was severance pay for their work as slaves. The Gemara states that if a slave runs away from his master he forfeits his rights to severance pay (*Kiddushin* 16b). This explains Moshe's behavior. For the Jews to have a right to collect the Egyptians' money, they had to leave with permission.

(*Parashas Derachim*)

> ... כִּי אֲשֶׁר רְאִיתֶם אֶת מִצְרַיִם הַיּוֹם לֹא תֹסִפוּ לִרְאֹתָם
> עוֹד עַד עוֹלָם. (י״ד:י״ג)
>
> ...that you saw the Egyptians is only today; you will not
> see them anymore forever. (14:13)

Rav Baruch Epstein, author of the classic *Torah Temimah*, wrote the following personal anecdote:

"Several decades ago, I spent the Shabbos of *parshas Beshalach* in the home of my uncle, the renown *Gaon*, Rav Naftali Berlin, known by the acronym "the Netziv". After Shabbos, I was sitting around the table with my uncle and other great scholars, when a townsman presented the following halachic question:

"More than twelve years ago, I had a bitter dispute with my business partner of many years, and swore in anger that I would never look at his face again. From that day on, I never put my eyes on him. Today that person died, and I want to look him in the face and ask for forgiveness. Is it permitted or not?'

"There was considerable discussion among the scholars, each one trying to bring proof to his view from the Talmud. When my turn came, I expressed amazement at the entire discussion that 'Why,' I exclaimed, 'only a few hours ago, we read the solution to this problem in the weekly Torah-reading." Everyone turned to me with a look of surprise. I then pointed out that initially Hashem promised the Jews that they would never again see the Egyptians. Yet later in this very same *parashah* (14:30) it is written that the Jews saw the Egyptians dead on the seashore. Thus we can infer that seeing a dead person is not considered 'seeing'! And furthermore, the Midrash (*Yalkut Shimoni, remez* 239) writes that the Jews recognized their former masters. This implies that they actually gazed at the Egyptians. Based upon this proof, the Netziv permitted the man to look at the face of the dead person."

(Tosefos Berachah)

וַיָּבֹאוּ בְנֵי יִשְׂרָאֵל בְּתוֹךְ הַיָּם בַּיַּבָּשָׁה וְהַמַּיִם לָהֶם חוֹמָה מִימִינָם וּמִשְּׂמֹאלָם. (י״ד:כ״ב)

The Jews entered into the sea, on the dry area; and the water was as a wall for them, on their right, and on their left. (14:22)

The Torah records in *pasuk* 22 that the Jews entered the dry area of the sea, and that the water was transformed into a wall. Surprisingly, the Torah seems to repeat the very same sentence in *pasuk* 29. However, there are two discrepancies. In the first *pasuk*, it is written "into the sea, on the dry area." The second time it says, "on the dry area, into the sea." Also, the first time the word חוֹמָה is spelled with a ו; the second time without one.

The Midrash (*Shemos Rabbah* 21:7) relates that at the moment of the splitting of the sea there were angels who protested the rescue of the Jews. They questioned why the Jews merited to be saved over the Egyptians. This fact is reflected in the *pasuk*. The word חמה is spelled without a ו, thus allowing it to be interpreted also as meaning anger (*Mechilta d'Rashbi*). Hashem responded to those angels and explained that the Jews deserved to be rescued in the merit of their trust and faith in Hashem.

One can suggest that there were two types of people among the Jews. There were those, such as the members of the tribe of Yehudah (see *Sotah* 37a), who jumped into the sea, trusting in Hashem that they would be saved. Others waited until the sea had dried. Therefore the Torah twice mentions the entry of the Jews into the sea, each time referring to a different group. The group that trusted in Hashem and entered the sea even before it split, is described by the Torah as going "into the sea, on the dry area," i.e. it became dry upon their entry. The other group waited until the sea was dry before they entered. Therefore the Torah writes concerning them that they went "on the dry area, into the sea." Also, only by the second group does the Torah write חמה without a ו , which means anger. The first group trusted in Hashem, and therefore deserved to be saved in the merit of their trust. The second group had an unanswered accusation against them: Why do they deserve to be saved more than the Egyptians.

(*Kol Eliyahu*)

... וַיַּרְא יִשְׂרָאֵל אֶת מִצְרַיִם מֵת עַל שְׂפַת הַיָּם. (י"ד:ל)

...the Jews saw the Egyptians lying dead on the seashore.(14:30)

The usual translation of the word "*mes*" is "dead". *Targum Yonasan*, however, explains this *pasuk* to mean that the Jews saw the Egyptians dying on the seashore. Mes is not commonly used in the present tense. Why did *Targum Yonasan* feel that this *pasuk* is one of those rare instances?

The Midrash (*Yalkut Shimoni, remez* 239) writes that Hashem caused the Egyptians to be washed ashore, in order that the Jews should not think that, just as they had come through on dry land, the Egyptians, too, were miraculously saved and had crossed to a different shore. Every Jew saw his former master dead on the shore and thus knew that the Egyptians had not been saved.

The Gemara writes that although water preserves a corpse, after the body is removed from the water it quickly becomes disfigured and cannot be legally identified (*Yevamos* 121a). It had to take several days for all the Jews to recognize their masters. In order that the bodies should still be identifiable to the Jews, Hashem caused the Egyptians to be alive when they were washed ashore, and they would die only a short while before being sighted by their former Jewish slaves.

(*Chidushei Maharil Diskin*)

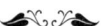

... בֵּין הָעַרְבַּיִם תֹּאכְלוּ בָשָׂר ... (ט״ז:י״ב)

...in the afternoon you shall eat meat... (16:12)

The Gemara states that when one vows not to eat meat he is still permitted to eat fowl (*Nedarim*, 54b). The reason for this is that since in vernacular speech people do not always use the two interchangeably, regarding the laws of vows, fowl is not considered meat. It is therefore difficult, why here, when Hashem intended to grant the Jews fowl [*slav*], He said that He will send them meat.

The Gemara (ibid.) reveals that it is unhealthy to consume fowl, but not animal meat, after one undergoes bloodletting. We can suggest that since meat and fowl differ with regard to this quality, therefore people do not interchange the two terms.

The Gemara states that the Jews did not perform circumcisions the forty years that they were in the desert, since the North Wind which is instrumental in healing wounds did not blow those years. From when did the wind stop blowing? One reason offered why the North Wind did not blow was in order not to disperse the Clouds of Glory that accompanied the Jews. These clouds appeared immediately upon the exodus of the Jews from Egypt (*Yevamos* 72a). It follows that the wind stopped blowing then too. Thus, when the Jews were informed of the arrival of the *slav*, they had already ceased bloodletting, since it was dangerous to let blood without the benefits of the North Wind.

It was suggested that since meat and fowl differ with respect to their being able to be eaten after bloodletting, fowl is not called meat. However, since in the desert there was no bloodletting done, in that era fowl was likewise designated as meat.

(*Toras Moshe*)

וַיֹּאמֶר ה' אֶל מֹשֶׁה כְּתֹב זֹאת זִכָּרוֹן בַּסֵּפֶר וְשִׂים בְּאָזְנֵי יְהוֹשֻׁעַ כִּי־מָחֹה אֶמְחֶה אֶת זֵכֶר עֲמָלֵק מִתַּחַת הַשָּׁמָיִם. (י"ז:י"ד)

> Hashem said to Moshe, "Write this as a reminder in the book **and place it in the ears of Yehoshua**, that I will obliterate the remembrance of Amalek from under the heaven." (17:14)

Hashem instructed Moshe to record in the Torah the obligation to obliterate the mention of Amalek. Moshe was also commanded to personally relay this obligation to Yehoshua. Yehoshua was able to see for himself this mitzvah in the Torah; what was the purpose of having it conveyed orally to Yehoshua?

The Gemara relates that David *HaMelech* sent his general, Yoav, to annihilate Amalek. Yoav killed only the males of Amalek. David confronted Yoav, and asked him why he did not fulfill the commandment of destroying every *zecher* [mention] of Amalek, which would include even the women. Yoav responded that his teacher had taught him that the requirement is to kill every *zachar* [male] of Amalek (*Bava Basra*, 21a).

The Torah is written without vowels. The word "זכר" can be properly read as *zecher* meaning "mention," but can also be erroneously read as *zachar* meaning "male," as Yoav's teacher had mistakenly done. To insure that Yehoshua would not err, Moshe was directed to orally tell Yehoshua to blot out any *zecher* of Amalek.

(*R' Chaim* of *Volozhin*, quoted by *Saaros Eliyahu*)

YISRO

וַיִּשְׁמַע יִתְרוֹ כֹהֵן מִדְיָן חֹתֵן מֹשֶׁה אֵת כָּל אֲשֶׁר עָשָׂה אֱלֹהִים לְמֹשֶׁה וּלְיִשְׂרָאֵל עַמּוֹ... (י"ח:א)

Yisro, the leader of Midian and the father-in-law of Moshe, heard about all that Hashem did for Moshe and the Jews his people... (18:1)

A QUESTION THAT CAN BE ASKED IS: WHY WAS IT NECESSARY TO mention that Yisro was the leader of Midian (see *Targum Onkelos*)?

The Gemara writes that in the era of David *HaMelech* and Shlomo *HaMelech* no Gentiles were accepted for conversion. In that era the Jews were at the apex of glory and success, and it was assumed that a Gentile would not sincerely convert but rather do so to participate in the success of the Jewish people (*Yevamos* 24b).

This being so, another question can be raised. Why did the Jews accept Yisro as a convert after the phenomenal success and glory which existed after the exodus from Egypt?

A similar question is raised: Shlomo *HaMelech* married the daughter of the king of Egypt after she converted. The Gemara asks: Why was this woman accepted as a convert considering the prohibition of accepting converts in that time? The Gemara replies that the reason for the prohibition did not apply to her. Ordinarily it was assumed one converted then for the sake of the glory. The daughter of the king of Egypt possessed all that glory beforehand; her conversion was assumed to be sincere (*Yevamos* 76a).

This explanation applies to Yisro as well. Yisro was the leader of Midian; he had no need for prestige and honor. Therefore his request to convert was sincere and he was accepted. The Torah points this out by prefacing the episode of Yisro's visit with the mention of his leadership. (*Aperion*)

וַיִּשְׁמַע יִתְרוֹ כֹהֵן מִדְיָן חֹתֵן מֹשֶׁה אֵת כָּל אֲשֶׁר עָשָׂה אֱלֹקִים לְמֹשֶׁה וּלְיִשְׂרָאֵל עַמּוֹ כִּי הוֹצִיא יְהוָה אֶת יִשְׂרָאֵל מִמִּצְרָיִם. (י"ח:א)

Yisro, the priest of Midian and the father-in-law of Moshe, heard about all that Hashem did for Moshe and the Jews his people; and that Hashem took the Jews out of Egypt. (18:1)

There are discrepancies between the first half of the *pasuk* and the second that require an explanation. In the first half, Hashem is referred to as *Elokim*, which always refers to Hashem acting in his role of strict justice (*middas hadin*); the second half has the word *Ado-noi*, which refers to Hashem when acting in a manner of mercy (*middas harachamim*). Also, in the first half it refers to the miracles which occurred to Moshe and the Jews; the second half only mentions the Jews.

This can be understood by suggesting that the two halves of the *pasuk* refer to different miracles. The beginning of the *pasuk* refers to the miracles of the war against Amalek and of the crossing of the Dead Sea; the second half refers to the actual exodus from Egypt.

The danger of the war against Amalek, and the danger at sea, also faced the tribe of Levi. In the combined merit of the tribe of Levi together with the merits of the other tribes, the Jewish people warranted to be saved. Therefore, Hashem's Name is written in a manner that indicates that even without mercy the Jews deserved to be saved. The Torah refers to the danger as having faced **Moshe** and the Jews — "**Moshe**" referring not only to himself personally, but rather to the whole tribe of Levi.

The actual exodus from Egypt did not benefit the tribe of Levi since they were not enslaved in Egypt. Only the rest of the Jewish nation benefited. Their merit alone did not entitle them to be rescued. It was only Hashem using his mercy (*middas harachamim*) which enabled them to leave. Therefore Hashem's Name of mercy is used. Also, since the miracles did not pertain to the tribe of Levi, the Torah omits mentioning "Moshe".

(*R' Yisrael Salanter*, quoted by *Ta'am VeDaas*.)

וַיִּשְׁמַע יִתְרוֹ כֹהֵן מִדְיָן חֹתֵן מֹשֶׁה אֵת כָּל אֲשֶׁר עָשָׂה אֱלֹקִים
לְמֹשֶׁה וּלְיִשְׂרָאֵל עַמּוֹ ... וַיִּקַּח ... אֶת צִפֹּרָה
אֵשֶׁת מֹשֶׁה אַחַר שִׁלּוּחֶיהָ (י״ח:א-ב)

Yisro heard all that Hashem did to Moshe and to his nation the Jews...And he took... Tzipporah, the wife of Moshe, after she had been sent away. (18:1-2)

Rashi explains that when the *pasuk* states that Yisro heard "all that Hashem did to Moshe," it refers to the miracles that Hashem did for the Jews, which include Moshe. This explanation is difficult to accept, since the word used for Hashem in this instance is *Elokim*, and the Name *Elokim* is used only when describing Hashem acting in a strict manner.

The Torah adds the phrase "after she had been sent away." The Midrash (*Mechilta*) explains that this refers to an incident which happened when Moshe met with Aharon upon going down to Egypt, and was advised by Aharon to send his wife back to Midian, and not to bring her with him to Egypt. The meeting of Moshe and Aharon is mentioned in *parashas Shemos*; why is this incident not mentioned there instead of here?

To answer these questions, three facts must be kept in mind. First, the Gemara writes that the original intention was for Moshe to be a Kohen. After a certain incident, Hashem became angry with Moshe and took away the right of *Kehunah*, and designated him a Levi (*Zevachim* 102a). Second, there is an opinion (*Rebbi Yehoshua*, mentioned in the *Mechilta*) that Moshe divorced Tzipporah prior to sending her home. Third, a Kohen is prohibited from marrying a divorced woman, even if she is his former wife (*Vayikra* 21:7).

Based upon these facts, the questions can be answered. Yisro knew that Moshe was destined to be a Kohen and would therefore not remarry Tzipporah. But after Yisro heard what "*Elokim*" — Hashem in his strict justice — had done to Moshe [removed from him the right to *Kehunah*], Yisro immediately brought Tzipporah back to Moshe, since Moshe was not forbidden to marry her.

(*Chanukas HaTorah*)

וַיֵּצֵא מֹשֶׁה לִקְרַאת חֹתְנוֹ וַיִּשְׁתַּחוּ וַיִּשַּׁק לוֹ... (י״ח:ז)

Moshe went out toward his father-in-law, and he bowed and kissed him (18:7)

The Midrash (*Mechilta*), quoted by Rashi, points out that the *pasuk* does not specify who bowed to whom.

The Gemara records that Moshe was extremely tall — ten *amos* tall (*Berachos* 54b)! In order for Moshe and Yisro, who was the average three *amos* tall, to kiss each other it was necessary for Moshe to bend or bow down to Yisro who was shorter. It is therefore obvious who bowed to whom, and is unnecessary for the Torah to mention it.

(*R' Yisrael Moshe HaKohen*, quoted by *Binyan Shlomo*)

עַתָּה שְׁמַע בְּקֹלִי אִיעָצְךָ וִיהִי אֱלֹקִים עִמָּךְ... (י״ח:י״ט)

> Now, listen to my voice, I will advise you,
> and Hashem will be with you... (18:19)

Yisro saw that his son-in-law was judging the Jews single-handedly. He chastised him that this task is exhausting and overwhelming, and advised him how to set up a judicial system, utilizing the various scholars among the Jews. Yisro then concluded, "And Hashem will be with you." What is the meaning of this vague statement?"

The Gemara states that if a prophet is overworked and overburdened then he will lose his ability to receive prophecy (*Sanhedrin* 17a).

Yisro advised Moshe to heed his advice in order that "Hashem will be with you." In light of the above, this remark can be understood as follows. Moshe was overworked. Yisro was warning him that he must reduce his workload or else Hashem will not be with him, since Hashem will not communicate with anyone who is not in the proper frame of mind.

(*Yalkut HaUrim*, in the name of *Maamar Avraham*)

MISHPATIM

אִם בְּגַפּוֹ יָבֹא בְּגַפּוֹ יֵצֵא אִם בַּעַל אִשָּׁה הוּא וְיָצְאָה אִשְׁתּוֹ עִמּוֹ. (כ"א:ג)

If he came alone, then he leaves alone; if he came with a wife, then his wife leaves with him. (21:3)

THERE ARE TWO WAYS IN WHICH A JEWISH SLAVE ACQUIRES HIS freedom from his master. One way, mentioned here, is that after six years of work he goes free. The other way is with the arrival Yovel, the Jubilee year of the Jewish calendar. In this *pasuk*, when mentioning the freedom acquired after six years, the Torah writes that a Jewish slave receives his freedom and leaves with his wife. When mentioning the freedom obtained by *Yovel* (*Vayikra* 25:41), the Torah adds that he shall leave with his children. Why are his children not mentioned here too?

The Gemara, quoted by Rashi, explains that although the Torah writes that a slave's wife leaves with him, it does not mean that she too had been in bondage. What the Torah means is that until the slave leaves his master, the master is required to support the wife and children of the slave (*Kiddushin* 22a). The Ramban explains that since the slave is unable to support his family, the Torah placed that moral obligation upon the master.

According to the strict letter of Jewish law, a father is only required to support his children up until the age of 6 (*Kesubos*

65b). If so, the master is also only required to support the children of the slave until they are 6 years old.

In this *parashah*, the Torah is discussing a master who acquires a slave who has a wife and children. The Torah states that at the conclusion of six years the master is no longer required to support the family of the slave. It is unnecessary to write that the master is then freed from support of the children, since his obligation was already terminated! Any children were at least six years old before the end of that period, and the master's obligation to them ended on their birthday.

The freedom of *Yovel* can occur soon after the buying of the slave, when the children are yet infants. Under such circumstances, the Torah writes that the master is freed from his obligation to the young children when *Yovel* arrives.

(*Toras Moshe*)

וְאִם אָמֹר יֹאמַר הָעֶבֶד אָהַבְתִּי אֶת אֲדֹנִי אֶת אִשְׁתִּי וְאֶת בָּנָי לֹא אֵצֵא חָפְשִׁי. וְהִגִּישׁוֹ אֲדֹנָיו אֶל הָאֱלֹהִים וְהִגִּישׁוֹ אֶל הַדֶּלֶת אוֹ אֶל הַמְּזוּזָה וְרָצַע אֲדֹנָיו אֶת אָזְנוֹ בַּמַּרְצֵעַ וַעֲבָדוֹ לְעֹלָם (כ"א:ה-ו)

> *If the slave declares, "I love my master, my wife, and my children; I do not want to go free!" His master shall bring him to the court; and he shall bring him to the door or the doorpost, and his master shall pirce his ear with an awl, and he shall serve him forever. (21:5-6)*

There is a well-known Midrash (*Mechilta*), quoted by Rashi, which states:

"Why did the Torah specify that the ear be pierced? Rabbi Yochanan ben Zakkai answered, 'A slave who was sold into slavery by *beis din* for stealing has his ear pierced because he did not heed the admonition of "Thou shalt not steal." A slave who sold himself into slavery out of poverty has his ear pierced because he did not heed Hashem's declaration of "You shall be my slaves" and not those of a human being.' "

The *Alshich* asks an obvious question on the reasons offered by the Midrash. Why doesn't the slave have his ear pierced as soon as he steals or sells himself into slavery? Why is it performed only after he chooses to remain with his master after the six-year period?

There is a simple answer pertaining to the person who steals. Initially, the selling of the thief into slavery is intended to be a punishment for not heeding the admonition of not to steal. However, if the slave requests to remain with his master after the six years, it proves that the slavery was not a punishment for him. Therefore, the new punishment of piercing the ear is administered.

There is a complex but fascinating way of explaining why the person who sells himself into slavery is later punished. The Rambam (*Avadim* 1:1) writes that a person who is extremely impoverished is permitted to sell himself into slavery. If so, a person who sells himself into slavery cannot be punished immediately since it is possible that he is very poor, and thus is acting appropriately. But why is he later punished? The Torah (*Re'eh* 15:14) states that a master must grant his slave gifts upon his receiving his freedom. How much must the gifts be worth? According to one opinion it is fifty *selaim* (*Kiddushin* 17a). Fifty *selaim* equals two hundred *zuz* (Rashbam, Bava Basra 165b). The Mishnah (*Pe'ah* 8:8) states that a person who has two hundred *zuz* is not considered poor and is prohibited to gather produce which the Torah designated for poor people (e.g. *leket, shich'chah, pe'ah,* etc.). Therefore, after a slave is freed, and has two hundred *zuz* in his possession, and nevertheless opts to remain in slavery, he is punished since he is decidedly not a poor person!

(*Levias Chein*)

וְהִגִּישׁוֹ אֲדֹנָיו אֶל הָאֱלֹהִים וְהִגִּישׁוֹ אֶל הַדֶּלֶת אוֹ אֶל הַמְּזוּזָה וְרָצַע אֲדֹנָיו אֶת אָזְנוֹ בַּמַּרְצֵעַ וַעֲבָדוֹ לְעֹלָם. (כ״א:ו)

His master shall bring him to the court; and he shall bring him to the door or to the doorpost, and his master shall pierce his ear with an awl, and he shall serve him forever (21:6)

The Midrash (*Mechilta*), quoted by Rashi, first suggests that the hole should be bored in the left ear of the slave. It concludes that through a *gezeirah shavah* we derive that the right ear is pierced.

This initial suggestion seems strange, since regarding Torah Law, the organ of choice is the one on the right. [Placing the *tefillin* on the left hand is derived from a special phrase.] Why should we assume otherwise with regard to this mitzvah?

The Midrash (*Sifri, VeZos HaBerachah*) explains that the words that emanated from Hashem on Mt. Sinai went out from "his right side" and therefore, since the Jews "were facing him," were heard by the Jews on their left side.

The Midrash (*Mechilta*), quoted by Rashi, states that the reason the ear, and not another organ, is pierced, is that on Mt. Sinai the ear heard Hashem's admonition not to steal. Nonetheless the person proceeded to steal and therefore the ear is pierced.

The original question can now be answered. The reason for the piercing is that the ear heard Hashem's word and disregarded it. Which ear heard it? The left ear! Therefore, if not for the *gezeirah shavah*, one would assume that the left ear should be pierced.

(*Chanukas HaTorah*)

כָּל אַלְמָנָה וְיָתוֹם לֹא תְעַנּוּן. אִם עַנֵּה תְעַנֶּה אֹתוֹ כִּי אִם
צָעֹק יִצְעַק אֵלַי שָׁמֹעַ אֶשְׁמַע צַעֲקָתוֹ. (כ"ב:כא-כב)

> *You shall not cause pain to any widow or orphan. If you [dare to] cause him pain — for if he shall cry out to me, I shall surely hear his outcry. (22: 21-22)*

The Torah states that **if** a widow or orphan prays to Hashem to be rescued from a tormentor, then Hashem will listen to her or his prayer.

Several *pesukim* later, the Torah writes that a lender is required to return an item held as security to a borrower daily if the borrower is in need of it (i.e. an only garment). The Torah then concludes this law by writing, "And it shall be **when** the borrower cries out to me in prayer then I shall listen to him, for I am compassionate" (22:26).

Two discrepancies strike us. Concerning a widow or orphan the Torah writes "**if** he shall cry out"; about the borrower the Torah writes "**when** he shall cry out." Also, regarding the laws of the borrower, the Torah concludes that Hashem will listen to the cries of the borrower **because He is compassionate**. No such phrase is written concerning the orphan.

The Gemara states that in a situation where a person can call a litigant to court, then he is forbidden to pray that Hashem enact judgment. In fact, the one who prays will be punished. However, if it involves a situation where the court will not accept his case, he is permitted to call to Hashem (*Bava Kamma* 93a).

If an orphan or widow is being oppressed, *beis din* is required to intercede on his or her behalf. Should the orphan pray to Hashem to punish the oppressor, he too will suffer. It is therefore improbable that the orphan will turn to Hashem. Thus the phrase "if" is used. Furthermore, the phrase "for I am compassionate" is not written after the mention of Hashem listening to the prayers of the orphan since the orphan will also suffer.

On the other hand, *beis din* does not intercede on behalf of the borrower to force the lender to return his collateral. Thus the borrower is free to cry to Hashem to mete out justice. The borrower will surely utilize this option, and therefore the term "when" is most appropriate. Also, since there will be no dire consequences for the one who cried out, the phrase "for I am compassionate" is written.

(*Binyan Shlomo*)

וַיִּקַּח מֹשֶׁה חֲצִי הַדָּם וַיָּשֶׂם בָּאַגָּנֹת וַחֲצִי הַדָּם זָרַק עַל הַמִּזְבֵּחַ (כ"ד:ו)

> *Moshe took half the blood and placed it in basins, and half the blood he sprinkled on the Altar. (24:6)*

The Midrash (*Vayikra Rabbah* Chap. 6), quoted by Rashi, writes that an angel divided the blood into two parts. What prompted the Midrash to veer from the simple understanding of the words?

The *Targum* (24:8) explains that the half of the blood that Moshe placed into basins was also subsequently spilled on the *Mizbe'ach*.

The halachah is that any blood, which is sprinkled on the *Mizbe'ach*, must issue directly from the animal to the bowl from which it will be sprinkled (see *Zevachim* 25a). If so, the blood must have spilled exactly half into one bowl and half into the other. This was impossible for Moshe to do since he had no way of knowing how much blood would eventually bleed from the animal. Only an angel could have known and done it. (*Chidushei Maharil Diskin*)

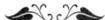

וְאֶל הַזְּקֵנִים אָמַר שְׁבוּ לָנוּ בָזֶה עַד אֲשֶׁר נָשׁוּב אֲלֵיכֶם וְהִנֵּה אַהֲרֹן וְחוּר עִמָּכֶם מִי בַעַל דְּבָרִים יִגַּשׁ אֲלֵהֶם (כ"ד:י"ד)

> *And to the elders he said, "Wait for us here until we return to you. Behold! Aharon and Chur are with you; whoever has a case should approach them." (24:14)*

Ramban explains this *pasuk* to mean that Moshe appointed the elders of the community in his stead to deal with all judicial matters until his return from Mt. Sinai.

Mishpatim / 119

The term "elders" generally refers to the seventy-one elders who comprised the *Sanhedrin* (see *Bamidbar* 11:16). Why was it necessary to have all of them to replace Moshe?

The Gemara states that Moshe had the authority equivalent to that of the *Sanhedrin* of seventy-one. He was permitted to issuel rulings on his own in all those cases that ordinarily only the *Sanhedrin* of seventy-one judges are permitted to deal with (*Sanhedrin* 13b).

Until Moshe went up to Mt. Sinai, he personally dealt with the cases that usually belong to the *Sanhedrin*. Now that he would be gone it was necessary to call those seventy-one elders, and advise them to be ready to replace him for the cases which require a *Sanhedrin* of seventy-one.

(*R' Yitzchak Zev Soloveitchik,* quoted by *Talelei Oros*)

Terumah

דַּבֵּר אֶל בְּנֵי יִשְׂרָאֵל וְיִקְחוּ לִי תְּרוּמָה... (כ״ה:ב)

Speak to the Jews, and let them take for Me a portion...(25:2)

HASHEM TOLD MOSHE TO INSTRUCT THE JEWS TO DONATE material for the Mishkan. Hashem included in his instruction that it should be "for Me." Rashi explains that this means "for the sake of My Name." This too is obscure.

The Gemara explains that the reason the Torah (in *Bamidbar, Parashas Nasso*) juxtaposed the laws of *terumah* and *maaser* with the laws of *sotah* is to teach us that whoever does not bring the required tithes to the Kohen will ultimately be punished by having a wife who will be a *sotah* (*Berachos* 63a).

One of the details of the laws of *sotah* is that the chapter dealing with the laws of *sotah*, which includes Hashem's Name, is scratched off a piece of parchment and mixed with water (*Bamidbar* 5:23).

This clarifies Rashi's words. Hashem requested that a Jew be scrupulous in the observance of the laws of donating to the Mishkan in order that he should not be punished by having a wife who is a *sotah* and thus cause Hashem's Name to be erased.

(*Chanukas HaTorah*)

דַּבֵּר אֶל בְּנֵי יִשְׂרָאֵל וְיִקְחוּ לִי תְּרוּמָה... (כ״ה:ב)

Speak to the Jews, and let them take for Me a portion...(25:2)

Hashem told Moshe to instruct the Jews to donate material for the Mishkan. Hashem included in his instruction that it should be "for Me." Rashi explains that this means "for the sake of my Name." This too is obscure.

The Mishnah (*Sotah* 37b) writes that in the Beis HaMikdash Hashem's Name was pronounced exactly the way it is written; outside of the Beis HaMikdash, Hashem's Name is pronounced as though it was written "*Ah-do-noi*." It follows then, that in the absence of a Beis HaMikdash, Hashem's Name will never be pronounced properly.

The purpose of these donations was to build a Mishkan, which had the sanctity and quality of the Beis HaMikdash. This is the intent of "for the sake of my Name." The Jews should donate toward the building of the Mishkan in order that Hashem's Name should be pronounced properly.

(*Peninim Yekarim*)

דַּבֵּר אֶל בְּנֵי יִשְׂרָאֵל וְיִקְחוּ לִי תְרוּמָה... (כ״ה:ב)

Speak to the Jews, and let them take for Me a portion...(25:2)

Hashem told Moshe to instruct the Jews to donate material for the Mishkan. Hashem included in his instruction that it should be "for Me". Rashi explains that this means "for the sake of my Name". This too is obscure.

In *Megillas Esther* (3:9) it is recorded that Haman offered ten thousand talents of silver to Achashveirosh to annihilate the

Jewish people. The Gemara reveals that Hashem saved the Jews from this decree many years before it materialized (*Megillah* 13b). The reason Hashem instructed the Jews to donate toward the building of the Mishkan was in order to provide them with a merit by which they would be saved from Haman's decree.

The Midrash (*Tanchuma, pararshas Ki Seitzei*), quoted by Rashi (*Shemos* 17:16), writes that "Hashem's Name is not whole until Amalek and his descendants are wiped out." By giving a donation now to the Mishkan, the Jews would cause that Haman, the descendant and successor of Amalek, would be killed, which would help that Hashem's Name "become whole."

(*Toras Moshe*)

דַּבֵּר אֶל בְּנֵי יִשְׂרָאֵל וְיִקְחוּ לִי תְּרוּמָה... (כ"ה:ב)

*Speak to the Jews, and let them
take for Me a portion...(25:2)*

Hashem instructed Moshe to inform the Jews that they should "**take** for Hashem a portion." The word "take" seems out of place. It would seem more appropriate to write that the Jews should **give** a portion, i.e. a donation for the Mishkan.

According to Jewish law, one of the methods whereby a man acquires a wife is by presenting her with a gift. If the woman gives the man a present, marriage has not taken place (*Kiddushin* 5b). However, if the man is a distinguished person, then even if the woman gives the man a present, the marriage takes place. This is based on the fact that the woman derives great satisfaction that so distinguished a person was willing to accept a present from her. The satisfaction generated by the man's acceptance constitutes a giving of a present on the part of the man (*Kiddushin* 7a).

This reasoning can be applied here too. If Hashem is willing to receive a present from us, it is considered as though we are taking a portion from Hashem and not vice versa. That is alluded to by the phrase "**take** for Me a portion." *(Alshich)*

וְעָשׂוּ לִי מִקְדָּשׁ... (כ"ה:ח)

They should construct a sanctuary for Me ... (25:8)

There is a well-known Midrash (*Pesikta Rabbasi*, Chap. 29, quoted by Rashi (*Succah*, 41a)) which states that the third Beis HaMikdash will be built by Hashem and descend into this world in a completed state.

It is written in *Megillas Eichah* (2:9) that the gates of the second Beis HaMikdash were not burned, but rather sunk into the ground. It is logical to assume that these gates were not destroyed in order to use them for the future third Beis HaMikdash. But if Hashem will construct the third Beis Hamikdash, why did Hashem cause that the gates should be stored in the ground?

There is a mitzvah to build a Beis Hamikdash, as is written in this *pasuk*. Hashem wanted to give the Jews the opportunity to perform this mitzvah even with regard to the third Beis HaMikdash. So what did Hashem do? He had the gates of the second Beis HaMikdash preserved in order that the Jews could place them on the future Beis HaMikdash. According to Jewish law (*Bava Basra* 53b), placing the doors on a building is considered as though somebody actually built the whole building. In this way, the Jews will be able to fulfill this precept even in the future.

In the Mussaf prayers of Yom Tov we say, "show us its [the Beis HaMikdash] building and make us happy in its restoration." Based on the above, the prayer can be explained as follows: Show us the building of the Beis HaMikdash, when it will descend from heaven, and make us rejoice by allowing us to participate in its restoration by adding gates, and thus fulfilling a mitzvah.

(*R' Yehoshua Leib Diskin,* quoted by *Siddur Ishei Yisrael*)

וְעָשִׂיתָ מְנֹרַת זָהָב טָהוֹר מִקְשָׁה תֵּיעָשֶׂה הַמְּנוֹרָה... (כ"ה:ל"א)

You should make a Menorah of pure gold, hammered out shall the Menorah be made...(25:31)

The Gerer Rebbe, Rav Avraham Mordechai Alter, related the following:

"For forty years I couldn't comprehend the following Midrash (*Bamidbar Rabbah* 15:10): 'When Hashem commanded Moshe to make the Menorah, Moshe asked Hashem how to do it...Hashem showed Moshe but he was still unable...Hashem then showed Moshe a Menorah made of fire, but he was still unable. Finally, Hashem told Moshe to instruct Betzalel to carve it; and Betzalel did it immediately.'

"What troubled me was: How could it be that Moshe found it too difficult to construct the Menorah and Betzalel had no difficulty at all? But then an event occurred which clarified everything.

"A short while ago, I went to visit my son-in-law, who was in a hospital in Warsaw recuperating from surgery that had some serious complications. I asked the surgeon for the details on his condition. The surgeon told me two stories:

" 'There was once a powerful monarch who owned an extremely precious diamond. There was a tiny flaw in the stone that the king wanted removed. However, all the diamond cutters were fearful of accepting the job due to the risk of possibly shattering the stone which was of enormous value. The king then sent for a simple artisan who did not realize what was at stake, and he removed the flaw easily.

" 'Similarly, Napoleon's wife was once having a very difficult childbirth, and all the midwives were afraid to be involved knowing well who her husband was, and what the consequences would be if perchance they harmed mother or child. Napoleon therefore summoned a simple peasant midwife who did not know that he was the emperor, and the child was delivered with ease.'

"The surgeon then said, 'The operation which I performed is always easy for me, and no complications arise. Only this time, upon realizing that I was operating on the son-in-law of the renowned and esteemed Gerer Rebbe, I became so nervous that complications arose.'

"Now I finally understand the above-mentioned Midrash. Moshe knew and understood the great holiness and secrets of the Menorah and all its parts. He therefore was gripped with paralysis and could not go ahead. Only Betzalel, who was not aware of all these details, was able to forge it with ease."

(*Likutei Yehudah*)

TETZAVEH

וְאַתָּה תְּצַוֶּה אֶת בְּנֵי יִשְׂרָאֵל וְיִקְחוּ **אֵלֶיךָ** שֶׁמֶן זַיִת זָךְ כָּתִית לַמָּאוֹר לְהַעֲלֹת נֵר תָּמִיד. בְּאֹהֶל מוֹעֵד מִחוּץ לַפָּרֹכֶת אֲשֶׁר עַל הָעֵדֻת יַעֲרֹךְ אֹתוֹ אַהֲרֹן וּבָנָיו מֵעֶרֶב עַד בֹּקֶר לִפְנֵי ה' **חֻקַּת עוֹלָם לְדֹרֹתָם**... (כ"ז:כ-כא)

> *You shall command the Jews that they should take **for you** pure, pressed olive oil for illumination, to kindle the lamp continually. In the Tent of Meeting, outside the Partition that is near the Testimonial-tablets, Aharon and his children shall arrange [for] it [to burn] from evening until morning before Hashem, **it is an eternal chok forever for their generations**... (27:20-21)*

IF ONE READS THE *PASUK* CAREFULLY, ONE IS STRUCK BY THE PHRASE "for you." The oil was not for Moshe's benefit at all; why then is it described as being "for you"?

The Midrash (*Mechilta, Bo,*1) states that Hashem spoke to Moshe only by day. The Ibn Ezra adds (*Bamidbar* 8:2) that as long as the fire of the Menorah was burning it was considered as day, and Hashem would communicate with him in the *Ohel Moed*.

This fact can explain the aforementioned problematic phrase. The light generated by the oil of the Menorah put Moshe in the proper frame of mind, and he could thus be spoken to even at night. This oil was in fact for Moshe's benefit, and can be labeled "for you."

Tetzaveh / 127

This practical benefit existed only as long as Moshe was living. After Moshe's demise there was no apparent benefit from the Menorah, since Hashem does not need the light of the Menorah. The mitzvah can then be called a *chok* — a mitzvah for which there is no rational basis. Therefore the *pasuk* concludes, "...it is a *chok* forever for your [future] generations." For future generations it is only a *chok*.

(*Meshech Chochmah*)

וְאַתָּה **הַקְרֵב אֵלֶיךָ** אֶת אַהֲרֹן אָחִיךָ וְאֶת בָּנָיו אִתּוֹ מִתּוֹךְ בְּנֵי יִשְׂרָאֵל לְכַהֲנוֹ לִי... (כ"ח:א)

You [Moshe] **bring near to you** *Aharon your brother and his sons with him, from among the Children of Israel, to be a Kohen for Me...(28:1)*

Moshe was instructed to bring his brother Aharon "near to him, to make him a Kohen." What does this "nearness" refer to?

The Gemara proves that Moshe at this point had the legal status of a Kohen Gadol (*Zevachim* 101b). Now was the moment that he was going to transfer that status to Aharon. The phrase "bring near to you" can be explained as meaning that Moshe should bring Aharon up to his level — i.e. to be the Kohen Gadol (see Ibn Ezra).

But a question still remains. The words of the *pasuk* imply that Moshe was the one who was going to elevate Aharon into a Kohen. Why did Moshe have the ability to make Aharon the Kohen Gadol?

Two legal entities are involved in appointing a Kohen Gadol: the king (*Tosefos, Zevachim* 18a) and the *Sanhedrin* of seventy-one elders (*Rambam, Sanhedrin* 5:1). Moshe had the authority of both these entities. He was a monarch (*Shemos Rabbah parashah* 2), and he had the legal authority of the *Sanhedrin* (*Sanhedrin* 16b). Therefore he was able to appoint Aharon to be the Kohen Gadol.

(*R' David Soloveitchik*, quoted by *Shai LeTorah*)

וְאַתָּה הַקְרֵב אֵלֶיךָ אֶת אַהֲרֹן אָחִיךָ וְאֶת בָּנָיו אִתּוֹ מִתּוֹךְ בְּנֵי יִשְׂרָאֵל לְכַהֲנוֹ לִי אַהֲרֹן נָדָב וַאֲבִיהוּא אֶלְעָזָר וְאִיתָמָר בְּנֵי אַהֲרֹן. (כ"ח:א)

*You [Moshe] **bring near to you** Aharon your brother and his sons with him, from among the Children of Israel, to be a Kohen for Me, Aharon and his sons **Nadav, Avihu, Elazar and Isamar.** (28:1)*

Hashem instructed Moshe to elevate Aharon and his sons into Kohanim. Hashem itemized the names of the sons in his instruction. What was the reason for that?

Originally all firstborn sons served as the Kohanim. After the firstborn sons participated in the sin of the *eigel hazahav,* the right of *Kehunah* was transferred to the tribe of Levi (*Rashi, Bamidbar* 3:12). Nadav was the firstborn of Aharon (*Bamidbar,* 3:2). The Torah states that all Levites, without exception, were not involved in the sin of the gold heifer (*Rashi, Shemos,* 32:26). This includes even Nadav, despite the fact that he was a firstborn.

If so, the following explanation is possible. Nadav was a Kohen beforehand by virtue of his being a firstborn. Aharon might have assumed that it was unnecessary for Nadav to undergo the new sanctification process. Therefore Hashem itemized the names of all the sons — including Nadav — to emphasize that each one had to be sanctified.

A reason as to why Nadav had to undergo this procedure can be offered. As long as the firstborn were Kohanim, only their own firstborn had the ability to also be Kohanim. Now a change was going to occur. All the offspring of the sons of Aharon were going to be Kohanim. This new aspect of *Kehunah* necessitated a new sanctification on the part of Nadav.

(*Chidushei Maharil Diskin*)

וְאֵלֶּה הַבְּגָדִים אֲשֶׁר יַעֲשׂוּ חֹשֶׁן וְאֵפוֹד וּמְעִיל וּכְתֹנֶת תַּשְׁבֵּץ... (כ״ח:ד)

> These are the garments which they should make for the Kohanim: a breastplate, an ephod, a robe, **a tunic of boxlike knit**...(28:4)

In one of the *Selichos* which are said only on Yom Kippur during the *Mussaf* prayers it is written that the *kesones* — the tunic of boxlike knit which the Kohen wore — was made out of *sha'atnez* — linen and wool together. This is startling, since it is written explicitly in the Torah (*Shemos* 28:39) that the tunic of the Kohen was made solely of linen!

This question was sent to the paramount commentator of the *machzor* — Rav Wolf Heidenheim. He replied as follows:

"The author based that prayer on an obscure opinion mentioned in the Midrash (*Yalkut Shimoni, Tzav, remez* 513) in the name of Rav Shimon. But how does Rav Shimon reconcile his statement with the explicit *pasuk*?

"The *kesones* was made from linen. The *me'il* — robe — which the Kohen wore on top of his tunic was made from wool (*Shemos*, 28:31). They were fastened together by the belt of the *ephod* (ibid., 29:5). According to the Gemara (*Yerushalmi, Klayim* 9:4, quoted by *Rema, Yorah Deah* 300:4), if one is wearing one garment of wool and another garment of linen, and the bottom garment cannot be removed without first removing the top one, this constitutes *sha'atnez*. Therefore, since the tunic of the Kohen could not be removed without first removing the robe it was considered *sha'atnez*!"

(Chasan *Sofer*, in *Kovetz Teshuvos Chasam Sofer* Chap. 48 [extract], and in *Toras Moshe*)

שִׁבְעַת יָמִים יִלְבָּשָׁם הַכֹּהֵן תַּחְתָּיו מִבָּנָיו אֲשֶׁר יָבֹא אֶל אֹהֶל מוֹעֵד לְשָׁרֵת בַּקֹּדֶשׁ. (כ״ט:ל)

For a seven-day period, the Kohen, who succeeds him [Aharon's] from his sons, who shall enter the Ohel Moed to serve in the sanctuary, shall don them. (29:30)

The son of Aharon, who succeeds him as Kohen Gadol, is sanctified for that position by wearing the special garments of the Kohen Gadol for a seven-day period. When the Torah describes the son of Aharon who replaces him in the position of Kohen Gadol, he is described as "the one who shall enter the *Ohel Moed* to serve in the Sanctuary." The Gemara, quoted by Rashi, explains that this refers to the service that was performed on Yom Kippur, which only the Kohen Gadol was permitted to do (*Yoma* 73a).

Why does the Torah write in a roundabout way? The Torah should describe him outright as "the future Kohen Gadol."

The Ra'avad (*Hil. Klei HaMikdash*, 4:13) posits that a Kohen Gadol who is being initiated is permitted to perform the daily services wearing the eight garments of the Kohen Gadol even before completing the seven days of initiation. He is only prohibited to perform the special Yom Kippur service of the Kohen Gadol before the end of his initiation.

This view clarifies the wording of the *pasuk*. The only activity for which seven days is imperative is the service of Yom Kippur. Therefore, when the Torah mentions the requirement of donning the garments for seven days, it describes the Kohen Gadol as the one who will perform the service on Yom Kippur.

(*Chidushei Maran Riz HaLevi*)

וְזֶה אֲשֶׁר תַּעֲשֶׂה עַל הַמִּזְבֵּחַ כְּבָשִׂים בְּנֵי שָׁנָה שְׁנַיִם לַיּוֹם תָּמִיד אֶת הַכֶּבֶשׂ הָאֶחָד תַּעֲשֶׂה בַבֹּקֶר וְאֵת הַכֶּבֶשׂ הַשֵּׁנִי תַּעֲשֶׂה בֵּין הָעַרְבָּיִם. (כ"ט:לח-לט)

This is what you shall offer upon the Mizbe'ach: two sheep within their first year every day, continually. You shall offer the first sheep in the morning and the second sheep you shall offer in the evening. (29:38-39)

The Torah discusses the two daily obligatory sacrifices, and describes the first sacrifice as being הָאֶחָד — the first one. Later, in *parashas Pinchas* (*Bamidbar* 28:4), when the Torah again describes those sacrifices, the Torah refers to the first one as אֶחָד, one sacrifice. This discrepancy calls for an explanation.

The Mishnah states that even if the morning daily offering was not brought, nevertheless the afternoon one may be brought (*Zevachim* 49a). This is only true after the *Mizbe'ach* has been inaugurated. Before that, if the morning one was not brought then the afternoon one could not be brought (*Menachos* 50a).

This fact explains the discrepancy. The *pasuk* here is discussing the inauguration process. If so, the morning offering must be the first one, and is described as such. *Parashas Pinchas* is discussing the offering after the *Mizbe'ach* was already inaugurated. Then the morning offering does not necessarily have to be the first one of the day, and is therefore only referred to as "one sheep."

(*Chidushei Maran Riz HaLevi*)

Ki Sisa

וְשָׁחַקְתָּ מִמֶּנָּה הָדֵק וְנָתַתָּה מִמֶּנָּה לִפְנֵי הָעֵדֻת בְּאֹהֶל מוֹעֵד... (ל׃ל״ו)

*You should grind **some of it** finely, and you should place **some of it** in front of the ark of testimony in the Ohel Moed...(30:36)*

Hashem commanded Moshe to gather several specific fragrances, grind them together, and make incense from them which would be offered daily in the *Ohel Moed*. In the instructions to grind the fragrances, the phrase "some of it" was said. What was meant by this phrase?

The Gemara prescribes the amount of *ketores* — incense — that is prepared at one time (*Kerisos* 6a). However, the Gemara adds that as long as the percentage of each ingredient is the same, one does not have to make the total amount prescribed (ibid. 6b). This explains this obscure phrase. It is informing us that it is not necessary to actually grind all the ingredients, but even only "some of it," i.e. part of it, suffices.

Further on in the *pasuk*, when mentioning the requirement to place the fragrance in the *Ohel Moed*, the phrase "some of it" is repeated. Here too it can be asked: To what is it referring?

One of the classic commentaries on *Rambam* — *Mishnah LaMelech* (*Temidin U'mussafin* 3:2) — suggests, that although post facto even if only a *kezayis* of incense is offered it suffices, nevertheless it is required that at the time of preparing the incense for sacrifice that there be the required daily *maneh* of incense. It can therefore be explained that the phrase "some of it" here too has a similar meaning. Although a *maneh* must be prepared, even if he offers only part of it — a *kezayis* — he has fulfilled his requirement.

(Chidushei Maran Riz HaLevi)

וַיִּפֶן וַיֵּרֶד מֹשֶׁה מִן הָהָר וּשְׁנֵי לֻחֹת הָעֵדֻת בְּיָדוֹ... (ל״ב:ט״ו)

Moshe turned and descended from the mountain, and the two Tablets of Testimony were in his hand...(32:15)

The Rambam (*Beis HaBechirah* 7:4) writes, that when a Kohen completes his work in the Beis HaMikdash and leaves, he is prohibited to leave with his back facing the Beis HaMikdash. Rather, he is required to walk out backwards, out of deference to the Presence of Hashem that is found in the Beis HaMikdash. This law can explain why Moshe "turned" as he descended. Hashem's Presence was on Mt. Sinai and required the same respect as the Beis HaMikdash. Therefore Moshe walked down the mountain in a "turned fashion," i.e. with his body facing the mountain.

However, this explanation seems to be contradicted from another *pasuk*. Earlier, in *parashas Yisro* (*Shemos* 19:14), after mentioning that Hashem spoke to Moshe on Mt. Sinai, the Torah writes that "Moshe descended from the mountain to go to the people," without mentioning that he "turned" as he descended. There too he was leaving Hashem's Presence and should have walked backwards as a sign of respect.

The solution to this lies in a careful reading of the words of the aforementioned Rambam. The Rambam prefaces his words by writing "when a Kohen completes his work." The requirement to walk backwards only applies after a Kohen has completed his services and is leaving for the day. Similarly, Moshe was only obligated to walk backwards after totally finishing his discussion with Hashem. The episode in *parashas Yisro* took place before the giving of the Torah, and Moshe had not yet finished conversing with Hashem. Therefore he left in a normal manner. *Parashas Ki Sisa* is describing Moshe's descent after the entire process of giving the Torah was completed. Moshe was taking final leave from Hashem. Thus Moshe left in a respectful manner — facing Hashem as he walked down the mountain.

(*R' Yitzchak Zev Soloveitchik*, quoted by *Shai LeTorah* [see also *Rabbeinu Chananel*])

וַיְמַהֵר מֹשֶׁה וַיִּקֹּד אַרְצָה וַיִּשְׁתָּחוּ. (ל"ד:ח)

Moshe hurried and kneeled and bowed on the ground. (34:8)

Rashi explains that Moshe hurried and bowed on the ground when he heard Hashem proclaim the Thirteen Attributes (*Middos*) of Mercy. Two questions can be asked. First, why did he bow? Secondly, why did he rush to bow?

The Mishnah records that when the Kohen Gadol would pronounce Hashem's Name in the Beis HaMikdash on Yom Kippur all the people who heard it would kneel and bow on the floor (*Yoma* 66a). It can be suggested that Moshe bowed for that reason. The first word Hashem said was His own Name. Therefore, upon hearing Hashem's Name, Moshe bowed on the floor.

The Rambam (*Avodas Yom HaKippurim*, 2:7) adds that the people would begin kneeling, bowing and saying a blessing as soon as the Kohen Gadol would begin saying Hashem's Name, and would finish simultaneously. This can explain the purpose of Moshe's rushing. He hurried in order to begin to kneel as soon as possible upon hearing Hashem's Name being pronounced.

(*Chidushei Maran Riz HaLevi*)

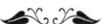

שְׁמָר לְךָ אֵת אֲשֶׁר אָנֹכִי מְצַוְּךָ **הַיּוֹם** הִנְנִי גֹרֵשׁ מִפָּנֶיךָ אֶת הָאֱמֹרִי וְהַכְּנַעֲנִי ... כִּי אֶת מִזְבְּחֹתָם תִּתֹּצוּן וְאֶת מַצֵּבֹתָם תְּשַׁבֵּרוּן וְאֶת אֲשֵׁרָיו תִּכְרֹתוּן. (ל"ד:י"א,יג)

> Be careful with that which I command you **today**. I will drive out before you the Amorite, the Canaanite, ...you must shatter their altars, smash their sacred pillars, and cut down their asheirah trees. (34: 11,13)

After the incident of the golden heifer, Hashem instructed the Jews to destroy the various idols of the nations that resided in Eretz Yisrael. One may ask: Why didn't Hashem relate this commandment on Mt. Sinai at the time of the giving of the Torah; why did He wait until now? Also, in the *pasuk* written above, what is the significance of the word "today" ["which I command you **today**"]?

If a person worships an object, it is regarded legally as an idol and must be destroyed. However, this is only true if one worships his own property. One cannot cause someone else's object to become prohibited. Based on this, the Gemara questions why the Jews were commanded to destroy the objects of worship of the residents of Eretz Yisroel; the Jews were the legal owners of Eretz Yisrael and the Gentiles could not therefore cause anything in Eretz Yisrael to become prohibited. The Gemara answers that since the Jews worshiped the golden heifer it proved that the Jews did not mind if the Gentiles worshiped the Jewish property, and therefore from then on the Gentiles had the legal ability to cause the property of the Jews to become prohibited (*Avodah Zarah* 53b).

With these words of the Gemara in mind, the questions can now be answered. The command to destroy the "idols" of Eretz Yisrael was only applicable after the sin of the golden heifer; thus it was not said on Mt. Sinai. This is also the meaning of the additional word "today." It was only "today" — after the incident of the golden heifer – that the forthcoming command was being given. (*Ohr Yekaros*)

שָׁלֹשׁ פְּעָמִים בַּשָּׁנָה יֵרָאֶה כָּל זְכוּרְךָ אֶת פְּנֵי הָאָדֹן ה' אֱלֹקֵי יִשְׂרָאֵל. כִּי אוֹרִישׁ גּוֹיִם מִפָּנֶיךָ וְהִרְחַבְתִּי אֶת גְּבֻלֶךָ וְלֹא **יַחְמֹד אִישׁ אֶת אַרְצְךָ** בַּעֲלֹתְךָ לֵרָאוֹת אֶת פְּנֵי ה' אֱלֹקֶיךָ שָׁלֹשׁ פְּעָמִים בַּשָּׁנָה. (ל"ד:כג-כד)

*Three times a year all your males shall appear before the Lord, Hashem — the G-d of Israel. For I shall banish nations before you, and broaden your boundary, **and no person shall covet your land** when you go up to appear before Hashem, your G-d, three times a year. (34:23-24)*

The Torah instructs the Jewish people to visit the Beis HaMikdash during the three *regalim* — Pesach, Shavuos, and Succos. Hashem allays the fears of the Jews by informing them that they need not worry that the neighboring Gentiles will steal their land during their absence.

The precept of being *oleh regel* — ascending to the Beis HaMikdash for Yom Tov — is mentioned earlier in *parashas* Mishpatim (*Shemos* 23:17). However, there is a noticeable difference between the two. In this *parashah* the Torah calms the Jews by guaranteeing them that their property will not be stolen during their absence. In *parashas Mishpatim* no soothing words are said. Why is this so?

The Gemara states that had the first *luchos* not been broken then no nation would have been able to subjugate the Jews (*Eruvin* 54a). This fact can explain the discrepancy between the two *pesukim*. *Parashas Mishpatim* relates mitzvos mentioned prior to the breaking of the first *luchos*. The Jews were invincible then and did not fear the Gentiles. The instructions in *parashas Ki Sisa* were given after the shattering of the *luchos*. The Jews now feared a possible takeover of their land, and had to be assured that no harm would befall their land while they were performing the mitzvah of *oleh regel*. (*Meshech Chochmah*)

וַיְהִי בְּרֶדֶת מֹשֶׁה מֵהַר סִינַי וּשְׁנֵי לֻחֹת הָעֵדֻת בְּיַד מֹשֶׁה בְּרִדְתּוֹ מִן הָהָר וּמֹשֶׁה לֹא יָדַע כִּי קָרַן עוֹר פָּנָיו בְּדַבְּרוֹ אִתּוֹ. (ל״ד:כ״ט)

> When Moshe descended from Mt. Sinai – with the two Tablets of Testimony in Moshe's hand as he descended from the mountain — Moshe did not know that the skin of his face had become radiant when Hashem spoke to him. (34:29)

The Midrash (*Tanchuma*, par. 37) asks: Why was Moshe granted the privilege of having his face become radiant. The Midrash answers that after he finished writing the Torah there remained a drop of ink in his quill which he smeared on his face and which caused it to shine.

Two questions arise. First, Hashem in His infinite wisdom knew precisely how much ink it would take to write the Torah. Why then was there surplus ink? Secondly, the question of the Midrash was **why** was Moshe privileged to such a reward. The answer of the Midrash seems to explain **how** Moshe's face began to shine but not **why**.

When the Torah (*Bamidbar* 12:3) describes Moshe as being extremely modest, the word ענו is written in an unusual manner — without a *yud*. Moshe, out of great humbleness, was reluctant to write about himself that he was humble, so he deliberately wrote it in an unusual manner. This answers our questions. Hashem filled the quill with enough ink to spell the word *anav* properly. There was a drop of extra ink because Moshe omitted that *yud*. Also, the fact that there was extra ink attested to the greatness of Moshe: The ink was there because Moshe was humble. It is because of this extraordinary act of humbleness that he was privileged that the remaining drop of ink caused his face to radiate.

(*Chanukas HaTorah, Ohr HaChaim*)

Vayakhel

שֵׁשֶׁת יָמִים תֵּעָשֶׂה מְלָאכָה וּבַיּוֹם הַשְּׁבִיעִי יִהְיֶה לָכֶם קֹדֶשׁ
שַׁבַּת שַׁבָּתוֹן לַה'... (ל"ה:ב)

Six days you may work, and the seventh day should be holy for you, a day of rest before Hashem... (35:2)

Moshe prefaced his instructions pertaining to the construction of the Mishkan with a mention of the precept of Shabbos. Many commentators ponder the reason for this.

The purpose of the Mishkan was that there should be a place in this physical world for Hashem to "reside" among the Jews. After the collective sin of the "golden heifer," Moshe was concerned that the Jews would not believe that Hashem would still want to reside among them, and thus would be reluctant to proceed with the building of the Mishkan. To prevent that from happening, Moshe mentioned the mitzvah of Shabbos. Shabbos is unique among the mitzvos in that it contains the quality of effecting forgiveness for those who observe it even for sins as severe as idol worship (*Shabbos* 118b). By remembering that they fulfill the mitzvah of Shabbos, the fears of the Jews would be allayed, since the sin of the "golden heifer" would also surely be forgiven through the observance of Shabbos. Moshe could now be confident that the Jews would believe that Hashem would descend to the Mishkan, and thus they would partake in its construction.

(*Imrei Shefer*)

וַיָּבֹאוּ הָאֲנָשִׁים עַל הַנָּשִׁים... (ל״ה:כ״ב)

The men came along with the women... (35:22)

The Torah records that the men accompanied the women as they went to present their donations toward the building of the Mishkan. What was the reason for this?

According to the Gemara, a representative of a charity fund is prohibited to accept a substantial gift from a woman without ascertaining that her husband is aware and agrees to it (*Bava Kamma* 119a). Here too the treasurer of the Mishkan would not have been permitted to accept the women's donations if their husbands had not accompanied them and expressed their approval.

(*Nachalas Yaakov, Tzafnas Pane'ach*)

וַיָּבֹאוּ הָאֲנָשִׁים עַל הַנָּשִׁים... (ל״ה:כ״ב)

The men came along with the women... (35:22)

The Mishnah states that a woman's earnings belong to her husband (*Kesubos* 65b). If so, how were the women able to donate toward the building of the Mishkan? Everything they owned belonged to their spouses.

The Gemara writes that the Sages instituted that a husband is required to support his wife, and in exchange the wife is required to hand over her earnings to her husband. However, since this institution is for the woman's benefit, she has a right to declare that she forgoes the husband's support and prefers instead to keep her earnings (*Kesubos* 58b).

In the desert, everyone received a heavenly sent portion of manna that provided their sustenance. Therefore the women did not need their husband's support and kept their earnings. From this money they donated towards the building of the Mishkan.

(R' Avraham Mordechai Alter (Gerer Rebbe),
quoted by Lukutei Yehudah)

וַיָּבֹאוּ הָאֲנָשִׁים **עַל** הַנָּשִׁים כֹּל נְדִיב לֵב הֵבִיאוּ... (ל״ה:כ״ב)

> *The men came along **after** the women, every generous person, and they brought... (35:22)*

The Torah mentions that the women donated towards the construction of the Mishkan before the men. If the Torah makes note of this there must be a reason why this occurred; it did not just so happen to be.

The Gemara explains that if a person who is required to perform a mitzvah does that mitzvah it is more laudable than if someone who is not obligated to perform that mitzvah does it (*Kiddushin* 31a). The logic behind this is that the performance of a mitzvah is more difficult for someone who is required to do it since he has to overcome the Evil Inclination that is trying to prevent him from doing the mitzvah.

The Torah writes that the **Bnei Yisrael** were commanded to build the Mishkan. This expression usually indicates that only the men were required to do so. If so, the women, who were not obligated to participate in the construction of the Mishkan, did not undergo an inner struggle with the Evil Inclination, and readily donated toward the building of the Mishkan. The men only arrived later with their donations after triumphing over their inner struggle. (*Imrei Shefer*)

וַיַּעַשׂ בְּצַלְאֵל אֶת הָאָרֹן עֲצֵי שִׁטִּים... (ל"ז:א)

Betzalel carved the Ark out of cedar wood... (37:1)

Betzalel was in charge of the making of all the vessels in the Mishkan. If so, why does the Torah only mention that the Ark was made by Betzalel?

The vessels of the Mishkan were permitted to be duplicated and replaced. In fact, some vessels were actually made over by others for the Beis HaMikdash. The Ark, however, was hidden at the time of the destruction of the first Beis HaMikdash and never replaced (*Yoma* 21b). The reason for this is that since the *luchos* were prohibited to be replaced, there was no purpose in replacing the Ark.

The Torah is now alluding to this fact. The only vessel that Betzalel made which will never be replaced is the Ark.

(*Meshech Chochmah*)

וַיָּבֵא אֶת הַבַּדִּים בַּטַּבָּעֹת עַל צַלְעֹת הָאָרֹן... (ל"ז:ה)

He placed the poles in the rings on the side of the Ark...(37:5)

When discussing the rings of the Table and Altar, the Torah describes them as being *"batim labadim"* — receptacles for the poles. However, that description is not used regarding the rings of the Ark. Why not?

The literal meaning of *"batim"* is "houses." A house is a place where its inhabitants are sometimes in residence and sometimes out. The poles of the Altar and Table were occasionally removed from their rings. Therefore the term *"batim"* is appropriate. The poles of the Ark were prohibited to be removed, thus rendering the term *"batim"* inappropriate.

(*Meshech Chochmah*)

Pekudei

וַיְהִי מְאַת כִּכַּר הַכֶּסֶף לָצֶקֶת אֵת אַדְנֵי הַקֹּדֶשׁ... (ל"ח:כ"ז)

The one hundred loaves of silver were used to pour the holy sockets... (38:27)

THE MIDRASH (*TANCHUMA*, PAR. 3) EXPLAINS THAT MOSHE GAVE an accounting of the silver, gold, and copper, mentioned in the previous *pesukim*, to the Jews. A careful reading will reveal that Moshe related to the Jews what was made from all the silver [the bases of the boards], but not what was made from the gold. Why not?

There is a difference as to how the gold and silver were obtained. Everyone was required to contribute a half-*shekel* of silver. The gold, on the other hand, was a voluntary contribution.

Moshe had a deep understanding of human nature. He understood that if the people were coerced to contribute silver, there would probably be those who would want an exact reckoning. The gold, however, was donated voluntarily by generous individuals, and they would not be demanding of Moshe to present an accounting.

However, if this logic is true, why did Moshe delineate what was done with the copper? The copper was also presented voluntarily. Here too the answer lies in understanding human nature. One who donates a low-cost contribution such as copper tends to want an accounting more than a giver of a generous donation. Stingy people are always seeking excuses not to give donations!

(Maayanah Shel Torah)

... וַיַּעֲשׂוּ אֶת בִּגְדֵי הַקֹּדֶשׁ אֲשֶׁר לְאַהֲרֹן כַּאֲשֶׁר צִוָּה ה' אֶת מֹשֶׁה. (ל"ט:א)

> ...they made Aharon's holy garments as Hashem commanded Moshe. (39:1)

After mentioning each of the garments of the Kohanim, the Torah writes that it was made "as Hashem commanded Moshe." This is not mentioned after each of the vessels of the Mishkan. What is the reason for this discrepancy?

Amongst the garments of the Kohanim was one [the belt] that contained *sha'atnez* — wool and linen together — that is ordinarily prohibited to be worn (see *Yoma* 12b). Moshe was the only person capable of transmitting this law; i.e. to wear such a garment. Although a prophet may transmit a message from Hashem to transgress a law of the Torah, it is only valid if it is a *hora'as sha'ah* — a temporary dictate. The clothes of the Kohen Gadol were of a permanent nature. Therefore only Moshe could deliver such a precept. This is what the Torah is pointing out — that this command was from Hashem to Moshe and therefore accepted.

(Meshech Chochmah)

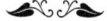

וַיַּעֲשׂוּ אֶת צִיץ נֵזֶר הַקֹּדֶשׁ זָהָב טָהוֹר וַיִּכְתְּבוּ עָלָיו מִכְתַּב פִּתּוּחֵי חוֹתָם קֹדֶשׁ לַה'. (ל"ט:ל)

They made the headplate, the holy crown, of pure gold, and they inscribed on it with a script like that of a signet ring the words "kodesh laShem." (39:30)

The Torah writes that "they" inscribed the words "*kodesh laShem*" on the *tzitz*. This seems to indicate that several people together wrote those words. Why was that so?

The Gemara (*Yoma* 38b) relates that Ben Kamtzar knew how to write with four quills simultaneously. He refused to teach this skill to anyone, and was sternly cursed by the Sages for this refusal.

One wonders what was so important about this skill that the Sages denigrated him for not passing on this skill to future generations. The *Tosefos Yom Tov* explains that if Hashem's Name is written in its entirety simultaneously then it is a glorification of His Name since it is not partially written even for a moment. Possessing the skill of writing with four quills enables one to write the four-letter Name of Hashem in one moment. By not passing on this skill, this glorification was lost. Therefore Ben Kamtzar was called wicked.

Based upon this it can be suggested that several people wrote the words "*kodesh laShem*" simultaneously, in order that those words should not be incomplete even for a moment. This is what the Torah is alluding to by using the plural form.

(*R' Avraham Mordechai Alter* [*Gerer Rebbe*], quoted by *Likutei Yehudah*)

וַתֵּכֶל כָּל עֲבֹדַת מִשְׁכַּן אֹהֶל מוֹעֵד וַיַּעֲשׂוּ בְּנֵי יִשְׂרָאֵל
כְּכֹל אֲשֶׁר צִוָּה ה' אֶת מֹשֶׁה כֵּן עָשׂוּ. (ל"ט:ל"ב)

All the work of the Sanctuary of the Ohel Moed was completed; and the Jewish people did all that Hashem commanded Moshe so did they do. (39:32)

The Gemara states that whoever is engaged in the performance of a mitzvah is exempt from the performance of other mitzvos (*Succah* 25a). Thus the Jews were exempt from the performance of all other mitzvos as long as they were involved in the construction of the Mishkan. This is corroborated by the fact that the Torah had to specify that the Jews should not desecrate the Shabbos in order to build the Mishkan, implying that all other laws did not have to be observed (see *Rashi, Shemos* 35:2).

After the completion of the building of the Mishkan, the Jews were once again obligated to perform all mitzvos. This explains the above *pasuk*. "And all the work of the Sanctuary of the *Ohel Moed* was completed," then, "and the Jewish people did all that Hashem commanded," i.e. they once again began fulfilling all of Hashem's mitzvos.

(*Imrei Shefer*)

וַיְבָרֶךְ אֹתָם מֹשֶׁה. (ל"ט:מ"ג)

...and Moshe blessed them. (39:43)

Rashi explains that Moshe blessed them with the classic words: וִיהִי נֹעַם ה' אֱלֹקֵינוּ עָלֵינוּ וכו'.

Rashi then adds that those words are taken from one of the eleven psalms that Moshe wrote. One wonders why Rashi found it important to mention where the blessing is found.

The Midrash (*Tehillim* Chap. 90) explains that the eleven psalms that Moshe composed are not included in the Torah since they are only words of prophecy and not words of Torah.

146 / Shabbos Delights

This clarifies Rashi's intention. It is surprising why the Torah does not mention what were the words of Moshe's blessing. Therefore Rashi adds that they are part of the eleven psalms which Moshe composed, and thus cannot be written in the Torah since they are only "words of prophecy."

(Gan Raveh)

וַיָּשֶׂם אֶת הַכִּיֹּר בֵּין אֹהֶל מוֹעֵד וּבֵין הַמִּזְבֵּחַ... (מ:ל)

> He placed the washbasin between the
> Ohel Moed and the Mizbe'ach... (40:30)

The order of the placement of vessels is usually listed with the inner vessels first. Yet here it seems that the Mizbe'ach was first set down and only afterwards the washbasin. Why?

Hashem instructed (40:6-7) to place the washbasin between the Ohel Moed and Mizbe'ach. This means that the place of the washbasin is determined in relation to the Ohel Moed and Mizbe'ach. Unless the Mizbe'ach was placed, there was no way of determining where the washbasin should be placed. Therefore the Mizbe'ach had to be placed first.

(R' Chaim Soloveitchik, Taamah D'Kra)

VAYIKRA

... וַיְדַבֵּר ה' אֵלָיו מֵאֹהֶל מוֹעֵד לֵאמֹר. (א:א)

...Hashem spoke to him from the Ohel Moed saying. (1:1)

THE MIDRASH (*SIFRA* 2:13), QUOTED BY RASHI, EXPLAINS THE word לֵאמֹר [literally: "to say"] to mean that Hashem instructed Moshe to present the laws of the offerings to the Jews Moshe is then to return and notify Him if the Jews willingly accepted those laws. This instruction is not found regarding any other set of laws in the Torah. What is so unique about the laws of offerings that Hashem wished to know if they were willingly accepted?

The Gemara explains that at the time of the giving of the Torah at Mt. Sinai the Jews were coerced into accepting observance of the laws of the Torah (*Shabbos* 88a).

The Gemara states that a *korban* must be brought willingly, without coercion, in order for it to be valid (*Rosh Hashanah* 6a). This answers our question. Hashem wanted that not only should each specific offering be brought willingly, but even the concept of bringing offerings should be accepted willingly by the Jews. Since the Torah as a whole had been pressed upon the Jews, Hashem instructed Moshe to specifically investigate if the laws of the offerings were acceptable to them.

There is an additional law regarding offerings. If there is any doubt as to one's consent, then he must orally express his willingness to bring the offering (ibid.). For this reason, Moshe was told to actually **hear** the words of consent from the Jews.

(Imrei Shefer)

... אֶל פֶּתַח אֹהֶל מוֹעֵד יַקְרִיב אֹתוֹ לִרְצֹנוֹ לִפְנֵי ה'. (א:ג)

...he shall bring it to the entrance of the Ohel Moed,
willingly, *before Hashem (1:3)*

The Torah stipulates that an offering must be brought willingly. The Gemara states that in a situation where one is required to bring an offering yet does not want to, *beis din* coerces him into (a) doing so and (b) declaring that he is doing it willingly (*Rosh Hashanah* 6a). This seems incomprehensible: How can it be considered "willingly" if he is being coerced?

The Gemara states that if a Gentile sent an offering to the Beis HaMikdash but did not include the requisite wine libation, *beis din* does not coerce the Gentile to send the wine, but purchases it with public funds (*Menachos* 73a). The *Shittah Mekubetzes* (ibid., note 4) points out that a Jew would be forced by *beis din* to provide the necessary wine. The reason for the discrepancy, explains the *Shittah Mekubetzes*, is that were the Gentile coerced it would not be considered "willingly." This needs clarification. If a Jew is coerced, why is it nevertheless considered as being voluntary?

A similar concept of a coerced declaration of willingness is found in regard to the laws of divorce. If one is obligated to divorce his wife and refuses to do so, *beis din* beats him into submission and also requires him to declare his willingness to divorce. Rambam (*Gerushin* 2:20) explains this seemingly meaningless declaration as follows. When halachah requires a Jew to divorce his wife, then since the inner will of every Jew is to obey the laws of the Torah, it is indeed his will to grant a divorce. The Evil Inclination is preventing him from actualizing his true will. Therefore *beis din* beats the Evil Inclination into submission. His subsequent declaration of willingness is sincere and a reflection of his true desire.

This explanation can be applied here. If a Jew who is required to bring an offering refuses to do so, it is only the Evil Inclination which hinders him. After being beaten, the Jew expresses his true desire which is to do what is right. With regard to a Gentile, his refusal indicates his true will. Any subsequent coerced declaration will not be a statement of his true will. (*Har Tzvi*)

The *pasuk* concludes that the offering is brought "in front of Hashem." This phrase seems superfluous. But in light of the above it can be suggested that this phrase refers to the preceding word "willingly." The Torah is saying that the offering should be brought even if the "willingness" is not apparent to us, but exists only "in front of Hashem." The case referred to is the one mentioned above, where a Jew is coerced by *beis din* to bring the offering. In such an instance, only Hashem is aware that there exists a sincere willingness to bring the offering.

(*Kesav Sofer*)

... וְהִקְרִיבוּ בְּנֵי אַהֲרֹן הַכֹּהֲנִים אֶת הַדָּם ... (א:ה)

... the sons of Aharon, the Kohanim, shall bring the blood... (1: 5)

The Gemara relates the following incident. In the era of the Judges, Eli *HaKohen* sought a Kohen to slaughter an animal as an offering. Shmuel *HaNavi* noticed and remarked that any Jew is permitted to perform the slaughter of the sacrificial animal. Eli questioned him as to the source of his statement. Shmuel replied that since the Torah only mentions that the Kohanim are the ones who receive the blood and bring it to the Altar, the implication is that prior to that stage, any Jew may perform the service. Eli commented that although Shmuel may be correct, he nevertheless transgressed the prohibition of deciding a halachic question in the presence of his teacher (*Berachos* 31b).

It is difficult to understand how Eli could not have been aware of this halachah. From when the Mishkan was erected in the wilderness, until that day, many offerings had been brought, with the slaughter not necessarily being done by a Kohen.

This can only be understood in light of an obscure Midrash (*Yalkut Shimoni, remez* 579), which states that in the Wilderness offerings had been required to be slaughtered by Kohanim. Since up until then it had been the custom to use a Kohen, Eli was unsure about the validity of using a non-Kohen in Eretz Yisrael.

But the Midrash itself warrants an explanation. Why was there a different law in the wilderness before the Jews entered Eretz Yisrael?

Tosefos (*Yoma* 32b) posits the reason why slaughter of an animal is permitted even by a non-Kohen. Since even nonsacrificial animals have ritual slaughter, the act of slaughter is not unique to the sacrificial process and therefore does not require a Kohen.

This only applied after the Jews were settled in Eretz Yisrael and were permitted to eat nonsacrificial meat. But when the Jews were in the Wilderness and ate only sacrificial meat (*Chullin* 16b), the act of slaughter did constitute a part of the sacrificial process, and thus required a Kohen to perform it.

(*Taam VeDaas* (*parashas Acharei*), Toldos Adam, Chap. 8)

אִם עֹלָה קָרְבָּנוֹ מִן הַבָּקָר ... (א:ג)
וְהִקְרִיבוּ בְּנֵי אַהֲרֹן הַכֹּהֲנִים אֶת הַדָּם ... (א:ה)
וְאִם מִן הָעוֹף עֹלָה קָרְבָּנוֹ לה' ... (א:י"ד) וְהִקְרִיבוֹ הַכֹּהֵן ... (א:ט"ו)

> *If one's **offering** is an elevation-offering from the cattle... (1:3)*
> *....the sons of Aharon, the **Kohanim**, shall bring the blood... (1:5)*
> *If one's **offering to Hashem** is an elevation-offering of fowl... (1:14) The **Kohen** shall bring it... (1:15)*

There are two inconsistencies in the *pesukim* between an elevation-offering of cattle to one of fowl. First, regarding cattle it says "offering," and regarding fowl it says "offering to Hashem". Second, by cattle it says "Kohanim" and by fowl it says "Kohen." What are the reasons for these differences?

Although no one eats any part of the *olah* [elevation-offering], the Kohen derives some benefit from a cattle *olah*: He keeps the hide. Since a part goes to a person, it does not say "an offering to Hashem." Likewise it says Kohanim, since the hide was divided among the Kohanim of that shift.

A fowl *olah* is entirely consumed by the Altar. Thus the phrase "offering to Hashem." Likewise only one Kohen benefited from the sacrifice: the one who actually did the *avodah* and earned a mitzvah for the service.

(*Panim Yafos*)

... וְהִזָּה מִן הַדָּם שֶׁבַע פְּעָמִים לִפְנֵי ה' אֶת פְּנֵי פָּרֹכֶת הַקֹּדֶשׁ. (ד:ו)

> ...he shall sprinkle some of the blood seven times before Hashem toward the Curtain of the Holy. (4:6)

Here, in connection to the offering of the Anointed Kohen, the term "Curtain of the Holy" is used. Later on, when discussing the communal offering, the term "Curtain" is written. Why the inconsistency?

The Mishnah (*Megillah* 1:9) explains that only a Kohen Gadol who had been anointed brought this offering. It follows then, that this offering was only brought in the days of the first Beis HaMikdash, when it was still possible to anoint with the oil, and not in the time of the second Beis HaMikdash.

Besides the unavailability of anointment oil in the era of the second Beis HaMikdash, the Ark with the *luchos* was missing. It can therefore be suggested that the Torah hints that the sacrifice of the Anointed Kohen will only be brought as long as there will be a Curtain of Holy, i.e. as long as the Ark will be there, and as such the Curtain will warrant the title "of Holy." But the communal offering was brought even in the era of the second Beis HaMikdash, when there was no Ark, thus appropriately not adding the words "of Holy" when mentioning its Curtain.

(*R' Chaim Berlin*, quoted in *MiShulchan Govoha*)

וְאֶת הַשֵּׁנִי יַעֲשֶׂה עֹלָה **כַּמִּשְׁפָּט**... (ה:י)

And he shall make the second one an elevation-offering **according to the law**... *(5:10)*

The Torah lists the sins for which a *korban asham*, a guilt-offering, is brought, and states that one should bring either a sheep or a goat for the offering. If one cannot afford that, he can instead bring two young doves, one as a *chatas* [sin-offering], and one as an *olah* [elevation-offering]. The Torah concludes and writes that he should make the *olah* "according to the law." What does that mean?

The Gemara explains that "according to the law" teaches that just as a *chatas* offering must be bought from ordinary, mundane money, and must be offered by day, and must be sacrificed with the right hand, likewise all these laws apply to this dove *olah* offering. The Gemara then asks: Why is it necessary to derive the requirement of its being offered by day from the *chatas*? There is a later *pasuk* from which it is derived that all offerings must be brought by day (*Chullin* 21a).

There are two textual versions regarding the Gemara's reply to this question. The version printed in today's Gemara's reads that although it was not really necessary to derive it from a *chatas*, still it is possible to derive it from there. There was another textual reading in the Gemara, which read that if not for this new derivation, one would think that the dove *olah* is an exception to the rule, and could be offered at night. About six hundred years ago, a letter of inquiry was sent to the noted Rashba: Why would one think that the dove *olah* is an exception? The Rashba responded that there is no logic to this and that it is a mistaken textual reading (*Responsa* of *Rashba*, 1:276).

We feel that there is an explanation for that reading. The Ibn Ezra (5:7) points out that a person of means brings only an *asham* offering while the poor person must add an *olah* offering. The reason for this, suggests the Ibn Ezra, is that an animal has fats which are totally consumed by the fire of the *Mizbe'ach*. A fowl has no fats, so instead an *olah*, which is also totally consumed, is brought. Based upon this, we can say that one might think that just as the fats of an animal burn all night on the *Mizbe'ach*, likewise this *olah*, which is its replacement, could also be sacrificed at night.[5]

(*Ohr Same'ach, Maaser Sheni* 7:3, and in the appendix)

---

5. EDITOR'S NOTE: There is an intriguing addendum to this explanation. In the introduction to *Minchas Baruch*, Rabbi Chaim Stein *shlit"a* quotes the author, Rav Baruch Ginzburg *zt"l*. Rav Ginzburg visited Rav Meir Simchah, author of *Ohr Same'ach*, and found him in an ecstatic mood. He had just thought of an original and beautiful explanation of a difficult Gemara. Furthermore, he continued, he dozed off right after, and dreamed that he was in Heaven with all the great scholars, and they were complaining that there were no longer scholars who can offer true explanations of the Gemara. Suddenly the Rashba stood up and said, "A scholar in Dvinsk (the town where Rav Meir Simchah, resided) just offered a truthful explanation better than I gave!" Rav Meir Simchah then told the above explanation to Rav Ginzburg, explaining that the Rashba was referring to this explanation.

It is interesting to note that the *Ohr Some'ach* concludes the explanation with the comment, "I am very happy that Hashem led me in the right path." In light of this story, it is understood why Rav Meir Simchah was confident that indeed he had gone on the right path with his explanation.

TZAV

צַו אֶת אַהֲרֹן וְאֶת בָּנָיו... (ו:ב)

Command Aharon and his sons ... (6:2)

IN THE PREVIOUS PARASHAH (*VAYIKRA*) THE PRECEPTS PERTAINING TO the offerings are addressed only to the "children of Aharon," and not to Aharon. This is the first time that Aharon's name is mentioned in this context. Why?

The previous *parashah* deals with various offerings, but none that were brought in the Wilderness. Since Aharon died before Bnei Yisrael entered the land, he brought offerings only in the Wilderness, therefore his name is not mentioned. This *pasuk* discusses the *olas tamid,* which was the only offering in the Wilderness (*Sifri, Bamidbar* 9:5), and therefore includes Aharon's name in the directive. (*Divrei Yehonasan*)

וּכְלִי חֶרֶשׂ אֲשֶׁר תְּבֻשַּׁל בּוֹ יִשָּׁבֵר וְאִם בִּכְלִי נְחֹשֶׁת בֻּשָּׁלָה וּמֹרַק וְשֻׁטַּף בַּמָּיִם (ו:כ״א)

An earthenware vessel in which it was cooked shall be broken. But if it was cooked in a copper vessel, that should be purged and rinsed in water. (6:21)

Any particles of an offering which remain past the time when they may be consumed are designated as "*nossar*" – left over. This pertains even to particles that were absorbed by the pot in which they were cooked, and they render the pot unusable. Purging a copper pot totally destroys those particles. This method is not feasible with regard to an earthen pot and therefore it must be shattered.

There is an opinion (see *Tosefos, Avodah Zara* 76a) that any food absorbed in a pot spoils overnight. Since spoiled food does not qualify as "*nossar,*" a different explanation is necessary according to this opinion as to why the Torah requires the purging or shattering of these pots.

The Mishnah (*Avos* 5:5) states that ten miracles occurred in the Beis HaMikdash. One of them was that the sacrificial meat did not spoil. Therefore, according to everyone, it was necessary to purge the pots in which the sacrificial meat was cooked.

(*Levias Chein*)

זֹאת הַתּוֹרָה לָעֹלָה לַמִּנְחָה לַחַטָּאת וְלָאָשָׁם וְלַמִּלּוּאִים וּלְזֶבַח הַשְּׁלָמִים. אֲשֶׁר צִוָּה ה' אֶת מֹשֶׁה בְּהַר סִינַי בְּיוֹם צַוֹּתוֹ אֶת בְּנֵי יִשְׂרָאֵל לְהַקְרִיב אֶת קָרְבְּנֵיהֶם לַה' **בְּמִדְבַּר סִינָי.** (ז:ל״ז,ל״ח)

> *T*his is the law of the elevation-offering, the meal-offering, the sin-offering, and the guilt-offering; and the inauguration-offerings, and the feast-offering; which Hashem commanded Moshe on Mt. Sinai, on the day He commanded the Jews to bring their offerings to Hashem **in the** Wilderness **of Sinai.** (7:37,38)

The concluding phrase, "in the Wilderness of Sinai," seems superfluous. Why is it written?

The Gemara derives from an earlier phrase in the *pasuk* — "on the day" — that offerings may only be brought during the daytime (*Zevachim* 98a). This rule only applies to major communal sacrificial altars, such as the Mishkan or Beis HaMikdash; on a private altar (*bamah*) one may bring offerings both by day and by night (*Zevachim* 120a, according to one opinion).

Private altars were only permitted during certain brief periods of Jewish history, i.e. during the years of conquest and settlement of the Land (*Zevachim* 112b). If so, the phrase "in the Wilderness of Sinai" can be understood as limiting the law of "during the daytime": Offerings are to be brought during the day only when the Jews were in the Wilderness of Sinai, but not during the years when they engaged in the conquest of Eretz Yisrael.

(*Meshech Chochmah*)

וַיַּקְרֵב מֹשֶׁה אֶת בְּנֵי אַהֲרֹן וַיַּלְבִּשֵׁם כֻּתֳּנֹת וַיַּחְגֹּר אֹתָם אַבְנֵט וַיַּחֲבֹשׁ לָהֶם מִגְבָּעוֹת כַּאֲשֶׁר צִוָּה ה' אֶת מֹשֶׁה. (ח:י"ג)

*Moshe drew the sons of Aharon near to him, and he dressed them in **Tunics**, and he girded them with a **Sash**, and he wrapped the **Headdresses** upon them, as Hashem commanded Moshe. (8:13)*

The Torah, in describing how Moshe dressed the Kohanim, refers to the Sash in singular form, but to all other garments in plural. This incongruity can be explained according to the Rambam (*Klei HaMikdash* 8:19) who writes that the Sash that was wrapped around the Kohen was thirty-two *amos* (approximately forty-eight feet) long. Since the Sash was very long, it fit all the Kohanim, and only one size was necessary. All the other garments required different sizes to fit all the sizes of the various Kohanim.

(*Meshech Chochmah*)

וַיַּקְרֵב מֹשֶׁה אֶת בְּנֵי אַהֲרֹן וַיַּלְבִּשֵׁם **כֻּתֳּנֹת** וַיַּחְגֹּר אֹתָם **אַבְנֵט** וַיַּחֲבֹשׁ לָהֶם **מִגְבָּעוֹת** כַּאֲשֶׁר צִוָּה ה' אֶת מֹשֶׁה. (ח:י״ג)

> Moshe drew the sons of Aharon near to him, and he dressed them with **Tunics**, and he girded them with a **Sash**, and he wrapped the **Headdresses** upon them, as Hashem commanded Moshe. (8:13)

Upon reading this *pasuk* one is struck by an anomaly. The Tunics and Headdresses are written in plural form, while the Sash is written in singular. Furthermore, earlier in *parashas Tetzaveh* (*Shemos* 28:40), the Torah writes that Moshe was commanded to make Tunics, Sashes, and Headdresses for the Kohanim; the "Sashes" also written in the plural There is an opinion in the Gemara (*Yerushalmi*, quoted by *Tosefos, Chagigah* 3a) that every Kohen received two of each item; thus using plural words when mentioning the garments is more appropriate.

One could answer that the Kohanim only donned one Sash during the inauguration period as opposed to the other garments. But even if this was so, what was the reason for it?

One can suggest that the purpose of having two of each of the garments was in order to use a better-quality garment while actually performing the sacrificial service, and one of lesser quality while removing the ashes of the *Mizbe'ach* (see *Rashi* earlier, 6:4). Likewise, during the inauguration period, the better garments were worn during the time of anointment, and the cheaper ones during the days they sat at the entrance to the *Ohel Moed* (see *pasuk* 35). However, the *Avnet*, which was made of sha'atnez, was only allowed to be worn during the time of service in the Mishkan or during the anointment (*Arachin* 3b), but not while the Kohanim were merely seated at the entrance to the *Ohel Moed*. Therefore, during the inauguration period only one Sash was donned: while being anointed.

(*Toras Moshe*)

וַיַּגֵּשׁ אֵת פַּר הַחַטָּאת וַיִּסְמֹךְ אַהֲרֹן וּבָנָיו
אֶת יְדֵיהֶם עַל רֹאשׁ פַּר הַחַטָּאת. (ח:י"ד)

He brought forward the sin-offering bull; Aharon and his sons leaned their hands on the head of the sin-offering bull. (8:14)

When the Torah mentions the placing of the hands of Aharon and his children on the head of the bull the Torah uses the singular *vayismach*. Later, in *pasuk* 18, when mentioning the placing of hands on the ram, the Torah uses the plural *vayismechu*. Why did the Torah differentiate between the two?

A simple answer can be offered. A bull has a large head and thus Aharon and his sons were able to simultaneously place their hands on the bull's head. Since it was done at one time, the word *vayismach* is used. A ram has a smaller head, which forced everyone to take turns placing their hands on it. Therefore the plural *vayismechu* is used.

(*Binyan Shlomo*)

SHEMINI

וַיֹּאמֶר מֹשֶׁה אֶל אַהֲרֹן קְרַב אֶל הַמִּזְבֵּחַ... (ט:ז)

Moshe said to Aharon, "Approach the altar..." (9:7)

ASHI QUOTES A MIDRASH (*SIFRA*) WHICH EXPLAINS THAT AHARON hesitated to approach the *Mizbe'ach*. Therefore Moshe told him, "Why are you hesitating to approach? You have been chosen for this task." If Aharon had been chosen for this, why then did he balk?

There is a law (*Orach Chaim* 53:16) that if one is requested to lead the prayer services he should decline the honor out of modesty. Only after being asked two or three times by the congregation should he accept the honor.

This halachah inspired Aharon's reaction. Aharon did not want to accept the honor of being the one to offer the animals on behalf of the entire nation. Moshe then told him to proceed immediately since he was chosen for the task. Moshe was referring to another halachah (ibid. 53:15), which states that if one is the regular appointed cantor, then he immediately proceeds to lead the prayer without delay. Therefore, Aharon, who was to do this task regularly, was instructed to proceed without delay.

(*Binyan Ariel*)

וַיֹּאמֶר מֹשֶׁה אֶל אַהֲרֹן קְרַב אֶל הַמִּזְבֵּחַ... (ט:ז)

Moshe said to Aharon, "Approach the altar..." (9:7)

Rashi quotes a Midrash (*Sifra*) which explains that out of modesty Aharon did not want to accept the honor of sacrificing on behalf of the nation. Moshe then told him to proceed since he was chosen "for that [reason]." What did he mean by that?

The Gemara states that originally Moshe was to have been the Kohen Gadol, but he lost that right as a punishment for demurring regarding Hashem's directive to lead the Jews out of Egypt. Even though Moshe's refusal stemmed from modesty, nevertheless it was inappropriate not to comply with Hashem's order (*Zevachim* 102a).

This sheds light on Moshe's remark. Moshe told Aharon not to refuse Hashem's directive since Aharon only received the right to be a Kohen as a result of a refusal [on the part of Moshe] of Hashem's order! (*Panim Yafos*)

וַתֵּצֵא אֵשׁ מִלִּפְנֵי ה' וַתֹּאכַל אוֹתָם וַיָּמֻתוּ לִפְנֵי ה'. (י:ב)

A fire went out from before Hashem and consumed them, and they died before Hashem. (10:2)

The Gemara states that two strands of fire emanated from the *Kodesh HaKadashim* and entered their nostrils and consumed them (*Sanhedrin* 52a). Why did they receive this unique punishment?

The Gemara says that the sons of Aharon were punished for teaching halachah in the presence of Moshe their mentor. Ordinarily, that sin is punishable by being bitten by a snake (*Eruvin* 63a). However, there were no snakes in the vicinity. Why not? The Midrash (*Devarim Rabbah* 7:9) says that when the Jews were in the Wilderness Hashem would send two strands of fire from the *Kodesh HaKadashim* that would incinerate the snakes.

If so, it was most appropriate that those two strands of fire should accomplish what the snakes ordinarily would; i.e. punish those who teach halachah in the presence of their mentor.

(*Tiferes Yehonasan*)

וַיִּקְרְבוּ וַיִּשָּׂאֻם בְּכֻתֳּנֹתָם אֶל מִחוּץ לַמַּחֲנֶה. (י:ה)

*They approached and carried them by their tunics
to the outside of the camp (10:5)*

Why does the Torah mention how they were carried out? The Ibn Ezra (*Shemos* 40:2) posits that the day on which this occurred was Shabbos. If so, it would have been prohibited to carry them out, since a corpse is *muktzah* and may not be moved. However, there is an opinion that one may move a corpse dressed in his clothing (*Shulchan Aruch* 311:4). The Torah mentions that they were wearing tunics to indicate that they were permitted to be carried on Shabbos.

(*Tiferes Yehonasan*)

וַיֹּאמֶר מֹשֶׁה אֶל אַהֲרֹן וּלְאֶלְעָזָר וּלְאִיתָמָר בָּנָיו רָאשֵׁיכֶם אַל תִּפְרָעוּ וּבִגְדֵיכֶם לֹא תִפְרֹמוּ... (י:ו)

*Moshe said to Aharon and to his sons Elazar
and Isamar, "Do not leave your heads unshorn
and do not rend your garments..." (10:6)*

The Gemara explains that although a mourner rends his clothing, the sons of Aharon were instructed not to do so, in order not to detract from the joyousness of the inauguration of the Mishkan (*Moed Kattan* 15a).

The Rambam (*Klei HaMikdash* 9:3) writes that the Torah prohibits tearing the clothing worn by the Kohanim for their service. Why were the sons of Aharon warned not to tear their clothing? They were anyway not allowed to tear the special clothing which they were then wearing.

One can suggest that the prohibition of tearing *bigdei Kehunah* is only if one tears the cloth itself, but not if one tears on the seam. Only permanent damage is prohibited. The *bigdei Kehunah* were required to be woven and therefore if the cloth was torn it could not be repaired. But a tear on the seam could be resewn, thus not being prohibited.

The word used here for tearing is *siframu*. Rashi explains that word to mean splits open at the seam (*Makkos* 22b). If so, our question is answered. They were warned not to unstitch their clothing although ordinarily it would be permitted. (*Marcheshes* Chap.2)

אַךְ אֶת זֶה לֹא תֹאכְלוּ מִמַּעֲלֵי הַגֵּרָה וּמִמַּפְרִסֵי הַפַּרְסָה אֶת הַגָּמָל כִּי מַעֲלֵה גֵרָה הוּא וּפַרְסָה אֵינֶנּוּ מַפְרִיס טָמֵא הוּא לָכֶם. וְאֶת הַשָּׁפָן כִּי מַעֲלֵה גֵרָה הוּא וּפַרְסָה לֹא יַפְרִיס טָמֵא הוּא לָכֶם. וְאֶת הָאַרְנֶבֶת כִּי מַעֲלַת גֵּרָה הִוא וּפַרְסָה לֹא הִפְרִיסָה טְמֵאָה הִוא לָכֶם. וְאֶת הַחֲזִיר כִּי מַפְרִיס פַּרְסָה הוּא וְשֹׁסַע שֶׁסַע פַּרְסָה וְהוּא גֵּרָה לֹא יִגָּר טָמֵא הוּא לָכֶם. (י"א:ד-ז)

> *But this is what you shall not eat from among those that bring up their cud or that have split hooves: the camel, for it brings up its cud, **but its hoof is not split** — it is unclean to you; and the hyrax, for it brings up its cud, **but its hoof is not split** — it is unclean to you; and the hare for it brings up its cud, **but its hoof is not split** — it is unclean to you; and the pig, for its hoof is split and its hoof is completely separated, but it does not chew its cud – it is unclean to you. (11:4-7)*

The Torah lists three animals that are prohibited to be eaten because they do not have split hooves. The phrase "but its hoof is not split" is slightly different with regard to each of these animals. In conjunction with the *gamal* (camel), the present tense is used; the *shafan* (hyrax) uses the future tense, and the *arneves* (hare) the past tense. What is the reason for this inconsistency?

The Midrash (*Midrash Rabbah* 13:5) states that each one of the animals mentioned here alludes to one of the countries in which the Jews were exiled. *Gamal* refers to Babylon, *shafan* is Media (which is synonymous with Persia, see *Megillah* 12a), and *arneves* is Greece.

Based on this, the unique phrases can now be explained. Babylon was an empire that lasted a short while — without much of a past or future (see *Yeshayahu* 23:13, and *Rashi* and *Malbim* there, and *Yeshayahu* 13:20). Therefore the phrase used regarding the *gamal* is in the present tense. The Persian Empire will last until the end of days (see *Avodah Zarah* 2); therefore the future tense is used regarding the *shafan*. The Greek Empire was an ancient empire, but once it was destroyed it never was rebuilt (see *Yoel* Chap. 4, *Daniel* Chap. 8, *Avodah Zarah* 8b). Therefore regarding the *arneves* the past tense is used.

(*Taamah D'Kra*)

TAZRIA

וּבִמְלֹאת יְמֵי טָהֳרָה לְבֵן אוֹ לְבַת... (י"ב:ו)

Upon completion of the days of her purity for a son or for a daughter... (12:6)

SEVERAL TIMES IN THIS PARASHAH, THE TORAH MENTIONS THE BIRTH of a "male" or "female" (*pesukim* 2,5,7). Yet here the infants are referred to as a "son" and "daughter." What is the reason for this difference?

The Torah uses "male" and "female" when mentioning birth. The Gemara states that until a baby is thirty days old one cannot assume that it will live; it is considered a possible stillborn (*Shabbos* 135b). One can infer from the Mishnah that a stillborn is not referred to as a "son" (*Nazir* 13a). Therefore the Torah does not refer to a newborn as a "son" or "daughter," but rather as merely a male or female.

This *pasuk*, however, is discussing the laws pertaining to the mother after the child is at least forty days old. Thus the terms "son" and "daughter" are appropriate.

(*Meshech Chochmah*)

וְהִקְרִיבוֹ לִפְנֵי ה' וְכִפֶּר עָלֶיהָ ... וְאִם לֹא תִמְצָא יָדָהּ דֵּי שֶׂה ...
וְכִפֶּר עָלֶיהָ הַכֹּהֵן וְטָהֵרָה. (י״ב:ז-ח)

> *He shall offer it before Hashem and atone for her... But if she cannot afford a sheep... and the Kohen shall provide atonement for her and she shall become purified. (12:7-8)*

When mentioning the offerings of the wealthy woman, the Torah writes "and [he] shall atone for her." Yet afterwards (*pasuk* 8) regarding the indigent woman it is written "and the **Kohen** shall provide atonement for her." Why is there a discrepancy in language?

A woman who has given birth is required to bring two offerings: an *olah* and a *chatas*. For a *chatas* one always brings a dove. But the animal used for this *olah* is a variable sin-offering. A rich woman brings a sheep, whereas a poor woman can bring a dove.

An impoverished woman can bring two doves — one as an *olah* and one as a *chatas*. The Kohen therefore has an active role in her purification, since he chooses which dove will be used for the *chatas* — the offering that purifies her. Therefore the Torah emphasizes that the Kohen is the one who is purifying her. In the case of the rich woman only one dove is used, thus the Kohen does not have a decisive role in the *chatas* offering. Therefore only the pronoun "he" is used.

(R' *Yosef Shaul Nathanson*, quoted by *Talelei Oros*)

אָדָם כִּי יִהְיֶה בְעוֹר בְּשָׂרוֹ שְׂאֵת ... (י״ג:ב)

> *If a person will have on the skin of his flesh a s'eis ... (13:2)*

Rav Avraham Mordechai Alter, the Rebbe of Ger, was asked the following question at a *sheva berachos*:

The Mishnah (*Negaim* 3:2) states that a newlywed who has a *nega* is not declared *tamei* during the seven festive days following his wedding. This seems puzzling since *negaim* appear as a punishment for sins (*Arachin* 16a), and yet the Gemara says that a newlywed is forgiven for all his sins (*Yerushalmi, Bikkurim* Chap. 3)!

Replied the Rebbe:

It is true that one is forgiven on the day of his wedding but the caliber of forgiveness is not greater than that of Yom Kippur. Yom Kippur only atones for sins between man and G-d, not for sins between man and his fellow man from whom he has not asked forgiveness (*Yoma* 85b). If so, a newlywed can have a *nega* due to a sin against a fellow Jew.

(*Rosh Golas Ariel*)

וְרָאָה הַכֹּהֵן וְהִנֵּה כִסְּתָה הַצָּרַעַת אֶת כָּל בְּשָׂרוֹ וְטִהַר אֶת הַנָּגַע כֻּלּוֹ הָפַךְ לָבָן טָהוֹר הוּא (י"ג:י"ג)

> The Kohen shall look and behold – the affliction has covered his entire flesh, then he shall declare the affliction to be pure; having turned completely white, it is pure. (13:13)

Is there a rational explanation why if only one hair of a person is white then he is defiled, yet paradoxically if his whole body turns white then he is pure?

The Torah instructs a *metzora* to sit in solitude so that he will contemplate why he was afflicted and that he must repent. If the *metzora* is not forced to think, there is a strong possibility that he will regard the affliction as occurring merely by chance, and not perceive it as a punishment from Hashem. When something so drastic and unusual happens, such as the entire body turning white, that in itself will cause him to repent without needing any external stimuli.

(*Chafetz Chaim*)

... וְטָמֵא טָמֵא יִקְרָא. (י"ג:מ"ה)

...he is to call out: "Contaminated, contaminated." (13:45)

The Gemara explains that the reason the *metzora* informs everyone of his defilement is to arouse them to pray on his behalf (*Shabbos* 67a). This explanation needs clarification: Why is he different from other sick people who are not required to ask others to pray for them? Furthermore, the Midrash (*Bereishis Rabbah* 53:14) states that a person's prayer on his own behalf is more effective than other people's prayers for him. Let the *metzora* pray for himself rather than ask others to do so.

The Zohar states that a *metzora's* prayers are not answered (53a). This elucidates the aforementioned Gemara. The *metzora* has to request others to pray on his behalf since his own prayers are not effective.

(*Yalkut HaUrim*)

וְהַבֶּגֶד כִּי יִהְיֶה בוֹ נֶגַע צָרַעַת בְּבֶגֶד צֶמֶר אוֹ בְּבֶגֶד פִּשְׁתִּים. אוֹ בִשְׁתִי אוֹ בְעֵרֶב **לַפִּשְׁתִּים וְלַצָּמֶר** ... (י"ג:מ"ז,מ"ח)

*If there be a tzara'as affliction in a garment, in a woolen garment or a linen garment, or in the warp or the woof **of the linen or the wool**... (13:47,48)*

Whenever the Torah mentions wool and linen together the wool is always mentioned first, except in this instance. Why?

The Mishnah (*Negaim* 11:8) mentions the opinion of Rabbi Yehudah who states that wool threads can become defiled through a *nega* only after they have been spun, whereas linen threads can be defiled at an earlier stage (see *Rashi, Shabbos* 27b). This explains why linen is mentioned first.

(*Taamah D'Kra*)

Tazria / 169

Metzora

וְצִוָּה הַכֹּהֵן וְלָקַח לַמִּטַּהֵר שְׁתֵּי צִפֳּרִים חַיּוֹת טְהֹרוֹת...(י״ד:ד)

The Kohen shall command; and for the person being purified there shall be taken two live, clean birds... (14:4)

THE GEMARA EXPLAINS THAT THE REASON BIRDS ARE PART OF THE purification process of the *metzora* is since *tzara'as* is a punishment for slanderous idle chatter, birds that constantly chatter are brought (*Arachin* 16b). However the Gemara does not explain the reason for two birds, or why one is slaughtered and one released.

The Gemara derives from a *pasuk* that a person's "occupation" should be "to be quiet," in order to avoid sins pertaining to speech. It further derives that this maxim does not apply to the study of Torah: the more words of Torah spoken the better (*Chullin* 89a).

This *derashah* explains the symbolism of this *pasuk*. One bird is slaughtered, symbolizing the need to be quiet, but the other bird is set free to teach us that there is a form of speech which is laudable.

(*Aperion* [extract])

וּמִיֶּתֶר הַשֶּׁמֶן אֲשֶׁר עַל כַּפּוֹ יִתֵּן הַכֹּהֵן עַל תְּנוּךְ אֹזֶן הַמִּטַּהֵר הַיְמָנִית וְעַל בֹּהֶן יָדוֹ הַיְמָנִית וְעַל בֹּהֶן רַגְלוֹ הַיְמָנִית **עַל דַּם** הָאָשָׁם. (י״ד:י״ז)
וְנָתַן הַכֹּהֵן מִן הַשֶּׁמֶן אֲשֶׁר עַל כַּפּוֹ עַל תְּנוּךְ אֹזֶן הַמִּטַּהֵר הַיְמָנִית וְעַל בֹּהֶן יָדוֹ הַיְמָנִית וְעַל בֹּהֶן רַגְלוֹ הַיְמָנִית **עַל מְקוֹם** דַּם הָאָשָׁם. (י״ד:כ״ח)

> *Some of the oil remaining on his palm, the Kohen shall put on the middle part of the right ear of the man being purified, on the thumb of his right hand and on the big toe of his right foot;* **on the blood** *of the guilt-offering. (14: 17)*
> *The Kohen shall place some of the oil that is on his palm upon the middle of the right ear of the person being purified, on the thumb of his right hand and on the big toe of his right foot –* **on the place** *of the guilt-offering's blood. (14:28)*

In describing the purification process of the *metzora*, the Torah instructs the Kohen to place blood of the guilt-offering on the right ear of the *metzora*, on his thumb and his big toe. Afterwards he should place oil on top of the blood.

Several *pesukim* later this instruction is repeated concerning an impoverished *metzora*. However, there it concludes by writing that the oil shall be put on the **place** where the blood was. The Gemara explains that this *pasuk* teaches us that the oil does not have to be poured on the actual blood, but rather on the spot where the blood had been placed (*Menachos* 10a). Why did the Torah see fit to teach us this when discussing the offering of the impoverished *metzora,* and not earlier regarding the one who is wealthy?

The Gemara states that a *metzora* may bring his *asham* offering on one day and pour the oil several days later (*Zevachim* 44b). Ideally it is best to perform them both on the same day. It is therefore logical to assume that a wealthy *metzora* does just that: pours the oil on the same day, when there is still blood left over on his hand. But an indigent person, who cannot readily afford to purchase oil, delays the pouring of the oil for several days. When it is finally poured, no blood remains; thus he merely pours on the place where the blood was.

(*Binyan Shlomo*)

וְאִם דַּל הוּא וְאֵין יָדוֹ מַשֶּׂגֶת... (י״ד:כ״א)

If he is poor and his means are not sufficient...(14:21)

The Gemara states that the sacrifice of the *metzora* is unique in that everyone agrees that a rich person does not fulfill his obligation by bringing the sacrifice of a pauper (*Yoma* 41b). Why is this so?

The Gemara explains that one reason *tzara'as* appears is in punishment for being stingy (*Arachin* 16a). If so, a wealthy person who offers a meager offering shows that he has not repented from his sin of miserliness, and therefore is not forgiven.

(*Meshech Chochmah* [14:51])

וְהַנּוֹתָר בַּשֶּׁמֶן אֲשֶׁר עַל כַּף הַכֹּהֵן יִתֵּן עַל רֹאשׁ הַמִּטַּהֵר וְכִפֶּר עָלָיו **הַכֹּהֵן** לִפְנֵי ה׳. (י״ד:י״ח)
וְהַנּוֹתָר מִן הַשֶּׁמֶן אֲשֶׁר עַל כַּף הַכֹּהֵן יִתֵּן עַל רֹאשׁ הַמִּטַּהֵר **לְכַפֵּר עָלָיו** לִפְנֵי ה׳. (י״ד:כ״ט)

And the rest of the oil that is on the Kohen's palm, he shall place upon the head of the person being purified; **and the Kohen will have provided him with atonement** *before Hashem. (14:18)*
And the rest of the oil that is on the Kohen's palm, he shall place upon the head of the person being purified; **to provide him atonement** *before Hashem. (14:29)*

When discussing the offering of the wealthy *metzora* (14:18), the Torah writes that after the placing of the oil the *metzo-*

ra will be forgiven, implying total atonement. Yet when mentioning the indigent *metzora* (14:29), the language implies that the oil is an integral part of the atonement process but not that the process is complete. Why is there a difference?

The Gemara states that one reason *tzara'as* appears is as a punishment for being haughty. It is understandable, although not condoned, if a wealthy individual is haughty (*Arachin* 16a) — he has what to be proud of (as the Torah warns, see *Devarim* 8:13-4). But it is especially despicable for a poor person to be haughty (*Pesachim* 113b). Therefore the full atonement is not granted to the poor person by merely pouring the oil.

(*Meshech Chochmah*)

דַּבְּרוּ אֶל בְּנֵי יִשְׂרָאֵל וַאֲמַרְתֶּם אֲלֵהֶם אִישׁ אִישׁ כִּי יִהְיֶה זָב מִבְּשָׂרוֹ זוֹבוֹ טָמֵא הוּא (ט"ו:ב)

> *Speak to the Children of Israel and say to them: Any man who will have a discharge from his flesh, his discharge is contaminated. (15:2)*

Moshe and Aharon were commanded to "speak to the Children of Israel," regarding a *zav* but not regarding a *metzora*. Why not?

A *metzora* is required to totally isolate himself from all three camps of the Jews. A *zav*, on the other hand, may reside among the Yisraelim; he is only prohibited from being near the Mishkan and near the Kohanim and Levites (*Pesachim* 67a). Therefore, since the *metzora* in a sense is alone and not part of the Jewish people, Moshe is not commanded to address the Jewish people concerning the *metzora*.

(*Meshech Chochmah*)

וְהַדָּוָה בְּנִדָּתָהּ (ט"ו:ל"ג)

And concerning a woman who suffers through her separation ... (15:33)

The Gemara mentions the opinion of the "Early Elders" who derive from this *pasuk* that when a woman is a *niddah* she should not apply make-up or adorn herself in any manner. Rabbi Akiva argues that if a *niddah* does not dress up it is possible that she will be ugly in the eyes of her husband who might then divorce her (*Shabbos* 64b). One can ask: Why were the Elders not troubled by Rabbi Akiva's concern?

The Mishnah documents a dispute as to what constitutes legal grounds for divorce. Beis Shammai say only if a woman is found to be immoral. Beis Hillel say even if she ruins his food. Rabbi Akiva says a husband may divorce his wife merely in order to marry a more attractive woman (*Gittin* 90a).

The Gemara can now be explained. The "Elders" mentioned in the Gemara are none other than "Shammai the Elder" and "Hillel the Elder." According to them a husband cannot divorce his wife merely if she is no longer attractive. Therefore they are not concerned if a *niddah* does not apply cosmetics. But Rabbi Akiva, who says that a lack of beauty is grounds for divorce, is concerned for the *niddah* and allows her to beautify herself.

(*Yalkut HaUrim*, in the name of *Zichron Yaakov*)

Acharei Mos

וַיְדַבֵּר ה' אֶל מֹשֶׁה ... וַיֹּאמֶר ה' אֶל מֹשֶׁה ... (ט״ז:א-ב)

*Hashem **spoke** to Moshe...*
*and Hashem **said** to Moshe... (16:1-2)*

SOMETIMES THE TORAH WRITES THAT HASHEM **SPOKE** TO MOSHE; other times it says that Hashem **said** to Moshe. This is the only place in the Torah where it is written that Hashem both "spoke" and "said" to Moshe. Why are both terms used here?

The Gemara states that when Moshe was given those mitzvos which are eternal the word *vayedaber* [he spoke] is used. The word *vayomer* [he said] is usually used by those mitzvos which were of a temporary nature (*Makkos* 11a).

This *parashah* is discussing two mitzvos simultaneously. One mitzvah applies to all Kohanim Gedolim throughout the generations. The Torah permits them to enter the Kodesh HaKadashim only on Yom Kippur, and only following the procedure given here. The other mitzvah was limited solely to Aharon *HaKohen*. According to the Midrash (*Vayikra Rabbah* Chap. 21), Aharon was permitted to enter the Kodesh HaKadashim anytime during the year as long as he followed the procedure enumerated here. Therefore, this *parashah* begins with the word *vayedaber* reflecting the eternal aspect of this mitzvah. But when Moshe is commanded to speak to Aharon it says *vayomer*, reflecting the temporal aspect of this mitzvah, which applied only to Aharon.   (*Taamah D'Kra*)

וְנָתַן אַהֲרֹן עַל שְׁנֵי הַשְּׂעִירִם גֹּרָלוֹת גּוֹרָל אֶחָד לַה' וְגוֹרָל אֶחָד לַעֲזָאזֵל. (ט״ז:ח)

Aharon shall place lots upon the two he-goats: one lot "for Hashem" and one lot "for Azazel." (16:8)

The cantillations under the words indicate the grouping of the words into phrases of the *pasuk*. There are also varying degrees of separations. The cantillation under the word "one" preceding the word "for Hashem" is of a lesser degree than the cantillation under the word "one" preceding the word "for Azazel," thus indicating that there is less of a separation between those two words. Why is that so?

The Gemara explains that there was a difference between the two lots. The lot for Azazel had only the word "Azazel" written on it, but the lot for Hashem had the words "*echad laShem*" [one for Hashem] written on it (*Yerushalmi, Yoma* 4:1).

This is reflected in the cantillations. Since the word "*echad*" was written together with the word "*laShem*" there is a lesser separation between the two. (*Tzafnas Pane'ach*)

... לִפְנֵי ה' תִּטְהָרוּ (ט״ז:ל)

...before Hashem you shall be purified. (16:30)

The Mishnah (*Keilim* 17:14) points out that on certain days duirng the week of Creation, objects were created from which vessels are made which can become *tamei* (defiled) On Sunday, the earth was created, and earthenware vessels can be defiled. On Tuesday, the trees were created, and wooden vessels can be defiled. On the other days, nothing that was created can become *tamei*. On Friday, animals and Man were created. Vessels made from their bones and skin can become *tamei*. On Monday, the heaven was created; on Wednesday, the sun and moon were created; and on Thursday, the fish and the birds were created, all of which cannot become *tamei*.

In the calendar system used today, Yom Kippur can only fall on Monday, Wednesday, Thursday, and Shabbos. It is most appropriate that the day of purification of the Jewish people falls on those days of unique purity!

(*Avnei Shoham*)

וְאִישׁ אִישׁ ... אֲשֶׁר יֹאכַל כָּל דָּם וְנָתַתִּי פָנַי בַּנֶּפֶשׁ הָאֹכֶלֶת אֶת הַדָּם **וְהִכְרַתִּי אֹתָהּ** מִקֶּרֶב עַמָּהּ. (י"ז:י)

> *Any man of the House of Israel ... who will consume any blood, I shall concentrate My attention upon the soul consuming the blood,* **and I will cut it off** *from his people. (17:10)*

Earlier, in *parashas Tzav* (7:25), when mentioning the punishment for eating nonkosher fat, the Torah writes "and the **soul** who eats it will be cut off." Here, upon discussing blood, the Torah writes "and **I will cut it off** [the soul]." Why is this act attributed to Hashem only in reference to blood?

The Gemara (*Makkos* 23b) states that people find the drinking of blood repulsive. Eating fat, however is enjoyable. Therefore, a person who drinks blood is doing so solely out of spite, and thus Hashem attributes the punishment to Himself. The one who eats fat is doing it for pleasure, and the punishment is therefore mentioned, but without indicating that Hashem is the One Who is punishing.

(*Meshech Chochmah*)

וְאִישׁ אִישׁ ... אֲשֶׁר יֹאכַל כָּל דָּם **וְנָתַתִּי פָנַי בַּנֶּפֶשׁ הָאֹכֶלֶת אֶת הַדָּם** וְהִכְרַתִּי אֹתָהּ מִקֶּרֶב עַמָּהּ. (י״ז:י)

> Any man of the House of Israel ... who will consume any blood, **I shall concentrate my attention** upon the soul consuming the blood, and I will cut it off from his people (17:10).

The *Midrash* (*Sifra*, 7:3), quoted by *Rashi*, interprets the phrase "I shall concentrate my attention" as meaning that Hashem says that He will "disengage Himself from his other activities and only concentrate on the one who sinned." Considering the fact that Hashem is Omnipotent, it is puzzling why Hashem has to cease paying attention to other matters in order to punish this individual.

The following explanation of Rashi's words can be suggested. Sometimes Hashem judges the entire world as one entity. In such an instance, the decision is based on the spiritual level of the majority of the people of the world. If the majority is deserving to be judged favorably, the entire world will be rewarded, even though a specific individual might not be deserving in his own right. Hashem therefore says that this sinner should not think that he will escape unpunished should Hashem judge the whole world together. Hashem will only focus on this sinner when judging him, and not perceive him as part of the whole world.

(*Imrei Shefer*)

אֶת מִשְׁפָּטַי תַּעֲשׂוּ וְאֶת חֻקֹּתַי תִּשְׁמְרוּ לָלֶכֶת בָּהֶם ... (י״ח:ד)

> Carry out My mishpatim and safeguard My chukos to follow them... (18:4)

The Torah commands a Jew to fulfill all the *mitzvos*, both *mishpatim*, mitzvos that are rational, such as the prohibitions against theft and murder, and also *chukim*, mitzvos that have no basis in logic, such as not eating pork and not wearing *sha'atnez*. One notices a difference in the wording the Torah uses regarding these mitzvos. When mentioning *mishpatim* it says "carry out" and when mentioning *chukim* it says "safeguard." Why is a different verb used?

The Rambam (*Shemoneh Perakim* Chap. 6) presents a seeming dispute between the Sages of the Gemara and the philosophers. From the writings of the Sages it appears that if one desires something forbidden and he refrains from sinning he is greater than one who never had the desire at all. Yet the philosophers write that one who does not even desire to sin is greater. The Rambam then writes that there is actually no disagreement between them. The philosophers are discussing *mishpatim*. Everyone would agree that one who naturally obeys them is loftier than one who has an urge to disobey them yet refrains. The Sages are talking about *chukim*. One is greater if he exercises self-control regarding these mitzvos than one who never had any urge at all.

This differentiation by the Rambam explains the wording of this *pasuk*. Telling a person to "carry out" *mishpatim* implies that he should do them out of his own volition. To "safeguard" *chukim* means to keep those laws only because Hashem told you so and you are heeding his command.

(*Aperion*)

Kedoshim

אִישׁ אִמּוֹ וְאָבִיו תִּירָאוּ וְאֶת שַׁבְּתֹתַי תִּשְׁמֹרוּ אֲנִי ה' אֱלֹקֵיכֶם. (י"ט:ג)

Every man: your mother and father shall you revere and My Sabbaths shall you observe, I am Hashem your G-d. (19:3)

THE GEMARA, QUOTED BY RASHI, STATES THAT THE TORAH juxtaposed the precept of honoring one's parents with the precept of observing Shabbos to teach that a child should not obey a parent who commands him to desecrate Shabbos, or to transgress any other transgression (*Bava Metzia* 32a). The *Sifsei Chachamim* explains that although the precept of Shabbos is more stringent than most mitzvos, and one cannot derive from it that all mitzvos override the mitzvah of obeying one's parents, nevertheless this can be derived from the concluding phrase "I am Hashem your G-d."

It is puzzling why the Torah singled out the stringent mitzvah of Shabbos to teach us that observing the mitzvos supersedes obeying parents. Had the Torah picked a lenient mitzvah, the lesson could have been taught without resorting to the additional phrase "I am Hashem your G-d."

According to Torah law, the forbidden labors of Shabbos are those *melachos* that were performed in the construction of the Mishkan and are performed for the very same purpose as they were done in the Mishkan. It is permitted to perform a *melachah* for another purpose [*melachah she'eino tzrichah legufo*] (*Shabbos* 94a, *Tosefos*). Maharik (*shoresh* 137) opines that it follows from this that if one does a *melachah* on Shabbos out of fear of being harmed by a Gentile, that work is considered as *melachah she'eino tzrichah legufo,* and is thus permitted. Likewise, wrote the Rav of Tchebin *zt"l*, if one does work on Shabbos out of respect for a parent's request it should be permitted.

Based upon this, we can explain the Midrash differently than the *Sifsei Chachamim*. In this instance the case of Shabbos is more lenient than all other mitzvos. The Torah picked the case of Shabbos to inform us that even though transgressing the Shabbos out of respect for parents fits into the category of *melachah she'eino tzrichah legufo*, nevertheless he should not obey his parents. If the Torah overrode the request of parents even in such a situation, surely one should not obey his parents to actually transgress any of the laws of the Torah.

(*Birkas Shimon*)

לֹא תִּגְנֹבוּ ... (י"ט:י"א)

You shall not steal ... (19:11)

The prohibition of theft is mentioned twice in the Torah. There is a difference in the subject between the two times. In *parashas Yisro* (*Shemos* 20:13) it is written in singular form [*lo signov*]; here it is written in plural form [*lo signovu*]. Why is this so?

The Gemara explains that the prohibition of stealing mentioned in *parashas Yisro* refers to kidnaping, and the prohibition of stealing mentioned here refers to theft of money. (*Sanhedrin* 86a)

A person who kidnaps receives capital punishment. Two people who kidnap together do not receive capital punishment. However if partners steal money they are both responsible. This halachah is being alluded to in the *pasuk*. The prohibition of kidnaping is written in singular since only if a person kidnaps on his own does he receive the death penalty. The prohibition of stealing is written in plural to signify that even if several people steal together they are all responsible.[6]　　　　　　　　(*Panim Yafos*)

וְלֹא תִשָּׁבְעוּ בִשְׁמִי לַשָּׁקֶר וְחִלַּלְתָּ אֶת שֵׁם אֱלֹקֶיךָ ... (י"ט:י"ב)

You shall not swear falsely by My Name, thereby desecrating the Name of your G-d...(19:12)

The word *sishav'u*, swear, is plural. The word *vechilalta*, desecrating (Hashem's Name), is singular. Why does the Torah make that change?

Rambam (*Shevuos*, 1:3) explains that included in the prohibition of swearing falsely are if he swears that he ate and he actually did not, and also if he swears that he will eat and ultimately does not. It seems that there is nevertheless a difference between the two. A desecration of Hashem's Name only occurs if one lies outrightly and swears falsely about a past event. If one swears about the future it is very possible that he originally intended to keep his word, and even if ultimately he fails to do so, it is not categorized as a desecration of Hashem's Name.

Thus the prohibition of swearing falsely is written in plural form since it includes two types of oaths. But the desecration of Hashem's Name is written in singular form since in only one of the two categories is there a desecration.

(*Meshech Chochmah*)

---

6. EDITOR'S NOTE: No source is found in the Gemara absolving partners in a kidnaping from capital punishment. Rav Chaim Kanievsky *shlit"a* wrote to me that the *Panim Yafos* considered kidnaping tantamount to murder, a crime where the Gemara does absolve partners.

לֹא תִקֹּם... (י״ט:י״ח)

You shall not take revenge... (19:18)

The Gemara (*Yoma* 22b) quotes Rav Yochanan as saying that a "Talmudic scholar who does not take revenge like a snake is not a true scholar." The Gemara asks: How is this statement reconciled with the *pasuk* that prohibits revenge? The Gemara answers by saying that the *pasuk* is referring only to money matters. For instance, if someone refused to lend him a tool, he should not pay him back in kind. But if someone aggravated him, the *talmid chacham* is permitted to take revenge. This answer is difficult to accept since revenge for aggravation also seems to be despicable. Furthermore, nowhere is it recorded that a snake takes revenge.

The Gemara intimates that a snake bites despite the fact that he derives no pleasure from it (*Taanis* 8a). Based upon this, a novel explanation of the previous Gemara can be offered. A scholar who was insulted must take revenge for the sake of the honor of the Torah that he embodies, but not for his own personal gain. Just as a snake receives no pleasure from his bite, but does so because Hashem so decreed after the primordial sin, so too the scholar should have no selfish motive in his revenge. Such revenge is laudable, and should be carried out. (*Chanukas HaTorah*)

כִּי אִישׁ אִישׁ אֲשֶׁר יְקַלֵּל אֶת אָבִיו וְאֶת אִמּוֹ מוֹת יוּמָת אָבִיו וְאִמּוֹ קִלֵּל דָּמָיו בּוֹ. (כ:ט)

For any man who will curse his father or mother shall be put to death; his father or his mother he has cursed, his blood is upon himself. (20:9)

The phrase "his blood is upon himself" appears to mean that if a person curses his parents then he is the cause of his own death. Why is that so?

The Gemara states that there are three partners in the creation of every person — the father, the mother, and Hashem (*Kiddushin* 30b). Therefore, when one curses his own parents, he is also cursing himself, since a part of his parents is in him. It is therefore only fitting that the curse should befall him. Thus he has caused his own death.

(Imrei Shefer)

וְאִישׁ אֲשֶׁר יִנְאַף אֶת אֵשֶׁת אִישׁ אֲשֶׁר יִנְאַף אֶת אֵשֶׁת רֵעֵהוּ
מוֹת יוּמַת הַנֹּאֵף וְהַנֹּאָפֶת. (כ:י)

> *A man who will commit adultery with a man's wife, who will commit adultery with his fellow's wife; the adulterer and the adulteress shall be put to death (20:10).*

There is an apparent redundancy in this *pasuk*: It says "who will commit adultery with a man's wife" and then continues "who will commit adultery with his fellow's wife." How can this be explained?

A woman whose husband suspects her of being unfaithful, and after being warned, nevertheless secludes herself with the suspected man, is required to drink the metaphysical "*sotah* water" which will cause her to die if she was unfaithful. However, if the husband himself was ever unfaithful then the waters will not be effective (*Sotah* 28a).

We can suggest that the intent of the Torah here is to inform us that when *beis din* condemns a person to death, it does so even if at one time the husband himself was unfaithful. The seeming redundant phrase is not describing the adulterer, but rather describing the husband of the adulteress! The *pasuk* thus implies that if a person has an illicit relationship with a woman whose husband had himself been unfaithful with "the wife of his friend," we are still commanded to put them to death. (*Imrei Shefer*)

Emor

וְקִדַּשְׁתּוֹ כִּי אֶת לֶחֶם אֱלֹקֶיךָ הוּא מַקְרִיב... (כ"א:ח)

*You shall sanctify **him**, for he offers the food of your G-d... (21:8)*

U NTIL THIS POINT, THE TORAH ALWAYS SAYS "YOU SHALL SANCTIFY **them**." Why is it written here "you shall sanctify **him**"? The Gemara states that from these words we derive that if a Kohen marries a woman prohibited to him, and he is not willing to divorce her, then *beis din* must force him to divorce her (*Yevamos* 88b). The Torah writes that the reason we are so harsh is because "he offers the food of your G-d." If so, one might mistakenly assume that if there are other eligible Kohanim who could bring sacrifices then *beis din* does not force him to divorce his wife. Therefore the Torah uses a singular term to inform us that the Torah demands that any Kohen who transgresses in this manner is coerced to divorce, regardless of the existence of other Kohanim. (*Ohr HaChaim*)

דַּבֵּר אֶל בְּנֵי יִשְׂרָאֵל... (כ"ג:ב)

Speak to the sons of Israel ... (23:2)

T here are several paragraphs which discuss the laws of the various Yamim Tovim. Most begin with Moshe being told to speak to the "sons of Israel." There are two exceptions — Shavuos and Yom Kippur. What is the reason for this inconsistency?

The Gemara (*Kiddushin* 36a), on an unrelated topic, states that the phrase "bnei Yisrael" refers only to the sons and not daughters. This rule may likewise be applied here and resolve our question.

This first paragraph, which mentions the "sons of Israel," is interpreted by the Midrash as referring to the sanctification of the month (see *Yalkut Shimoni, Emor, remez* 683). Since sanctifying the month is referred to as an act of *beis din* (see *Rosh Hashanah* 25b), then women, who are disqualified from being judges, are exempt from this law. Therefore the phrase "sons of Israel" is aptly used. Likewise, since women are exempt from the mitzvos of *sefiras ha'omer*, shofar, and succah, there too the phrase "sons of Israel" is mentioned., However, both men and women are equally obligated in the laws of Shavuos and Yom Kippur; thus that phrase does not appear there. (*Panim Yafos*)

דַּבֵּר אֶל בְּנֵי יִשְׂרָאֵל לֵאמֹר בַּחֹדֶשׁ הַשְּׁבִיעִי בְּאֶחָד לַחֹדֶשׁ יִהְיֶה לָכֶם שַׁבָּתוֹן זִכְרוֹן תְּרוּעָה מִקְרָא קֹדֶשׁ. (כ״ג:כ״ד)

> *Speak to the Children of Israel saying: In the seventh month, on the first of the month, there shall be a rest day for you, **a remembrance of shofar blasts**, a holy convocation (23:24)*

Here the Torah writes that on Rosh Hashanah there is merely **a remembrance of shofar blasts**. Later (*Bamidbar* 29:1), the Torah writes that the shofar is actually blown on Rosh Hashanah. The Gemara (*Rosh Hashanah* 29b) reconciles the two *pesukim* and says that if Rosh Hashanah falls on a weekday the shofar is actually blown, but if Rosh Hashanah falls on Shabbos then the shofar is only mentioned. [Although the prohibition of blowing the shofar on Shabbos is actually of Rabbinical origin, the Torah is alluding to this future prohibition.]

Most years Rosh Hashanah falls on a weekday. Thus it would seem most appropriate that the *pasuk* which dictates the requirement to blow shofar should be written in conjunction with the essential paragraph in the Torah which deals with the mitzvos of Rosh Hashanah. Yet this is not the case. The main *parashah* of Rosh Hashanah is here, and the law of the *remembrance* of the shofar is written here. Later the Torah writes the command of blowing the shofar in its discussion of the sacrifice. Why is this so?

The Gemara relates that in the year that the Jews left Egypt the holiday of Pesach started on a Thursday (*Shabbos* 87b). According to the system of holidays it follows then that the forthcoming Rosh Hashanah fell on Shabbos (see *Tur* Chap. 428).

Therefore, since that year Rosh Hashanah was on a Shabbos, the Torah first alluded to the laws of Rosh Hashanah relevant to that year, which is merely a remembrance of shofar.

This also explains another seeming incongruity. The Torah completes its discussion of the laws of the various holidays with *pasuk* 37. Two *pesukim* later it adds the laws of the Four Species that are taken on Succos. Why didn't the Torah include those laws in the laws of Succos? Rosh Hashanah that first year fell on Shabbos, Succos began exactly two weeks later. The Four Species are not taken on Shabbos. The Torah alludes to this by not mentioning the laws of the Four Species together with the rest of the laws of Succos, but rather by adding them later.

(*Kehillas Yitzchak* [extract])

כָּל מְלָאכָה לֹא תַעֲשׂוּ חֻקַּת עוֹלָם לְדֹרֹתֵיכֶם בְּכֹל מֹשְׁבֹתֵיכֶם (כ״ג:ל״א)

> *You shall not do any work; it is an eternal decree throughout your generations in all your dwelling places. (23:31)*

With regard to the laws of Yom Kippur, after mentioning the prohibition of work, the Torah writes that it is an eternal decree for all generations. This is not mentioned after the prohibition of eating (*pasuk* 32). Why not?

The Gemara (*Moed Kattan* 9a) relates that the First Beis HaMikdash was inaugurated on Yom Kippur, and that in honor of that the Jews saw fit to celebrate and eat and drink on that day.

It can be suggested that the Torah omitted writing that the prohibition of eating on Yom Kippur is eternal, to allude to that one time in Jewish history that it would be permitted.

(*Meshech Chochmah*)

דַּבֵּר אֶל בְּנֵי יִשְׂרָאֵל לֵאמֹר בַּחֲמִשָּׁה עָשָׂר יוֹם לַחֹדֶשׁ הַשְּׁבִיעִי הַזֶּה חַג הַסֻּכּוֹת שִׁבְעַת יָמִים לַה'. (כ״ג:ל״ד)

> *Speak to the Children of Israel, saying: On the fifteenth day of this seventh month is the Festival of Succos, a seven-day period for Hashem. (23:34)*

The festival of Succos is mentioned four times in the Torah. The first two times (*parashas Mishpatim*, and *parshas Ki Sisa*) it is referred to as the "festival of the ingathering [of the crop]." Only the last two times (*parashas Emor* and *parashas Re'eh*) is it called the festival of Succos. Why didn't the Torah always refer to it by its common name?

The Vilna Gaon (in his commentary to *Shir HaShirim* 1:4) posits that the original Clouds of Glory which accompanied the Jews upon their exodus from Egypt departed when they sinned with the Golden Calf, and only returned on the fifteenth of Tishrei when they began the construction of the Mishkan. The festival of Succos was designated to be on the fifteenth of Tishrei to commemorate the return of the Clouds of Glory.

It follows from the words of the Vilna Gaon that before the departure and return of the Clouds the holiday of "the fifteenth day of Tishrei" did not include the mitzvah of dwelling in a succah, which is meant to commemorate that event. The first two mentions of this holiday were written prior to that event, thus not being able to be called Succos. The last times take place afterwards, when dwelling in a succah was part of the mitzvah, therefore warranting being called Succos.

(*Meshech Chochmah*)

מִחוּץ לְפָרֹכֶת הָעֵדֻת בְּאֹהֶל מוֹעֵד יַעֲרֹךְ אֹתוֹ אַהֲרֹן מֵעֶרֶב עַד בֹּקֶר לִפְנֵי ה' תָּמִיד... (כ"ד:ג)

Outside the Curtain of the Testimony, in the Ohel Moed, Aharon shall arrange it, from evening to morning, before Hashem, continually... (24:3)

The Torah here refers to the *Paroches* as the "Curtain **of** the Testimony (Ark)." Yet earlier, in *parashas Tetzave* (*Shemos* 27:21), it is referred to as the "Curtain that is **on** the Ark." How can this inconsistency be explained?

Here this phrase follows the mention of the laws of Yom Tov. The Gemara (*Yoma* 54a) states that on Yom Tov the *Paroches* was pulled aside and the *Cherubim* were shown to the public. If so, it is appropriate that here the *Paroches* is not referred to as being on the Ark.

This also explains why here the Torah mentions only Aharon, and earlier (ibid.) Aharon and his children are mentioned. The Gemara (*Yerushalmi, Chagigah* 2:4) writes that the Kohen Gadol would perform the services in the Mishkan only on Shabbos and Yom Tov. Therefore, the service which is mentioned here, and is mentioned in conjunction with Shabbos and Yom Tov, only mentions the name of Aharon, the Kohen Gadol.

(*Meshech Chochmah*)

BEHAR

וְשָׁבְתָה הָאָרֶץ שַׁבָּת לַה' (כ"ה:ב)

...the land shall observe a Sabbath rest for Hashem. (25:2).

THE MIDRASH (SIFRA 1:2), QUOTED BY RASHI, POINTS OUT THAT the Torah describes Shabbos and *Shemittah* with the same phrase: that it is "a Sabbath rest for Hashem". But the Midrash does not explain the meaning of this enigmatic phrase.

There is a fundamental difference between Shabbos and Yom Tov. Every seventh day is automatically Shabbos. But it is the Jewish people who ultimately decide on which day the Yamim Tovim will fall. The day designated as the first of the new month effects the day the Yom Tov of that month will be (*Beitzah*, 17a).

There is a parallel difference between *Shemittah* and *Yovel*. It is absolutely prohibited to work the land during *Shemittah*. But the agricultural prohibitions of *Yovel* go into effect only if certain conditions are met [freeing of slaves, returning of land, etc.] (*Rosh Hashanah* 9b).

This is the intention of the Midrash. The very same phrase — "a Shabbos **for Hashem**" — is written regarding both Shabbos and *Shemittah*, implying that they are both determined by Hashem and not by humans. Regarding *Yovel* (*pasuk* 25:12) and

Yom Tov (earlier, 23:7) the phrase "it is holy ... **for you**" [...קֹדֶשׁ לָכֶם] is used, implying that the Jews determine which day should be holy.

Likewise there is a parallel between the themes. Both *Shemittah* and Shabbos proclaim that Hashem is the Creator and Owner of the world. On *Yovel*, the slaves are given their freedom, similar to the exodus from Egypt, which is the theme of Yom Tov.

(Meshech Chochmah)

...שָׂדְךָ לֹא תִזְרָע וְכַרְמְךָ לֹא תִזְמֹר (כ״ה:ד)

...your field you shall not sow and your vineyard
you shall not prune. (25:4)

The prohibitions of *Shemittah* are all written in singular form (לֹא תִזְרָע, לֹא תִזְמֹר). When discussing *Yovel* (25:11), the very same prohibitions are written in the plural form (לֹא תִזְרָעוּ לֹא תִבְצְרוּ). How can this inconsistency be explained?

The Gemara explains that the requirement to observe the laws of *Yovel* only applies when a majority of the Jewish people reside in Eretz Yisrael. If the majority of the nation live outside of Eretz Yisrael, every remaining Jew is exempt (*Arachin* 32b).

This halachah is reflected in the wording of the *pesukim*. The laws of *Yovel* are written in plural since they apply only when most of the Jews are in Eretz Yisrael. The requirement to observe *Shemittah* is incumbent even on a lone Jew residing in Eretz Yisrael; therefore it is written in the singular.

(Har Tzvi, in the name of R' Zev Frank)

וְהָיְתָה שַׁבַּת הָאָרֶץ לָכֶם לְאָכְלָה ... וְלִבְהֶמְתְּךָ וְלַחַיָּה
אֲשֶׁר בְּאַרְצֶךָ... (כ"ה:ו,ז)

> *The Sabbath produce of the land shall be yours to eat...*
> *And for your animal and for the beast*
> *that is in your land... (25:6,7)*

The Gemara states that a person is required to first feed his animal and only afterwards may he eat (*Berachos* 40a). It is puzzling that the Torah mentions the permissibility of a person to eat *Shemittah* produce before that of an animal.

Sefer Rav Tov qualifies the aforementioned Gemara and claims that it only applies if the animal and person have their own respective foods. But if there is only food fit for human consumption then the person takes precedence.

The Rambam (*Shemittah* 5:5), quoting a *Tosefta* (*Sheviis* 5:13), states that it is from this *pasuk* that we derive that although it is prohibited to feed an animal sacred *Shemittah* food which is fit for human consumption, nevertheless if the animal takes it by himself one is not required to take it away. Thus we see that this *pasuk* is discussing food fit for humans. This being the case, the wording of the *pasuk* is accurate, since in this instance a person may eat before an animal.

(*Gan Raveh*, in name of *Yalkut HaGershuni*)

...וּקְרָאתֶם דְּרוֹר בָּאָרֶץ לְכָל יֹשְׁבֶיהָ...וְאִישׁ אֶל מִשְׁפַּחְתּוֹ תָּשֻׁבוּ (כ"ה:י)

> *...and proclaim freedom throughout the land*
> *for all its inhabitants... and you shall return*
> *each man to his family (25:10).*

The Torah states that the *Yovel* year is a year of freedom for all; i.e. that every Jewish slave is freed (*Rashi*). If so, why does the Torah repeat that "people return to their family," which also refers to the freeing of slaves (*Rashi*)?

The Rambam (*Shemittah* 10:14) states that at the beginning of the *Yovel* year the slaves cease working, but do not yet return home. Only after the blowing of the shofar on Yom Kippur do the fields return to their original owners and the slaves to their families.

This is alluded to in the *pasuk*. The first phrase refers to the first stage of cessation of slavery. The end of the *pasuk* alludes to the second stage of *Yovel*, which is the actual return of the slaves to their homes.

(*R' David Soloveitchik, quoted by Shai LeTorah*)

... וּקְרָאתֶם דְּרוֹר בָּאָרֶץ לְכָל יֹשְׁבֶיהָ ... (כ"ה:י)

...and proclaim freedom throughout the land for all its inhabitants... (25:10)

Yovel is the year when all the Jewish slaves are freed. However, the phrase "all its inhabitants" seems awkward, since only slaves are freed, not masters.

The following answer can be suggested. The Gemara (*Kiddushin* 20a) states that if someone buys a slave it is as if he bought a master for himself. The basis for this statement is that the Torah has strict regulations how to treat one's slave. This being so, when one's slave is freed, in a sense the master himself is being freed from being "enslaved" to his slave.

(*Pnei Yehoshua, quoted by Zichron Yaakov*)

... וְאֶבֶן מַשְׂכִּית לֹא תִתְּנוּ בְּאַרְצְכֶם לְהִשְׁתַּחֲוֹת עָלֶיהָ ...
אֶת שַׁבְּתֹתַי תִּשְׁמֹרוּ וּמִקְדָּשִׁי תִּירָאוּ ... (כ"ו:א-ב)

> ...and in your land you shall not place a flooring stone upon which to prostrate oneself... My Sabbaths shall you observe and My Sanctuary shall you revere... (26:1-2).

Rashi writes that one is permitted to bow down on a stone floor only in the Beis HaMikdash. One wonders why the Torah made an exception of the Beis HaMikdash. Another question that comes to mind is: What is the connection between the laws of Shabbos and Mikdash that the Torah juxtaposed them?

The following explanation clarifies everything. The floor of the Beis HaMikdash was covered with blood from the slaughtered animals. It was necessary to wash the floor to retain the glory of the Mikdash. Had there been an earthen floor, it would have remained soiled on Shabbos, since washing an earthen floor is prohibited on Shabbos. Therefore Hashem commanded to make a floor of stones, even though it would mean that the Jews would bow on it.

The *pesukim* should be understood as follows: "Do not bow on a stone floor in your land" — but bow in the Beis HaMikdash on a stone floor. Why? — "Observe My Shabbos" — in order that the Shabbos not be desecrated. And do not ask why the Mikdash should be washed at all on Shabbos, since "Revere My Sanctuary" — one should keep the Mikdash in a state of reverence.

(*Chasam Sofer*, commentary on *Shabbos* 69b, quoted by *Pardes Yosef*)

BECHUKOSAI

וְנָתַתִּי גִשְׁמֵיכֶם בְּעִתָּם וְנָתְנָה הָאָרֶץ יְבוּלָהּ... (כ"ו:ד)

I will provide your rains in their time, **and the land will give** its produce... (26:4).

THE TORAH PROMISES THAT IF THE JEWS WILL OBSERVE THE LAWS of the Torah the rain will fall in its proper time, and the land will give forth its produce. One notices a difference in the language used by the *pasuk*. The fall of the rain is directly attributed to Hashem ["I will provide your rains "], whereas the growth of the produce is attributed to the land ["**the land** will give its produce"]. Why did the Torah write in such a manner?

The Gemara states that three activities remain solely in the hands of Hashem, and were not given over to an intermediary. They are: the granting of rain, childbirth, and the resurrection of the dead (*Taanis* 2a).

This explains the language used by the *pasuk*. The giving of rain is emphasized as being from Hashem since no intermediary is involved, as opposed to produce which has an intermediary.

(*R' David Soloveitchik*, quoted by *Shai LeTorah*)

... וַאֲכַלְתֶּם לַחְמְכֶם לָשֹׂבַע ... (כ"ו:ה)

...you will eat your bread to satiety...(26:5)

The Midrash (*Sifra* 1:7), quoted by Rashi, explains that the *pasuk* is informing us that although the Jews will eat only a little bit of food they will nevertheless be satiated. One wonders what is the purpose of this blessing being that the Jews will be blessed with an extraordinary bountiful amount of food (see *pesukim* 4,5).

The Midrash (quoted by *Tosefos, Kesubos* 104a) informs us that the consumption of delicacies is an impediment for success in the study of Torah! The less one eats the more one will be a true Torah scholar. The special blessing being expressed here in our *pasuk* is that the Jews will be satisfied even though they will not have to eat much and thus be greater Torah luminaries.

(Chasam Sofer on Chumash)

... וְנָפְלוּ אֹיְבֵיכֶם לִפְנֵיכֶם לֶחָרֶב (כ"ו:ח)

*...and your enemies will fall **before you** by the sword (26:8).*

The Midrash (*Sifra* 2:4), quoted by Rashi, states that the meaning of "will fall before you" is that the enemies shall fall before the Jews in an "unnatural manner." However, the Midrash remains cryptic and does not explain to what it is referring.

It is recorded (*I Shmuel* 17:49) that Goliath fell forwards "on his face." The Midrash (*Yalkut Shimoni, remez* 127) explains that Hashem intentionally caused Goliath to fall forwards on his face and not backwards as usually happens, in order that David be spared the bother of walking the extra distance to sever Goliath's head.

We can suggest that this is the intention of the blessing here. The Jews shall benefit that their enemies will fall forwards upon being killed, which is unusual, and not backwards. (*Chanukas HaTorah*)

... וְנַסְתֶּם וְאֵין רֹדֵף אֶתְכֶם. (כ״ו:י״ז)

...you will flee with no one pursuing you. (26:17)

The Torah warns the Jews of terrible events that shall befall them if they sin. One of the threats is that they will flee with no one pursuing them. Superficially this does not appear to be that threatening, since it is better to be fleeing without someone pursuing than with someone pursuing.

It is written that Hashem seeks out the one who is being pursued and helps him (*Koheles* 3:15). The Midrash (*Vayikra Rabbah* 27:5) adds that Hashem will always help the one who is being pursued, even if it is a *rasha* being chased by a *tzaddik*.

This changes the whole picture. The Torah is indeed writing a horrific curse. If someone would be pursuing the Jews, then, as evil as the Jews might be, Hashem would rescue them. But now that no one is chasing after them there is no hope.

This also explains a later *pasuk* (26:37) which states that "they shall stumble one upon the other ... and no one will be pursuing them, and they will not recover." It is because no one will be pursuing them that there is no hope for them and they will not recover.

(*Chanukas HaTorah*)

... וְאָפוּ עֶשֶׂר נָשִׁים לַחְמְכֶם בְּתַנּוּר אֶחָד וְהֵשִׁיבוּ לַחְמְכֶם בַּמִּשְׁקָל וַאֲכַלְתֶּם וְלֹא תִשְׂבָּעוּ. (כ״ו:כ״ו)

...ten women will bake your bread in one oven, and they will bring back your bread by weight; you will eat and not be sated. (26:26)

The Gemara (*Bava Metzia* 30a) states that something which is viewed with envy will come to harm. Likewise, something which is already measured and weighed cannot become bountiful (ibid. 42a). This offers a new explanation of our *pasuk*. Since the bread will be baked by many women, and thus be in the public eye, plus the bread will be weighed, therefore they will eat and not be sated. This is in contradistinction to the times of blessing, when even a little bit of food is satisfying ["blessed in their stomach" — *Rashi* 26:5].

(*Divrei Shaul*)

וַהֲשִׁמּוֹתִי אֶת מִקְדְּשֵׁיכֶם וְלֹא אָרִיחַ בְּרֵיחַ נִיחֹחֲכֶם. (כ״ו:ל״א)

> ...I will make your sanctuaries desolate; I will not savor your satisfying aromas. (26:31)

The end of this *pasuk* seems redundant. Hashem threatens the Jews that he will desolate the Mikdash, and that he will not savor the satisfying aromas of the offerings. If the Beis HaMikdash will be destroyed, it follows that there will no longer be any offerings with their rich aroma!

The Gemara (*Yoma* 39b) records that the aroma of the *ketores* [incense-offering] was so pervasive that even for hundreds of years after the cessation of the incense-offering, its scent could be detected in the air.

This engenders a new explanation of the *pasuk*. The Torah is warning that the Beis HaMikdash will be destroyed and not in existence for such a long period of time that even the fragrance of the *ketores* will cease to be in the air!

(*Maharil Diskin*)

BAMIDBAR

וַיְדַבֵּר ה' אֶל מֹשֶׁה בְּמִדְבַּר סִינַי בְּאֹהֶל מוֹעֵד **בְּאֶחָד לַחֹדֶשׁ הַשֵּׁנִי**
בַּשָּׁנָה הַשֵּׁנִית לְצֵאתָם מֵאֶרֶץ מִצְרַיִם לֵאמֹר.
שְׂאוּ אֶת רֹאשׁ כָּל עֲדַת בְּנֵי יִשְׂרָאֵל... (א:א-ב)

*Hashem spoke to Moshe in the Wilderness of Sinai, in the
Ohel Moed, **on the first day of the second month**,
in the second year of their exodus from Egypt, saying,
"Take a census of the entire Jewish community..." (1:1-2)*

AT THE BEGINNING OF THE SECOND YEAR FOLLOWING THE EXODUS from Egypt, Hashem instructed Moshe to count the Jews. What was the purpose of that census? They had already been counted as recently as seven months earlier. Rashi suggests that because the Jews were dear to Him, Hashem would count them upon unique occasions. Since Hashem intended for His Divine Presence to manifest itself, He counted them first.

Rashi, previously (*Vayikra* 9:23), explains that the Divine Presence appeared on the first day of *Nissan*, the day the Mishkan was erected. Why did Hashem wait one month before counting the Jews, and not count them the day the Divine Presence appeared?

The Gemara states that one is not legally considered a resident of a city until he has dwelled there for at least thirty days (*Bava Basra* 8a). This concept can be applied here. Until one month had elapsed, the appearance of Hashem's Presence there was not considered permanent and it had not been considered a special occasion to warrant counting the Jews. It was only after Hashem's Presence had resided in the Mishkan for thirty days that Moshe was told to count the Jews.

(Bi'urei Maharia)

שְׂאוּ אֶת רֹאשׁ כָּל עֲדַת בְּנֵי יִשְׂרָאֵל לְמִשְׁפְּחֹתָם לְבֵית אֲבֹתָם בְּמִסְפַּר שֵׁמוֹת כָּל זָכָר **לְגֻלְגְּלֹתָם**. (א:ב)

> *Take a census of the entire Jewish community, by families, following the paternal line, according to the names of each male; **take a head count** (1:2).*

When instructing Moshe to count all the Jews, with the exception of the tribe of Levi, Hashem used the word לְגֻלְגְּלֹתָם — which means "take a head count." Later (3:15), when instructing Moshe to count the tribe of Levi, that word was not mentioned. Why not?

The *Gemara* mentions a halachic discussion concerning a baby born with two heads. One point stated is that such a baby is a *treifah* — mortally ill child, who will not survive till its first birthday (*Menachos* 37a).

This fact resolves the discrepancy. Included in the instructions, which Moshe received about the first count, was a clause that he should only count those above the age of 20. There cannot be a two-headed person that age; thus the word לְגֻלְגְּלֹתָם can be used, without concern that a two-headed individual might be counted as two since it has two heads. But the tribe of Levi was counted from the age of one month (*Bamidbar* 3:15). There could be a two-headed baby that age, and a mistake might ensue if that term would be used!

(Tiferes Yehonasan)

There is a simpler explanation offered to explain the discrepancy. The Midrash (*Tanchuma* par. 16), quoted by Rashi, relates that when Moshe was ordered to count the tribe of Levi, which included the infants, he expressed his discomfort at entering other people's homes. Hashem told him not to be concerned, and ultimately Moshe stood at the entrance of each tent, and a Divine voice emanated from within and informed him of the number of infants residing inside. Thus, unlike the rest of the tribes, the tribe of Levi did not have an actual head count, and did not qualify having the word לְגֻלְגְּלֹתָם said in conjunction with its count.

(*Responsa Binyan Shlomo*)

לִבְנֵי דָן תּוֹלְדֹתָם לְמִשְׁפְּחֹתָם לְבֵית אֲבֹתָם ...
לִבְנֵי אָשֵׁר תּוֹלְדֹתָם לְמִשְׁפְּחֹתָם לְבֵית אֲבֹתָם ...
בְּנֵי נַפְתָּלִי תּוֹלְדֹתָם לְמִשְׁפְּחֹתָם לְבֵית אֲבֹתָם ... (א:ל״ח,מ,מ״ב)

To the sons *of Don, their births according to their families, according to the house of their fathers ...*
To the sons *of Asher, their births according to their families, according to the house of their fathers ...*
The sons *of Naftali, their births according to their families, according to the house of their fathers (1:38,40,42)*

When recording the number of people of the different tribes, the Torah states "**to** the sons of etc." But with regard to the last tribe to be listed, Naftali, it merely says "the sons of etc." Why was the word "to" omitted?

The following scenario can be suggested to explain the discrepancy. The manner in which the count was done was that Moshe went from tent to tent and wrote down the names of its residents, and to which tribe they belong. After that was completed, he organized the names according to their tribes and then he counted them. Therefore they searched through the list for every name from a particular tribe, and copied it onto a list consisting only of members of that tribe, and then counted them. This was done for all the tribes. However, for the last tribe, Naftali, there was no need to start a new separate list, since any remaining names belonged to the members of Naftali.

The phrase "to the sons" connotes that the names should be added to the list of the members of that tribe. Since the names of the members of Naftali were not added to any list, the word "to" is omitted.

(*Ari z"l*, quoted by *Pardes Yosef*; see also *Gan Raveh*)

וַיֹּאמֶר ה' אֶל מֹשֶׁה פְּקֹד כָּל בְּכֹר זָכָר לִבְנֵי יִשְׂרָאֵל מִבֶּן חֹדֶשׁ וָמָעְלָה... (ג:מ)

Hashem said to Moshe, "Count every male first-born of the Jews, from one month of age and up..." (3:40).

Moshe was instructed to count all the firstborn who were at least one month old. Rashi explains that the count began at one month to insure that only babies who are viable would be counted. According to halachah, up until that age a newborn's health is still fragile, and it cannot be assumed that it will survive. Likewise, earlier (3:15) Moshe was told to count all the Levites who were over one month of age. Rashi offers the same reason given here. But there is an almost imperceptible difference in the language used. With regard to the firstborn Rashi writes "מִשֶּׁיֵּצֵא מִכְּלַל סְפֵק נְפָלִים," there should not be any **possibly** unviable children included in the count, and concerning the Levites he writes "מִשֶּׁיֵּצֵא מִכְּלַל נְפָלִים," there should not be any unviable children, omitting the word סְפֵק. Why didn't Rashi use the same phrase in both places?

The Midrash (*Rabbah*, par. 3) relates that when Moshe was ordered to count the infants of the tribe of Levi, he expressed his discomfort at entering other people's homes. Hashem responded that he need not be concerned. Ultimately Moshe stood at the entrance of each tent, and a Divine voice emanated and told him the number of infants residing inside. Since Hashem did the counting of the Levites, the purpose of disregarding newborns was to avoid including those babies which He **definitely** knew would not live thirty days. But the firstborn babies were counted by Moshe (see *Rabbah*, par. 4), who did not know which would live. Thus the purpose of his count can rightfully be stated as disregarding those who **might possibly** not live.

(*Levias Chein*)

נָשֹׂא אֶת רֹאשׁ בְּנֵי קְהָת מִתּוֹךְ בְּנֵי לֵוִי לְמִשְׁפְּחֹתָם לְבֵית אֲבֹתָם. מִבֶּן שְׁלֹשִׁים שָׁנָה וָמַעְלָה וְעַד בֶּן חֲמִשִּׁים שָׁנָה כָּל בָּא לַצָּבָא **לַעֲשׂוֹת מְלָאכָה** בְּאֹהֶל מוֹעֵד. (ד:ב,ג)

> "Take a census of the descendants of Kehas, among
> the Levites. Take it by families, following the paternal line.
> It shall include those from 30 to 50 years old,
> all who enter service **to work** in the Ohel Moed "(4:2,3)

This *parashah* lists the various families of the tribe of Levi, and their work assignments while en route. One notices that in conjunction with the family of Kehas, when mentioning "work" the word מְלָאכָה is used, whereas in connection with the families of Gershon (*pasuk* 25) and Merari (*pasuk* 29) the word עֲבוֹדָה is used. Why is this so?

The prohibited activities of Shabbos are called מְלָאכוֹת. The duty of the members of the family of Kehas was to carry their load on their shoulders in a public domain, which is one of the *melachos* of Shabbos. Thus the word *melachah* is appropriate to describe their work. The families of Gershon and Merari had animals carry their assigned workload. According to the Torah, one may lead an animal that has a load on it. Therefore, the word *melachah* is not used, but is replaced by the word *avodah*.

(*Meshech Chochmah*)

וְעַל מִזְבַּח הַזָּהָב יִפְרְשׂוּ בֶּגֶד תְּכֵלֶת וְכִסּוּ אֹתוֹ בְּמִכְסֵה עוֹר תָּחַשׁ...
וְדִשְּׁנוּ אֶת הַמִּזְבֵּחַ וּפָרְשׂוּ עָלָיו בֶּגֶד אַרְגָּמָן. (ד:י״א,י״ג)

> They shall spread a cloth of turquoise wool on the Golden Mizbe'ach, and then cover it with a covering of tachash hide ... **They shall remove all the ashes from the Copper Mizbe'ach**, and place a cloth of purple wool over it (4:11,13).

There were two Altars in the Mishkan: one of copper and on it the offerings were burned; and one of gold, upon which the incense was burned. In the instructions to the Levites regarding carrying the sacrificial vessels during their travels, it was stated that the Copper *Mizbe'ach* should be cleared of its ashes before being covered (see *Rashi* 4:13). But no such instruction was given about the Golden *Mizbe'ach*. What could the reason have been?

The Mishnah (*Tamid* 3:9) states that every day the Golden *Mizbe'ach* would be cleaned of all its ashes. The Gemara explains that a fistful of ashes would be removed every day from the Copper *Mizbe'ach* as part of the sacrificial service, implying that the rest remained (*Yoma* 24a).

Thus the Copper *Mizbe'ach* had a large amount of ashes piled up which needed to be removed before traveling. But the Golden *Mizbe'ach*, being cleaned every day, was already void of ashes.

(Responsa Binyan Shlomo)

NASSO

זֹאת עֲבֹדַת מִשְׁפְּחֹת בְּנֵי מְרָרִי ... (ה':ל"ג)

This is the service of the families of the sons of Merari ... (4:33)

THE TORAH DIVIDES THE TASK OF DISMANTLING AND CARRYING THE Mishkan among the three major families of the tribe of Levi — Kehas, Gershon, and Merari. At the end of *parashas Bamidbar* and at the beginning of *parashas Nasso*, the Torah assigns specific duties to each of these families. The first family to be assigned its duties is that of Kehas. The concluding *pasuk* listing these duties is 4:16. In the Torah, the letter *pei* [which indicates the end of a paragraph] follows that *pasuk*. After the Torah concludes listing the jobs of Gershon (*pasuk* 28), we find the letter *samech*, which likewise indicates the end of a paragraph. Surprisingly, after *pasuk* 33, which concludes the listing of the duties of Merari, there is no letter signifying the conclusion of a paragraph. Why is this so?

The Midrash (*Sifra*, *parshasa* 1, Chap. 1, par. 9) states that the paragraphs in the Torah follow exactly how Hashem related it to Moshe. Hashem paused at the end of every paragraph to enable Moshe to review that which he had heard, and to digest the information.

Based on this Midrash, the following explanation is offered. After Hashem delineated the tasks required of Kehas, He paused to give Moshe time to memorize them. The same was true for Gershon. But after He related Merari's duties to Moshe, Hashem did not pause. The reason is that it was easy for Moshe to recall what was required of Merari. How? By process of elimination. He knew that any duties which Hashem had not assigned to Kehas and Gershon had to belong to Merari. *(Taamah D'Kra)*

עַל פִּי ה' פָּקַד אוֹתָם בְּיַד מֹשֶׁה אִישׁ אִישׁ עַל עֲבֹדָתוֹ וְעַל מַשָּׂאוֹ וּפְקֻדָיו אֲשֶׁר צִוָּה ה' אֶת מֹשֶׁה. (ד:מ"ט)

*According to the **word of Hashem** he appointed them, by the hand of Moshe, every person to his work and burden; his appointments were in accordance with that which Hashem **commanded** to Moshe (4:49).*

This *pasuk* twice mentions that the appointments of the various Levite families to their specific tasks were carried out upon the orders of Hashem. The commentaries (see *Rashi* and *Ohr HaChaim*) explain that this refers to two different aspects of their jobs. The first half of the *pasuk* alludes to the actual jobs the Jews had to perform; the second half to the requirement that the Levites working in the *Mishkan* had to be between the ages of 30 and 50. Both of these directives originated from Hashem.

The word used in the Torah for command is *tzivah*. Accordingly, we find the word *tzivah* at the end of this *pasuk*. The *pasuk* begins, however, with the phrase "al pi Hashem" [according to the word of Hashem], not the usual *tzivah*. What is the reason for this departure from the general pattern; and why does it occur in the same *pasuk* as *tzivah*?

With one exception, the miscellany of tasks and laws associated with the Mishkan only applied while the Jews were in the

Wilderness and had a Mishkan. Ramban (*Sefer HaMitzvos, shoresh* 3) posits that the law that the Levites had to be between 30 to 50 years of age to serve in the Mishkan was in effect both in the Mishkan and later in the Beis HaMikdash.

The Midrash (*Sifra, Baraisa D'Rebbi Yishmael,* 6) states that if the verb *tzivah* is used in conjunction with the issuance of a law, the Torah is indicating that the edict applies to all future generations as well.

The choice of language in the *pasuk* can now be understood. The end of the *pasuk* refers to the command concerning the age of the Levites who served in the Mishkan, and it applied to the future Beis HaMikdash. That law is forever, therefore the verb *tzivah* is employed. The beginning of the *pasuk* alludes to the various tasks that existed only while the Jews were in the Wilderness; therefore, *tzivah* is not used. (*Chidushei Maran Riz HaLevi*)

וַיַּעֲשׂוּ כֵן בְּנֵי יִשְׂרָאֵל וַיְשַׁלְּחוּ אוֹתָם אֶל מִחוּץ לַמַּחֲנֶה כַּאֲשֶׁר **דִּבֶּר** ה' אֶל מֹשֶׁה כֵּן עָשׂוּ בְּנֵי יִשְׂרָאֵל. (ה:ד)

*And the Jews did so. They sent the metzoraim out of the camp; the Jews did exactly as Hashem **told** Moshe should be done. (5:4)*

In all other places in the Torah, where Hashem commands and the Jews obey, the Torah writes, "And the Jews did as Hashem **commanded**" [see *Shemos* 12:3, 39:32; *Bamidbar* 9:5]. Here, although the Jews were commanded to send any *metzora* out of the camp (*pasuk* 2), the *pasuk* states that the Jews did as "Hashem **told** them to do." Why the inconsistency?

The Midrash (*Sifri, Bamidbar,* 1) states that the word *tzav*, or any derivative of it, implies a directive that people would be reluctant to carry out without being urged to do so. *Tzav* tells us that the Jews had to obey even though it might not have been to their liking.

Nasso / 207

Jews who were not *tamei* did not need to be persuaded to remove a *metzora* from their midst in the Jewish camp; they were more than happy to do so. Opposition might have come from the metzoraim themselves. However, the Gemara (*Berachos* 5b) explains that all the halachic aspects pertaining to a *metzora* were aspects of a process of atonement. Consequently, even the metzoraim were happy to be sent from the camp! In fact, it is recorded in the Midrash (*Sifri* ibid.) that there was no resistance to the implementation of this law. This explains why the word *tzav* is not written here. Since all the Jews were happy to fulfill this particular command it would have been inappropriate to use the expression "as Hashem commanded them." Instead we find "as Hashem told them" which does not imply that they were made to do the mitzvah.

(*Meshech Chochmah*)

דַּבֵּר אֶל בְּנֵי יִשְׂרָאֵל וְאָמַרְתָּ אֲלֵהֶם אִישׁ אִישׁ כִּי תִשְׂטֶה אִשְׁתּוֹ וּמָעֲלָה בוֹ מָעַל... (ה:י״ב)

Speak to the Jews and say to them, "If any man's wife goes astray, and acts treacherously toward him..." (5:12).

Moshe was told to inform the Jews of all laws pertaining to a *sotah*. The Midrash (*Lekach Tov*) comments that the purpose of their knowing these laws was for future generations. The implication of this statement is that the Jews of that era did not have a need for these laws. Why not? Was there no possibility of *sotah* in their time?

The Gemara relates that the manna had miraculous qualities. For instance, if a woman were unfaithful, the next morning her portion of manna would not fall near her husband's residence but rather near her father's house (*Yoma*, 75a)! In light of this, the Midrash can be understood. The purpose of the process that the *sotah* had to undergo was to determine whether or not she had actually been unfaithful. The Jews of Moshe's time did not need this method; where the manna fell was ample proof. The laws of *sotah* were only necessary for subsequent generations.

(*Tiferes Yehonasan*)

אִישׁ אִישׁ כִּי תִשְׂטֶה אִשְׁתּוֹ ...
וְהֵבִיא הָאִישׁ אֶת אִשְׁתּוֹ אֶל הַכֹּהֵן ... (ה:י״ב,ט״ו)

*If any man's wife goes astray...
that man shall bring his wife to the Kohen ... (5:12,15)*

The Torah writes that if a man suspects his wife of infidelity, he must bring her to a Kohen, and she undergoes a special test to determine the truth. The Torah then elaborates on the details of this test. This section which deals with the laws of a *sotah* follows a discussion of the requirement to give certain gifts to a Kohen. The Gemara, quoted by Rashi, comments that the Torah juxtaposed these two sections to teach us that one who refrains from going to a Kohen to give him the required gifts will be cursed: He will have to go to a Kohen because his wife will be a *sotah* (*Berachos* 63b). This is astonishing. Every human is endowed with free will to choose between good and bad, yet this Gemara appears to be saying that Hashem will cause a man's wife to sin in order to punish him!

The story of Chanah the mother of Shmuel *HaNavi* is found in the beginning of *sefer Shmuel*. The Gemara (*Berachos* 31b) explains this chapter in detail. The Gemara relates that Chanah challenged Hashem: "If You don't accept my prayers and grant me a child, I will seclude myself with a strange man in front of my husband Elkanah, who will then force me to undergo the *sotah* test. And it is written in Your Torah that a faithful woman who undergoes that test will be rewarded and bear a child if she was barren until then!" (*Berachos* 31b)

Based on this Gemara, we suggest that a person who does not give the required gifts to the Kohen will be punished that he will be childless. In order to have children he will have to resort to Chanah's plan: have his wife behave like a *sotah* and bring her to a Kohen as a result of which she will conceive. This is the intention of the

Gemara when it says that his wife will have to be brought to a Kohen as a result of which she will conceive. This is the intention of the Gemara when it says that his wife will have to be brought to a Kohen. It does not intend to imply that his wife will actually have sinned.

Although it is not stated explicitly anywhere that a person who does not bring his gifts to a Kohen will be punished with childlessness, there is a partial proof for it. One of the blessings the Kohanim gave the Jews is *vi'chuneka*. The Midrash (*Lekach Tov*) interprets this as meaning that the Jews will have children. It is therefore probable that a person who does not benefit a Kohen will not receive the benefit of his blessings, one of them being to have children.

(*Binyan Ariel*)

קָרְבָּנוֹ קַעֲרַת כֶּסֶף אַחַת ... מִזְרָק אֶחָד כֶּסֶף ... שְׁנֵיהֶם מְלֵאִים סֹלֶת בְּלוּלָה בַשֶּׁמֶן לְמִנְחָה. כַּף אַחַת עֲשָׂרָה זָהָב מְלֵאָה קְטֹרֶת ... זֹאת חֲנֻכַּת הַמִּזְבֵּחַ בְּיוֹם הִמָּשַׁח אֹתוֹ מֵאֵת נְשִׂיאֵי יִשְׂרָאֵל קַעֲרֹת כֶּסֶף שְׁתֵּים עֶשְׂרֵה מִזְרְקֵי כֶסֶף שְׁנֵים עָשָׂר כַּפּוֹת זָהָב שְׁתֵּים עֶשְׂרֵה... כַּפּוֹת זָהָב שְׁתֵּים עֶשְׂרֵה מְלֵאֹת קְטֹרֶת ... (ז:ע"ט,פ,פ"ד,פ"ו)

> *His offering was one silver bowl... one silver basin... both of them filled with fine flour, mixed with oil for a meal-offering. One gold ladle of ten shekels filled with incense ... This was the dedication of the Mizbe'ach, on the day it was anointed, from the Nesiim of Israel, twelve silver bowls, twelve silver basins, and twelve gold ladles ... There were twelve gold ladles filled with incense ... (7:79,80,84,86).*

On each of the days following the inauguration of the Mishkan, one of the twelve *Nesiim* brought offerings on the *Mizbe'ach*. The offerings were identical. Describing the sacrifices of each *Nasi*, the Torah writes, "His offering was one silver bowl...and one silver basin... both were filled with fine flour mixed with oil ...[and] one ladle of ten *shekels* filled with incense."

The Torah then sums up, and states (7:84), "... there were twelve silver bowls, twelve silver basins." No mention of their contents is made. Why this omission? Furthermore, the Torah also totals the incense bowls and states (7:86), "There were twelve gold ladles filled with incense..." Here the Torah does mention the contents of the ladles. Why did the Torah mention theses contents and not that of the bowls and basins?

The answer is to be found in a careful reading of the beginning of *pasuk* 84, where it is written, "This was the dedication offering of the *Mizbe'ach* from the *Nesiim* of Israel on the day it was anointed." The *pasuk* then continues and lists the sum of their offerings. The Torah is not merely totaling the amount subsequently brought by the *Nesiim*. It is informing us exactly what occurred. On the day of the inauguration of the Mishkan, all of the *Nesiim* arrived with their respective offerings. Hashem told Moshe that beginning the following day one *Nasi* should bring his offering each day. When the Torah states that there were "twelve silver bowls, etc.," it refers to the amount that the *Nesiim* brought with them on the inauguration day. [See earlier in *pesukim* 10 and 11, and in Rashi's commentary there.]

The Mishnah (*Me'ilah*, 2:8) states a law, that if a person consecrates flour for an offering, and then places the flour in a *kli shareis* (a vessel designated to be used with offerings), that flour must be offered before the end of the night, or else it will be disqualified. The Gemara points out, that although this disqualification, *linah* (where the components of the offering are left beyond their prescribed time), applies to many types of offerings, the *ketores* is an exception. There is no issue of *linah* with *ketores* (*Shevuos* 11a).

The *Nesiim* were well aware of this law. Although they all appeared at the inauguration of the Mishkan with their offerings, they realized that perhaps Hashem would not accept them all on that day. Consequently, they did not place the flour in the sacrificial trays and bowls; it would have been disqualified if it were not brought that day. Not so the *ketores*. Even if they did not offer it that day, it could be offered days later. Therefore, even though they were unsure, they placed the *ketores* in the incense spoons. That is why the Torah mentions the *ketores* but not the flour; the flour was not brought that day! (*Yesod Ohel Moed*, quoted by *Gan Raveh*. The *Chidushei HaGriz* [stencil] writes this in the name of *R' Elazar Moshe Horowitz zt"l*)

BEHA'ALOSCHA

דַּבֵּר אֶל אַהֲרֹן וְאָמַרְתָּ אֵלָיו **בְּהַעֲלֹתְךָ** אֶת הַנֵּרֹת אֶל מוּל פְּנֵי הַמְּנוֹרָה יָאִירוּ שִׁבְעַת הַנֵּרוֹת. (ח:ב)

"Speak to Aharon and say to him, when you kindle the lamps, toward the face of the Menorah shall the seven lamps cast light." (8:2).

THE MIDRASH (*SIFRI*), QUOTED BY RASHI, DERIVES FROM THE WORD *"beha'aloscha"* that the Kohen stood on steps when he lit the Menorah. Why was this necessary? The Menorah was three *amos* high (*Menachos* 28b); and according to the Gemara (*Yoma* 31a) the height of an average person is three *amos*! It should not have been a problem for Aharon to light the Menorah without standing on steps.

The Mishnah states that a Kohen Gadol is prohibited to raise his hand above the *tzitz* which he wore on his forehead (*Sotah* 38a). In keeping with this law, Aharon, who was the Kohen Gadol, could not light the Menorah while standing on the ground; he would have had to reach above his head. Thus the use of a step.

(*Panim Yafos*)

> וַיַּעַשׂ כֵּן אַהֲרֹן אֶל מוּל פְּנֵי הַמְּנוֹרָה הֶעֱלָה נֵרֹתֶיהָ כַּאֲשֶׁר
> צִוָּה ה' אֶת מֹשֶׁה. (ח:ג)

Aharon did so; toward the face of the Menorah he kindled its lamps, as Hashem commanded Moshe. (8:3)

Rashi explains that the Torah is teaching us that Aharon was worthy of praise — he did exactly as he was told; he did not diverge in the slightest from Hashem's instructions. This interpretation seems odd, since it would be totally out of character for a person of Aharon's stature not to obey Hashem's directions. Why then is he being singled out for praise?

The Midrash (*Yalkut Shimoni, Va'eira, remez* 181) informs us that Aharon was exceedingly tall. Although there were steps available upon which the Kohen would stand to light the Menorah, Aharon had no need of these steps. Even so, because Hashem instructed the Kohanim to use them, Aharon followed the exact instructions and likewise used the steps. For this he deserved special praise.

This explanation is alluded to in the *pasuk*, which says that Aharon was "*he'elah*" the wicks. This verb has two meanings — kindling and a step — implying that he stood on steps when lighting the candles. *(Maharil Diskin, Siach Yitzchak)*

> וְכִי יָגוּר אִתְּכֶם גֵּר וְעָשָׂה פֶסַח לַה' כְּחֻקַּת הַפֶּסַח וּכְמִשְׁפָּטוֹ
> כֵּן יַעֲשֶׂה חֻקָּה אַחַת יִהְיֶה לָכֶם וְלַגֵּר וּלְאֶזְרַח הָאָרֶץ. (ט:י״ד)

When a convert shall dwell with you, and he shall make a pesach-offering to Hashem, according to the decree of the pesach-offering and its law so shall he do; one decree shall be for you, both for the convert and the native of the Land. (9:14)

The Torah states that both one born a Jew and one who is a convert are required to bring the *pesach*-offering. The phrase used to describe a person who was born a Jew is "native of the Land." In every other instance in the Torah a Jew from birth is referred to merely as a "native." Why is this law unique that the Torah adds the words "of the Land"?

The Gemara declares that a person who does not own property in Eretz Yisrael is exempt from the mitzvah of *oleh regel* – journeying to the Beis HaMikdash and bringing offerings there on the Yamim Tovim of Pesach, Shavuos, and Succos (*Pesachim* 8b). *Tosefos* (ibid. 3b) adds that not only is he exempt from being *oleh regel*, he is also exempt from bringing the *pesach*-offering.

This is the key to understanding the *pasuk*. The Torah is alluding to the law posited by *Tosefos*. Only a "native of the Land"— a Jew who owns property — is required to bring the *pesach*-offering. One who does not is exempt. The Torah teaches that law by adding that phrase only here and in no other place.

(*Meshech Chochmah*)

וַיֹּאמֶר מֹשֶׁה לְחֹבָב בֶּן רְעוּאֵל הַמִּדְיָנִי חֹתֵן מֹשֶׁה נֹסְעִים אֲנַחְנוּ אֶל הַמָּקוֹם אֲשֶׁר אָמַר ה' אֹתוֹ אֶתֵּן לָכֶם לְכָה אִתָּנוּ וְהֵטַבְנוּ לָךְ כִּי ה' דִּבֶּר טוֹב עַל יִשְׂרָאֵל. (י:כ"ט)

And Moshe said to his father-in-law, Chovav the son of Reuel the Midianite, "We are journeying to the place of which Hashem has said, 'I shall give it to you.' Go with us, and we shall treat you well, **for Hashem has spoken of good for Israel."** *(10:29)*

Hashem promised the Jewish people that they would vanquish the residents of Eretz Yisrael, and take control of the Land. Consequently, Moshe was confident that the Jews would conquer Eretz Yisrael, and he invited Yisro to join the Jewish people and reside there. However, in his invitation, Moshe uttered an obscure phrase, and said, "...for Hashem has spoken of good for Israel." What is the meaning of this phrase?

Rambam (*Yesodei HaTorah* 10:4) states that if a *Navi* proclaims in the name of Hashem that a certain calamity will occur, and it does not occur, this does not disprove the validity of the *Navi*. It is possible that Hashem first communicated to the *Navi* and told him that something terrible would occur, but subsequently, in His attribute of mercy, rescinded his decree; or perhaps the object of the misfortune repented and was forgiven. One can therefore ask why Moshe was so sure that the residents of Eretz Yisrael would be sent from the Land. Although Hashem promised it would happen, he could have taken pity on them and allowed them to remain.

Rambam (ibid.) also states that if Hashem ever promises that something beneficial will happen, he will never retract his promise. There were two aspects to Hashem's promise to the Jews: It was detrimental to the inhabitants living in Eretz Yisrael; it was beneficial to the Jews. The latter was the source of Moshe's confidence. Since the promise of inheriting Eretz Yisrael contained an element of good, Moshe knew that it was irrevocable.

This explains the obscure phrase mentioned above. Moshe was trying to persuade Chovav (Yisro) to join with the Jews. His appeal was based on the belief that the Jews would capture Eretz Yisrael and rid it of its former inhabitants. This was definitely going to happen because it was a promise that was beneficial to the Jews: "...for Hashem has spoken of good for Israel." With these words Moshe was emphasizing that the promise was good for the Jewish people and therefore not retractable.

(*Meshech Chochmah*)

וְעַתָּה נַפְשֵׁנוּ יְבֵשָׁה אֵין כֹּל בִּלְתִּי אֶל הַמָּן עֵינֵינוּ. (י"א:ו)

> But now our life is parched, with nothing but the manna before our eyes. (11:6)

The Gemara states that seeing the food one eats adds to the sensation of fullness that one has after eating; therefore blind people never feel totally full. It also states that although one could taste in the manna whatever flavors one desired, it never changed its appearance (*Yoma* 74b).

This begets a possible explanation of this *pasuk*. The Jews complained that they see nothing but the manna in front of their eyes, and therefore they are never satiated!

(*Likutei Ritzba*)

וַיָּקָם הָעָם כָּל הַיּוֹם הַהוּא וְכָל הַלַּיְלָה וְכֹל יוֹם הַמָּחֳרָת וַיַּאַסְפוּ אֶת הַשְּׂלָו הַמַּמְעִיט אָסַף עֲשָׂרָה חֳמָרִים... (י"א:ל"ב)

> The people rose up all that day and all the night, and all the next day, and gathered up the slav. The one with the least gathered in ten chomers... (11:32)

There is an amazing calculation that explains why the least amount gathered was ten *chomers*.

The *slav* fell on the outskirts of the camp of the Jews. Those living near the perimeter could pick an abundance of it. The Jews living in the center were the worst off, and they picked ten *chomers*. Why?

The Gemara states that a person can walk ten *parsa'os* in twelve hours (*Pesachim* 93b). Since the Jews had three of these time periods to gather the *slav* — day, night, and day — they were able to travel thirty *parsa'os*. There is another Gemara which says that the length of the Jewish camp was three *parsa'os*

(*Berachos* 54b). Consequently, someone who lived in the middle of the camp [one and a half *parsa'os* from the edge] had to walk a total of three *parsa'os* in order to leave the camp to pick *slav* and return home. Since they walked a total of thirty *parsa'os*, the people living in the middle of the camp were able to make ten trips and gather ten *chomers*!

(*Kol Eliyahu*)

SHELACH

שְׁלַח לְךָ אֲנָשִׁים וְיָתֻרוּ אֶת אֶרֶץ כְּנַעַן אֲשֶׁר אֲנִי נֹתֵן לִבְנֵי יִשְׂרָאֵל... (י״ג:ב)

Send forth men and let them spy out the Land of Canaan that I give to the children of Israel... (13:2)

Rashi quotes a Midrash (*Tanchuma* par. 5) which explains that the Torah juxtaposed the episode of the *meraglim* with the story of Miriam's slander of Moshe and her punishment to point out the gravity of the spies' sin. After they witnessed how Hashem afflicted Miriam with a plague for speaking slander, they nevertheless committed slander themselves!

Rashi seems to emphasize that the sin of the *meraglim* was all the worse because they actually witnessed what occurred to Miriam. If they had merely heard about Miriam's punishment, they would not have been held to account so strongly. Why is this so?

The Gemara reveals that Hashem sometimes causes a person to suffer in this world in order to increase his reward in Olam Haba. This is referred to as *yesurin shel ahavah* (*Berachos* 5a). It further states (ibid. 5b) that a plague that befalls a person is sometimes a punishment, and sometimes *yesurin shel ahavah*. If no one notices that the plague befell the person, then it is *yesurin shel ahavah*. If people see it happen, it is a punishment.

We can now appreciate Rashi's choice of words. The Torah is condemning the *meraglim* for not having learned a lesson from Miriam's punishment. Such criticism is valid only if they had actually been able to see the effect of the plague on Miriam; only if the plague is visible to others is it a punishment. If the spies had merely heard about it, they would have been correct to assume that Miriam was not punished for slander, but, instead, she was the beneficiary of *yesurin shel ahavah*. Rashi, as precise as ever, therefore wrote that the *meraglim* saw the plague.

(*Chanukas HaTorah*)

... וַיִּקְרָא מֹשֶׁה לְהוֹשֵׁעַ בִּן נוּן יְהוֹשֻׁעַ. (י"ג:ט"ז)

...and Moshe called Hoshea bin Nun [a new name] — Yehoshua. (13:16)

Rashi explains that the name Yehoshua alludes to the fact that Moshe prayed on behalf of Yehoshua; he prayed that Yehoshua would not participate in the slandering of Eretz Yisrael. Certainly Moshe was concerned about the spiritual welfare of all the *Nesiim* who went on the spy mission. Why did he only pray for Yehoshua? One could say that he never suspected that the other *Nesiim* would speak badly about Eretz Yisrael; he suspected only Yehoshua. But Yehoshua was on the same spiritual plane as the other *Nesiim*. Why would he be more suspect than the others?

Analyses of the possible motives that Yehoshua and the other *Nesiim* might have had leads to an understanding of this matter. The Zohar (*Shelach* p.158a) states that the *Nesiim* were biased in not wanting to enter Eretz Yisrael: They assumed that they would no longer head their respective tribes after the Jews entered. Yehoshua, on the other hand, had an altruistic reason for impeding the advance of the Jews. He knew that his beloved teacher Moshe was not permitted to enter the Land and would die before the people did so. As long as he could somehow prevent the Jews from entering the Land, Moshe would remain alive!

Although it would seem that the *Nesiim* were in a worse position than Yehoshua since their motives were selfish, they did have an advantage over him. If they would pause to examine themselves they would have realized what their motive was, and immediately desisted from such a shameful act. Yehoshua thought he was doing a noble act. Nothing would cause him to regret dissuading the Jews from entering Eretz Yisrael.

Moshe understood all this. He had faith that the *Nesiim*, in their honesty, would eventually realize the motive for their actions, and desist from slandering Eretz Yisrael. For Yehoshua, however, there was no solution except to pray for Divine help. That is why Moshe prayed only for Yehoshua.

(*Kehillas Yitzchak,* in the name of *R' Yaakov Yosef*)

וַיֵּלְכוּ וַיָּבֹאוּ אֶל מֹשֶׁה וְאֶל אַהֲרֹן וְאֶל כָּל עֲדַת בְּנֵי יִשְׂרָאֵל... (י״ג:כ״ו)

> They [the meraglim] went and came back to Moshe and to Aharon and the entire assembly of the children of Israel... (13:26)

In the previous *pasuk* the Torah mentions that the *meraglim* returned from their journey. It seems out of place for the Torah to write in this *pasuk* that the *meraglim* went to Eretz Yisrael after it had already mentioned their return. Rashi explains that the Torah is revealing that just as they spoke evil of Eretz Yisrael when they came, likewise when they departed they already had evil designs to slander Eretz Yisrael.

Earlier in the *parashah* (13:3), when the *Nesiim* are sent to spy out Eretz Yisrael, the Torah describes them as *anashim*. Rashi explains that wherever this is found in the Torah it is a title of distinction. We must, therefore, assume that at that point in time they were righteous people. It seems that Rashi is contradicting himself. Earlier he writes that they were righteous when they left Eretz Yisrael and had no evil plans; here he writes that when they went out they already planned slander.

The Gemara states that sometimes Hashem punishes people for planning to do evil, and sometimes He does not (*Kiddushin* 40a). The rule is as follows: If a person eventually carries out his evil plan, then he is also punished for the planning itself; however, if the plan never comes to fruition, he is not punished for it.

We can now resolve the apparent contradiction. Before the *meraglim* departed for Eretz Yisrael, they already planned to speak ill of it. Nevertheless, the Torah describes them as *anashim*; they had not done anything wrong yet so their plan was not held against them. Later, after they returned and actually slandered Eretz Yisrael, the Torah speaks derogatorily about their planning per se.

(*R' Avrohom Mordechai Alter — Gerer Rebbe*,
quoted by *Likutei Yehudah*)

וַיְסַפְּרוּ לוֹ וַיֹּאמְרוּ בָּאנוּ אֶל הָאָרֶץ אֲשֶׁר שְׁלַחְתָּנוּ...
וְהֶעָרִים בְּצֻרוֹת ... (י״ג:כ״ז-כ״ח)

> They reported to him and said: We arrived at the Land to which you sent us... and the cities are betzuros... (13:27-28)

The *meraglim*, upon their return, complained that the cities in Eretz Yisrael are *betzuros*. What is the meaning of *betzuros*? The *Targum Onkeles* explains that it means round. This explanation is puzzling. How would the fact that the cities were round dissuade the Jews from entering Eretz Yisrael?

In *parashas Metzora* (14:34), Hashem informed the Jews that houses in Eretz Yisrael could contract *tzara'as* and such a house had to be demolished. The Midrash (*Vayikra Rabbah* 17:6, quoted by Rashi) adds that this was good news for the Jews. Many of the inhabitants of Eretz Yisrael would hide gold treasures in the walls of their houses. If a house became afflicted with *tzara'as*, it meant that there was a treasure hidden in its walls and the Jewish owner would find it after destroying the house.

The Mishnah (*Negaim* 12:1) lists several types of houses to which the laws of *tzara'as* do not apply. One such house is a round house. If a round house is infected with *tzara'as* it is not demolished.

We can now understand what the *meraglim* were conveying. The Jews were happy to have heard from Hashem that great treasures awaited them in Eretz Yisrael. But the *meraglim* were in effect telling them, "Don't expect any great treasures! The houses in Eretz Yisrael are round and their walls will not have to be thrown down!"

(*Hilula D'Pischa*, quoted by *Zichron Yisrael*)

וְהֵמַתָּה אֶת הָעָם הַזֶּה כְּאִישׁ אֶחָד... (י"ד:ט"ו)

Yet you killed this people like a single man... (14:15)

When Moshe protested Hashem's intention to annihilate the Jewish nation, he used the phrase "like a single man." It seems superfluous, but surely Moshe intended to add to his defense of the Jews with these words. What did he have in mind?

The Gemara states that there is a difference between the way Hashem acts toward the community and toward an individual. If an individual sins twice, Hashem will forgive him, but he will not be forgiven the third time. A communal sin will be forgiven even a third time, but it will not be forgiven the fourth time [quote of the Gemara (*Yoma* 86a) according to text of *Rif* and *Rambam*].

The Midrash (*Tanchuma, Korach* Chap. 4) comments that the episode of the *meraglim* was the third time that the Jewish community sinned against Hashem. The first time was with the *eigel hazahav* (*Shemos* 32); the second, the story of the *misonenim*, complainers (*Bamidbar* 11). According to the *Gemara*, then, the Jews deserved to be forgiven for the sin of the *meraglim*; this was only their third communal sin.

This is what Moshe meant by the expression "like a single man." He was complaining that Hashem was treating the nation as if it were an individual.

(*Gan Raveh*, in name of *Mishkenos Yaakov*)

וַיִּהְיוּ בְנֵי יִשְׂרָאֵל בַּמִּדְבָּר וַיִּמְצְאוּ אִישׁ מְקֹשֵׁשׁ עֵצִים בְּיוֹם הַשַּׁבָּת (ט״ו:ל״ב)

And the children of Israel were in the Wilderness, and they found a man gathering wood on Shabbos. (15:32)

All the events recorded in this *parashah* occurred while the Jews were in the Wilderness. Why then was it necessary for the episode of the wood-gatherer on Shabbos to begin with the phrase "and the Jews were in the Wilderness"?

The Gemara (*Shabbos* 96b) relates that the wood-gatherer transgressed the prohibition of transporting an item four cubits in *reshus harabim*. This might seem odd, as a desert does not qualify as a *reshus harabim* since people do not usually travel there. However, the Gemara states that when the Jewish people were in the Wilderness, after their exodus from Egypt, it qualified as a *reshus harabim*, due to the vast number of people found there at the time (*Shabbos* 6b).

Therefore, to prevent one from wondering why the wood gatherer was punished, the Torah mentions that the Jewish people were then found in the Wilderness, thus qualifying it as a *reshus harabim*.

(*Ohr HaChaim*)

Shelach / 223

KORACH

וַיִּקַּח קֹרַח... (ט"ז:א)

Korach separated himself [from the rest of the community]... (16:1)

Rashi quotes a Midrash (*Tanchuma* par. 1) which explains that the cause of Korach's dispute was Moshe's appointment of Elitzaphun ben Uziel as *Nasi* of the descendants of Kehas; Korach felt that the position was rightfully his. This appointment occurred some time before Korach's protest. One wonders why he waited and did not argue against Moshe immediately.

The Zohar (*Shelach* p. 158a) reveals that the *Nesiim* tried to thwart the Jews' entrance into Eretz Yisrael because they knew they would keep their positions as *Nesiim* only in the Wilderness. Once the people entered Eretz Yisrael others would be appointed in their stead.

It may be inferred from the words of the Zohar that it was generally assumed that all people in high positions would be replaced once the Jews entered Eretz Yisrael. Based on this inference we can suggest the following. Elitzaphun was appointed before the sin of the *eigel hazahav* when the Jews expected to enter Eretz Yisrael very shortly. At that time Korach did not care about the appointment; he assumed he would replace Elitzaphun when the

Jews entered Eretz Yisrael. Later, after it was decreed that the Jews should spend forty years in the Wilderness, Korach became upset. He did not know if he would ever see the day when he would be the *Nasi*. (*Binyan Ariel*)

וַיִּחַר לְמֹשֶׁה מְאֹד וַיֹּאמֶר אֶל ה' אַל תֵּפֶן אֶל מִנְחָתָם... (ט״ז:ט״ו)

*This **distressed** Moshe greatly and he said to Hashem, "Do not turn to their gift-offering..." (16:15)*

The Torah uses the word *vayichar* when describing Moshe's emotion. The usual translation of the word is "angry." Rashi, however, explains it as meaning "distressed." Why did Rashi depart from the usual explanation?

It is evident from the Gemara that it is not proper for one to pray while in a state of anger (*Eruvin* 65a). Yet here Moshe prayed to Hashem not to accept the offering of the Jews. It must therefore be that Moshe was not angry, but rather distressed.

(*Imrei Shefer*)

וּקְחוּ אִישׁ מַחְתָּתוֹ וּנְתַתֶּם עֲלֵיהֶם קְטֹרֶת וְהִקְרַבְתֶּם לִפְנֵי ה' אִישׁ מַחְתָּתוֹ חֲמִשִּׁים וּמָאתַיִם מַחְתֹּת וְאַתָּה וְאַהֲרֹן **אִישׁ מַחְתָּתוֹ**. (ט״ז:י״ז)

*Let each man take his fire-pan and you shall place incense on them, and you will offer before Hashem each man his fire-pan, and you and Aharon **each man with his fire-pan**. (16:17)*

Korach and his colleagues were instructed to bring their own fire-pans. Aharon was also so instructed. It appears that Aharon was not permitted to bring the communal fire-pan that he generally used. Why not?

We learn that the original vessels of the Mishkan had to be consecrated with oil prior to their first use (*Shemos* 40:9). All subsequent vessels became sanctified automatically upon being used once (*Sanhedrin* 16b).

Although Aharon generally used an original communal fire-pan when offering the *ketores*, Moshe now instructed him to use his own private fire-pan. If Aharon would use the communal fire-pan and live, people might claim that his offering was accepted because the fire-pan had been consecrated, and not because Aharon's claim to *Kehunah* was valid.

(Meshech Chochmah)

וַתִּפְתַּח הָאָרֶץ אֶת פִּיהָ וַתִּבְלַע אֹתָם וְאֶת בָּתֵּיהֶם וְאֵת כָּל הָאָדָם אֲשֶׁר לְקֹרַח וְאֵת כָּל הָרְכוּשׁ. (ט״ז:ל״ב)

> *The earth opened its mouth and swallowed them and their households, and all the people who were with Korach,* **and the entire wealth** *(16:32)*

The Torah records that the ground swallowed up Korach's conspirators and their property. A careful reading reveals that the Torah does not write "their entire wealth" but rather "the entire wealth." Why?

We can suggest that Korach and his conspirators acquired the status of an *ir hanidachas* by challenging the Divine appointment of Aharon. This would explain why their wives and children were also killed [see Rambam (*Avodas Kochavim* 4:6), who writes that even the women and children of an *ir hanidachas* are killed].

It follows, then, that although the sons of Korach repented and were not swallowed up, nevertheless their property was destroyed, just as the property of *tzaddikim* is destroyed in an *ir hanidachas* [see Rambam, ibid. 4:7]. Therefore it is written "the entire wealth"; to include even the property of the children of Korach.

(Meshech Chochmah)

וַתִּפְתַּח הָאָרֶץ אֶת פִּיהָ וַתִּבְלַע אֹתָם וְאֶת בָּתֵּיהֶם... (ט״ז:ל״ב)

The earth opened its mouth and swallowed them and their houses... (16:32)

Earlier in *pasuk* 27 their abodes are referred to as "tents." Here the Torah calls them "houses." Why does the Torah describe them differently?

A tent is a portable temporary residence. A house connotes a permanent dwelling place. When the Jews were in the desert, moving from place to place, their homes were referred to as tents. However, once Korach and his followers were swallowed in the ground their tents became their graves, permanent resting-places. Their places of residence were then called houses.

(*Imrei Shefer*)

וַיִּלֹּנוּ כָּל עֲדַת בְּנֵי יִשְׂרָאֵל מִמָּחֳרָת עַל מֹשֶׁה וְעַל אַהֲרֹן לֵאמֹר אַתֶּם הֲמִתֶּם אֶת עַם ה'... וַיִּפְנוּ אֶל אֹהֶל מוֹעֵד וְהִנֵּה כִסָּהוּ הֶעָנָן וַיֵּרָא כְּבוֹד ה'. וַיָּבֹא מֹשֶׁה וְאַהֲרֹן אֶל פְּנֵי אֹהֶל מוֹעֵד. (י״ז:ו-ח)

The entire assembly of the children of Israel complained on the morrow against Moshe and Aharon saying, "You have killed the people of Hashem"... they turned to the Ohel Moed, and behold it was covered with a cloud, and the glory of Hashem appeared. Moshe and Aharon entered the Ohel Moed. (17:6-8)

The commentaries explain that the people were blaming Moshe and Aharon for causing the death of so many Jews. Although the accomplices of Korach deserved death, the masses felt that Moshe was at fault for subjecting them to a test that would result in their death.

The Gemara reveals that a person who causes another person to be punished will not be privileged to be "in Hashem's enclosure" (*Shabbos* 149b). This Gemara illuminates the sequence of *pesukim* here. The people were accusing Moshe of causing the death of Korach's colleagues. Hashem appeared in the *Ohel Moed*, and Moshe and Aharon entered the *Ohel Moed* to be enveloped in that Divine cloud. This proved that Moshe and Aharon were innocent of the accusations. Had they been the cause of the punishment they would not have been allowed to be in such intimate "contact" with Hashem.[7]

(*Be'er Yosef*, in the name of *R' Eliyahu Meir Leibowitz*)

---

7. EDITOR'S NOTE: In the Torah these *pesukim* are followed by a space, which indicates the end of a paragraph. This seems out of place since these *pesukim* appear to be a mere prelude to what follows, where Hashem responds with anger to the complaints of the Jews. The preceding explanation also answers this. These *pesukim* do comprise an integral unit: the complaint of the Jews and the response of Hashem to their complaint. Hashem did not respond verbally, but with an action that demonstrated the innocence of Moshe and Aharon.

CHUKAS

וַיְדַבֵּר ה' אֶל מֹשֶׁה וְאֶל אַהֲרֹן לֵאמֹר. זֹאת חֻקַּת הַתּוֹרָה אֲשֶׁר צִוָּה ה' לֵאמֹר דַּבֵּר אֶל בְּנֵי יִשְׂרָאֵל וְיִקְחוּ אֵלֶיךָ פָרָה אֲדֻמָּה תְּמִימָה... (י״ט:א-ב)

> *Hashem spoke to Moshe and Aharon saying, "This is the decree of the Torah which Hashem has commanded saying: Speak to the Children of Israel, and they shall take to you a completely red cow... (19:1-2)*

THE ORDER OF THE WORDS SEEMS ODD. IT SHOULD FIRST HAVE stated "speak to the children of Israel" and afterwards "This is the decree of the Torah etc." Why was it reversed?

The Gemara (*Tosefta, Sanhedrin* Chap. 3) states that only a "*beis din* of seventy-one" [the highest judicial authority] can authorize the burning of a *parah adumah*. The Gemara (*Sanhedrin* 16a) also says that Moshe had vested in him the authority of a "*beis din* of seventy-one."

This explains the order of the phrases. It is part of the statutes of the Torah that Moshe be the one to "speak to the children of Israel" and instruct them to burn the red cow; otherwise it would not be permitted.[8]

(*Chidushei Maran Riz HaLevi*)

---

8. ADDENDUM: This explanation sheds light on the purpose of the dividing line that is found in the Chumash after the word *dabeir*. The Torah is pointing out that the word *dabeir* is connected to the previous phrase "this is the decree of the Torah" and teaches that it is essential for Moshe to do the talking and instructing.
(*Ya'er Hapsik*)

... וְשָׁחַט אֹתָהּ לְפָנָיו. (י״ט:ג)

... and someone shall slaughter it in his presence. (19:3)

Targum Yonasan adds, that just like every animal that undergoes *shechitah* (ritual slaughter) has its internal organs checked to assure that it is not a *tereifah*, so too the *parah adumah* was checked. This statement seems to contradict the law (see *Chullin* 11a) that the *parah adumah* had to be burned entirely intact; it could not be dissected prior to its burning. In order to inspect for *tereifus*, one would have to cut up the animal and check the internal organs. It follows, then, that according to the Gemara this inspection could not take place.

Tosefos (*Shabbos* 22b) quotes an amazing Midrash (*Meleches HaMishkan* Chap. 14) which declares that the miraculous cloud which accompanied the Jews in the desert had an x-ray quality. A person was able to see through the walls of a closed container and know what was inside! If so, there is no contradiction between *Targum Yonasan* and the Gemara. The Jews were able to check for *tereifus* without dismembering the *parah adumah*. They merely looked at it, and were able to see whether or not the internal organs had blemishes which rendered them *tereifah*!

However, *Targum Yonasan* still seems to contradict yet another Gemara. There is an axiom in Jewish law — *holchin achar harov* [we follow the majority]. Whenever something is under question as to its characteristics, we assume that it has the same qualities as the majority of its kind, and we do not suspect that this specific case is an exception. The Gemara queries where in the Torah is there a source for this principle. One suggestion given is that the laws of *parah adumah* are based on this principle. The *parah adumah* could not be a *tereifah*. Yet, as mentioned earlier, it could not be dismembered to check for *tereifus*. How can that be? It must be that the Torah allows us to rely upon the *rov* principle, and we can assume that since most animals are not *tereifah*, this animal also is not *tereifah* (*Chullin* 11a). This Gemara clearly assumes that the *parah adumah* was not checked for *tereifus*. This contradicts *Targum Yonasan* wrote.

However, this seeming discrepancy can easily be resolved. *Targum Yonasan* is referring specifically to the *parah adumah* of the era when the Jews were in the Wilderness. That particular cow was checked against *tereifus* with the "x-rays" of the "clouds." The proof of the Gemara to the *rov* principle is from every subsequent *parah adumah,* which could not be checked in this manner, and must have been valid due to the *rov* principle.

(R' Chaim Berlin zt"l, quoted in Har Tzvi)

וְכִבֶּס הָאֹסֵף אֶת אֵפֶר הַפָּרָה אֶת בְּגָדָיו... (י"ט:י)

The one who gathered the ash of the cow shall immerse his clothing... (19:10)

The Torah states that the collector of the ashes should immerse his clothing, and refers to his clothing as **es begadav**. However, when the Torah states (*pasuk* 7) that the Kohen who cast the various ingredients into the *parah adumah* amalgam should also immerse his clothes, it simply writes "*begadav*," omitting the word *es*. This discrepancy begs an explanation.

The Gemara teaches us, that when the Torah writes the word *es* preceding a noun, it can convey a message of "including something, which is subordinate to that noun" (*Bava Kamma* 41b). Applying that rule here, it can be suggested that the word *es* teaches that not only does the clothing of the collector have to be immersed, but also all ornaments which are attached to the clothing [and are subordinate to it] should be immersed.

The Mishnah (*Parah* 4:1) states that the Kohen who was involved in producing the *parah adumah* solution wore standard clothing of the Kohanim — the four simple white garments described in the Torah. That Kohen was prohibited to wear anything more than that. It can now be understood why the Torah omitted the word *es*. Since that Kohen wore no additional ornaments, the word *es* is superfluous. (*Taamah D'Kra*)

וְלָמָה הֶעֱלִיתֻנוּ מִמִּצְרַיִם לְהָבִיא אֹתָנוּ אֶל הַמָּקוֹם הָרָע הַזֶּה לֹא מְקוֹם זֶרַע וּתְאֵנָה וְגֶפֶן וְרִמּוֹן... (כ:ה)

> *Why did you take us out of Egypt and bring us to this evil place? It is not a place of seed, or fig, grape, or pomegranate... (20:5)*

The Jews seemed to be complaining that they did not reach the desired land of the "seven species" which they had been promised. Yet they omitted two of the seven: olive oil and [date] honey [*seed* encompasses the two species of wheat and barley]. What was the reason for that?

The Torah mentions that the manna that the Jews ate in the desert tasted like honey and like oil [see *Shemos* 16:31, and *Bamidbar* 11: 8]. If so, the Jews could not justifiably protest that they did not arrive at a Land that had oil and honey.

This also explains the conduct of the *meraglim* who brought back only figs and pomegranates, but not olives and dates. There was nothing novel about them; their taste was found in the manna. (*Meshech Chochmah*)

וְהָיָה אִם נָשַׁךְ הַנָּחָשׁ אֶת אִישׁ וְהִבִּיט אֶל נְחַשׁ הַנְּחֹשֶׁת וָחָי. (כ"א:ט)

> *...it was that if the serpent bit a man, he would stare at the copper serpent, and live. (21:9)*

The words *vayehi* and *vehayah* both mean "and it was." The Gemara (*Megillah* 10b) states the rule as to when each word is used. When prefacing a sorrowful event, the Torah will write *vayehi*; a happy event, *vehayah* will be used. If so, it is incomprehensible why the Torah wrote the word *vehayah* here. Surely the biting of a serpent is an adverse event, and therefore the Torah should have written *vayehi*.

In the previous *pasuk* (21:8) we read that Hashem told Moshe that whoever is bitten by a serpent and thereupon stares at the copper serpent will definitely live. This implies that even a person who was deathly ill from another cause, if a serpent bit him and he would then look at the copper serpent, he would be totally healed from all life-threatening maladies. Such a person would be overjoyed if a serpent bit him! Therefore, since for some people snakebite was a joyous occasion, the Torah used the word *vehaya*h.

(Meshech Chochmah)

כִּי חֶשְׁבּוֹן עִיר סִיחֹן מֶלֶךְ הָאֱמֹרִי הִוא וְהוּא נִלְחַם בְּמֶלֶךְ מוֹאָב הָרִאשׁוֹן וַיִּקַּח אֶת כָּל אַרְצוֹ מִיָּדוֹ עַד אַרְנֹן. (כ״א:כ״ו)

> *For Cheshbon was then a city of Sichon, king of the Amorite, and he had warred against the first king of Moav and took all his land from his control, until Arnon. (21:26)*

Rashi explains that the Torah relates the history of the city of Cheshbon in order to clarify why the Jews were allowed to capture it. Cheshbon originally belonged to Moav and could not be attacked by the Jews, under the prohibition "Do not distress Moav." However, Sichon attacked Moav and captured Cheshbon. The Jews were permitted to attack Sichon, which they did, and thus captured Cheshbon from them.

This explains a puzzling phrase in the Siddur. In the Shabbos-morning prayer, psalm 136 lists many acts of kindness by Hashem toward the Jewish people while they were in the Wilderness, with each stanza ending off with *ki le'olam chasdo*. Included among them is that He smote great and powerful kings, and that He gave their land to the Jews for an inheritance. It is written there וְנָתַן אַרְצָם לְנַחֲלָה, "He gave their land for an inheritance" and then a new stanza נַחֲלָה לְיִשְׂרָאֵל עַבְדּוֹ, "an inheritance to the Jewish people His servant." Superficially the second stanza seems redundant. But in light of the above, it can be explained that the first phrase means that He smote the mighty kings of Moav and gave their land to Sichon. The second phrase means that He then gave that land to the Jewish people. The special praise here is that He gave it to the Jews in a roundabout manner to allow them to conquer it.

(*Siddur Maggid Tzedek*)

Balak

וַיַּרְא בָּלָק בֶּן צִפּוֹר אֵת כָּל אֲשֶׁר עָשָׂה יִשְׂרָאֵל... (כ״ב:ב)

Balak the son of Tzippor saw all that Israel had done... (22:2)

THE *BAAL HATURIM* EXPLAINS THAT BALAK SAW HASHEM STOP THE motion of the sun for a period of time for the benefit of Moshe (see *Taanis* 20a), and this is what he feared. However, no reason is offered why this so frightened Balak.

The Gemara states that Hashem is angered for one second every day, and whoever utters a curse in that time frame will have his wish fulfilled. That second is at sunrise, and is almost impossible to compute. The only one who was able to was Bilaam (*Berachos* 7a).

Balak depended on Bilaam being able to curse the Jews. If Moshe could stop the sun from setting and rising, Bilaam would not have the opportunity to curse the Jews. This is what Balak feared most.

(*Satmar Rebbe zt"l*, quoted by *Talelei Oros*)

> וַיִּשְׁלַח מַלְאָכִים אֶל בִּלְעָם בֶּן בְּעוֹר פְּתוֹרָה אֲשֶׁר עַל הַנָּהָר
> אֶרֶץ בְּנֵי עַמּוֹ לִקְרֹא לוֹ... (כ״ב:ה)

He sent emissaries to Bilaam the son of Beor, to Pesor, which is by the river, of his native land, to summon him... (22:5)

Why did the Torah find it important to mention that Pesor is by a river?

Bilaam prophesied even though he was not in Eretz Yisrael. How could that be? We know that Hashem appears to people only in Eretz Yisrael. The Midrash (*Yalkut Shimoni*, beg. of *Yechezkel*) already asked this question about the prophet Yechezkel. The answer given there is that Yechezkel prophesied near a river, and since a river cannot become defiled, Hashem appears there to his prophets.

The Torah is forestalling the above question by mentioning that Bilaam was situated near a river. By being there he was able to prophesy despite being outside the Land.

(*Tiferes Yehonasan*)

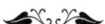

> וַיִּפְתַּח ה' אֶת פִּי הָאָתוֹן וַתֹּאמֶר לְבִלְעָם מֶה עָשִׂיתִי לְךָ כִּי
> הִכִּיתָנִי זֶה שָׁלֹשׁ רְגָלִים. (כ״ב:כ״ח)

Hashem opened the mouth of the she-donkey, and it said to Bilaam, "What have I done to you that you struck me three times?" (22:28)

The donkey complained to Bilaam for hitting her three times. The word the donkey used for "times" was *regalim*. The Midrash (*Tanchuma* par. 9) explains that this unusual word was placed in the donkey's mouth by Hashem to convey an indirect message. *Regalim* usually refers to the three Yamim Tovim which are mentioned in the Torah — Pesach, Shavuos, and Succos.

Hashem was pointing out to Bilaam that by cursing and annihilating the Jewish nation he would be wiping out a nation who observes the three *regalim*.

A question that comes to mind when seeing this Midrash [quoted by Rashi] is: Why did Hashem pick this specific mitzvah? There are hundreds of mitzvos that the Jews perform and which they would not be doing if they were destroyed. What is unique about this mitzvah that only it was mentioned to Bilaam? To answer this question, one must be apprised of two other Midrashim.

First, there is a Midrash, which states: Hashem said to Bilaam, "If you decimate the Jewish people, who will observe My precepts? I have already asked the other nations if they wish to accept My laws and they refused." To which Bilaam replied, "I will observe Your precepts in their stead!"

Second, the Gemara states that Bilaam was blind in one eye, and also limped on one foot (*Sanhedrin* 105b). According to halachah (*Chagigah* 2a), one maimed in this way is exempt from fulfilling the mitzvah of *oleh regel*.

With the above information, we can now comprehend the first Midrash mentioned. Hashem complained to Bilaam that the Torah would not be observed if the Jews were killed. Bilaam replied that he would observe the Torah in place of Israel. To refute Bilaam, Hashem mentioned *oleh regel* — a mitzvah that would not be applicable to Bilaam. Although there are other mitzvos that Bilaam might not be able to perform, this mitzvah was chosen since there is also within it an implied denigration of Bilaam. The inability of Bilaam to perform this mitzvah stemmed from his physical impairment; the mentioning of this mitzvah therefore underscored this fault.

(R' Kopel of Lublin, quoted by Nofes Tzufim)

... וַיַּעַל בָּלָק וּבִלְעָם פָּר וָאַיִל בַּמִּזְבֵּחַ. (כ"ג:ב)

Balak and Bilaam brought up a bull and a ram on each mizbe'ach. (23:2)

The Torah relates that three times Bilaam had altars built and offerings brought. However, Bilaam's involvement with the actual offering is mentioned only regarding the first sacrifice. This implies that the other two times Bilaam did not take part in the actual sacrificing. Why was this so?

Bilaam referred to himself as *shesum ha'ayin* (24:3). The Gemara explains this to mean that he was blind in one eye (*Niddah* 31a). After bringing the first series of offerings, Bilaam had a degrading thought about Hashem and as a punishment was blinded in one eye.

A person who is physically blemished is prohibited from sacrificing an animal, even on a private altar (*Zevachim* 16a). Blindness, even in one eye, is considered a blemish and is disqualifying (ibid. 68b). This also applies to a Gentile (*Bereishis Rabbah* Chap. 30, par. 6).

Knowing all this, the riddle is solved. In the first round of offerings Bilaam was an active participant. Immediately afterwards he was blinded and was thereafter ineligible from taking part. Therefore, the following two times only Balak participated and only his name is mentioned.

(*Taamah D'Kra* [extract])

וַיִּשָּׂא בִלְעָם אֶת עֵינָיו וַיַּרְא אֶת יִשְׂרָאֵל שֹׁכֵן לִשְׁבָטָיו ... (כ"ד:ב)

Bilaam raised his eyes and saw Yisrael dwelling according to its tribes... (24:2)

The Gemara, quoted by Rashi, explains that Bilaam was impressed upon noticing that the entrances of the tents of the

Jews did not face each other in order that one should not peek into the tent of his neighbor (*Bava Basra* 60a).

What prompted the Gemara to offer this explanation?

The Rashbam (ibid.) states that the camp of Yisrael was legally considered a communal courtyard, unlike the camp of the Levites which was a public place. If so, in the camp of the Levites it was permitted to have doors facing each other, as in every public place. Thus Bilaam must have noticed also the difference between the camp of Yisrael and that of the Levites.

This is expressed in the *pasuk*, when it says, "And Bilaam lifted his eyes and saw Yisrael..." i.e. the camp of Yisrael and not of Levi [otherwise the *pasuk* should have written, "and he saw them..."]. The Gemara understood that this was the only difference between the two camps that he could have seen.

(*Chidushei Rabbeinu Yosef M'Slutzk*)

וַיִּהְיוּ הַמֵּתִים בַּמַּגֵּפָה אַרְבָּעָה וְעֶשְׂרִים אָלֶף. (כ"ה:ט)

The number of those who died in the plague was twenty-four thousand. (25:9)

If one looks at the *ta'amim* (cantillations) of this *pasuk*, one sees an *esnachta* on the word *bamageifah*. This seems inconsistent with the rules of *ta'amim*. An *esnachta* is only placed on a word that separates two separate sentences within one *pasuk*. This *pasuk* cannot be split into two independent sentences; why then is there an *esnachta*?

Hashem decreed that twenty-four thousand Jews should die in the plague. However, the Gemara states that this era was one of great mercy from Hashem toward the Jews, and that He mitigated this decree. Hashem declared that all those who were destined anyway to die in this period of time should be included in this quota. This would result in fewer Jews perishing due to the plague (*Sanhedrin* 105b).

We can suggest that this is alluded to by the *ta'am*. The *pasuk* is conveying a message different than its superficial one. It should be understood as two separate statements as indicated by the *ta'am*. The first statement is "*vayiheyu hameisim bamageifah*": all those who were supposed to die anyway now died in the plague. The next statement is "*arba'ah ve'esrim alef*": the total of all people who died was twenty-four thousand.

(*Kehillas Yitzchak*, in the name of *R' Shraga Feivel of Smargon*)

[There is an amazing story behind this explanation. The composer of this *dvar Torah*, Rav Shraga Feivel, lived in the same time as the renowned Vilna Gaon. After his death, Rav Shraga Feivel appeared to his son in a dream, and revealed that he was on his way to appear to the Vilna Gaon to bring him "heavenly greetings." The Vilna Gaon was thus privileged due to his having recently said a novel and true explanation on a passage in the Torah. And why was Reb Shraga privileged to be the conveyor of these "greetings"? Because he too once said an authentic original explanation of a *pasuk*. "What was that explanation?" asked the son. Reb Shraga then told him the above explanation!

(*Kehillas Yitzchak*)]

Pinchas

פִּינְחָס בֶּן אֶלְעָזָר בֶּן אַהֲרֹן הַכֹּהֵן ... (כ״ה:י״א)

Pinchas the son of Elazar son of Aharon the Kohen... (25:11)

THE GEMARA, QUOTED BY RASHI, RELATES THAT AFTER PINCHAS killed Zimri, the populace criticized Pinchas and said, "Did you see that? Pinchas's grandfather [Yisro] worshiped idols, and yet Pinchas killed the *Nasi* of one of the tribes of the Jewish nation!" Therefore, continues the Gemara, to offset that complaint the Torah mentioned his other illustrious lineage — that he was a grandson of Aharon *HaKohen* (*Sanhedrin* 82b).

It is difficult to comprehend why the people expressed themselves the way they did. If they opined that Pinchas acted improperly, why voice specific resentment that the killer of the *Nasi* is a descendant of an idol worshiper? On the other hand, if they felt that the action taken by Pinchas was justified, why did they belittle him? Being a descendant of an idol worshiper does not disqualify him from being allowed to kill a *Nasi* rightfully.

The Gemara states that the sin which Zimri committed is not one which is tried by a court (*Sanhedrin* 82a). Likewise, if a similar situation would arise and one would ask *beis din* whether or not to kill the perpetrator of the sin, he would be advised to refrain from killing. However, if one Jew sees another having marital relations with a Gentile woman in public, and is incensed, he is permitted to kill the sinner. This is only permitted if the observer is motivated to his action out of great love of Hashem. If the viewer has a prior grudge against the sinner, he is prohibited to utilize this opportunity and kill the sinner for his own ulterior motive.

Now we can understand the people's reaction. They grumbled that it could not be that the grandson of an idol worshiper is so concerned with Hashem's honor and so upset by Zimri's sin that it should lead him to kill Zimri. It must be that Pinchas used this opportunity to settle an old score. If this would be true, then Pinchas's act would be a despicable one. Therefore the Torah writes that Pinchas is a grandson of Aharon the Kohen, who loved Hashem dearly. This trait which was passed down to Pinchas is what motivated him to act zealously at the crucial moment. The Torah is testifying that Pinchas acted solely "for the sake of Hashem" when he killed Zimri.

(*Beis Yitzchak*, in the name of *R' Moshe Mendel*)

לָכֵן אֱמֹר הִנְנִי נֹתֵן לוֹ אֶת בְּרִיתִי שָׁלוֹם. וְהָיְתָה לוֹ וּלְזַרְעוֹ אַחֲרָיו בְּרִית כְּהֻנַּת עוֹלָם... (כ״ה:י״ב,י״ג)

> *Therefore say: I give him My covenant of peace. It shall be for him and for his descendants a covenant of eternal priesthood... (25:12,13)*

Hashem rewarded Pinchas with a "covenant of peace" for his heroic action. The Torah does not explain what this covenant is. One might suggest that this refers to his achieving the status of a Kohen. But this is not so, since the Torah mentions the "covenant of eternal priesthood" as a separate reward. If so, what is this "covenant of peace?"

The Gemara (*Sanhedrin* 82a) states that Moshe did not make a move when Zimri committed his terrible sin. Instead,

Pinchas took the initiative. Although the act of Pinchas per se was laudable, nevertheless since it contradicted Moshe's response to the situation it was tantamount to "teaching laws in the presence of one's mentor" which is usually considered irreverent and thus prohibited. More so, the Gemara states R' Chiya bar Abba's opinion that one who has the audacity to teach the laws of Torah in front of his Rebbi deserves to be bitten by a snake (*Eruvin* 63a)!

Pinchas was concerned that his action might result in the punishment mentioned in the Gemara — being bitten by a snake. Hashem therefore allayed his fears and promised him a "covenant of peace." This meant that the snakes would be at peace with him and would not bite him. The Torah (*Bereishis* 3:15) relates that after *Adam HaRishon* sinned, Hashem caused an eternal enmity between man and snake. A "covenant of peace" denotes that these two age-old archenemies would make peace and would not attack one another. Pinchas need not worry about snakebites.

The Gemara (ibid.) mentions two other punishments that "one who teaches law in front of his Rebbi" deserves. One is that he will die without leaving descendants. The other one is that he will be lowered from his level of greatness. In light of this, Hashem's other blessing can be fully appreciated. Hashem promised Pinchas that he and his descendants would be Kohanim forever. The implication of this is that his stature will increase — he will be a Kohen; and that he will have descendants. This is the exact opposite of the two aforementioned punishments! Hashem was promising Pinchas that none of these punishments would befall him. In this specific instance, a terrible sin was being committed and thereby Hashem's honor was being desecrated; therefore Pinchas was correct in taking the initiative even in front of his Rebbi.

(*Kehillas Yitzchak*, in the name of
R' Ben-tzion of Shkod; *Tosefos Berachah*)

רְאוּבֵן בְּכוֹר יִשְׂרָאֵל בְּנֵי רְאוּבֵן חֲנוֹךְ מִשְׁפַּחַת הַחֲנֹכִי . (כ״ו:ה)

Reuven was Yisrael's firstborn; the descendants of Reuven are the Chanochite family from Chanoch... (26:5)

The Midrash (*Yalkut Shimoni, remez* 773), quoted by Rashi, explains the reason why the Torah wrote the name of the families in this manner — adding a *hei* at the beginning of the name, and a *yud* at the end. The Jews classified themselves according to tribes, and the criterion was patrilineal descent. The Gentiles derided the Jews and claimed that having lived in bondage so many years under the Egyptians it was inevitable that the Jewish women had been defiled by the Egyptian men, and that many Jews were fathered by Egyptians. To quell this rumor, Hashem added the letters *yud* and *hei* to the names of the designated Jewish families. The letters *yud* and *hei* combined comprise one of Hashem's Names. The message it conveys is that Hashem is testifying that the Jews are actually descendants of those families.

The commentator Alshich poses the following question on the Midrash. Why didn't Hashem add the letters *yud* and *hei* at an earlier point when mentioning the Jewish families; why did Hashem wait until now?

This same Midrash also writes that in order to squash those malicious rumors, Hashem caused all children born in Egypt to look exactly like their fathers! Consequently, everyone believed that they were the children of their Jewish fathers. Herein lies the answer to the question of the Alshich. This miracle was beneficial only as long as the fathers were alive, and the striking resemblance between father and son was evident. Once the fathers died the proof vanished. Therefore, until now, Hashem did not have to testify in his Torah by writing *yud-hei*; there was living proof to this. It was only now after forty years of being in the Wilderness, with all the fathers dead, that Hashem had to attest to the fact that these Jews were bona fide members of the tribes they belonged to.

(*Levias Chein*)

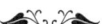

אָבִינוּ מֵת בַּמִּדְבָּר וְהוּא לֹא הָיָה בְּתוֹךְ הָעֵדָה הַנּוֹעָדִים עַל ה' בַּעֲדַת קֹרַח כִּי בְחֶטְאוֹ מֵת וּבָנִים לֹא הָיוּ לוֹ. (כ"ז:ג)

> *"Our father died in the Wilderness, but he was not among the group that banded together against Hashem in the company of Korach; he died because of his own sin, and he had no sons (27:3).*

Why did the daughters of Tzelaphchad mention that their father had not been part of Korach's followers? Did it affect their claim?

The Gemara distinguishes between the estate of one who is killed by *beis din* and one who is killed by the king. The estate of the former is passed down to his inheritors, while the king appropriates the estate of one whom he has killed (*Sanhedrin* 48b).

Korach's followers challenged the authority of Moshe, who had the legal status of a king (see *Devarim* 33:5). Thus, when they were punished and died, they were considered as having been killed by the king, and their property was confiscated. Therefore the daughters of Tzelaphchad claimed that their father had not died for that reason, but rather for a different sin, which entitled them to an inheritance.

(*Meshech Chochmah*)

כֵּן בְּנוֹת צְלָפְחָד דֹּבְרֹת נָתֹן תִּתֵּן לָהֶם אֲחֻזַּת נַחֲלָה בְּתוֹךְ אֲחֵי אֲבִיהֶם ... (כ"ז:ז)

> *The daughters of Tzelaphchad have a just claim; give **them** a hereditary portion of land alongside their father's brothers... (27:7)*

The word "them" in the above *pasuk* is written in Hebrew as *lahem*. Anyone with even an elementary knowledge of

Hebrew grammar knows that the feminine form of "them" is *lahen* [with a *nun* at the end]; the masculine form is *lahem*. Hashem is discussing the daughters of Tzelaphchad in this *pasuk*. Why then did Hashem refer to them as *lahem*?

The Torah (*Bereishis* 36:24) mentions a person called Anah. It is questionable whether Anah was a man or a woman. *Tosefos* (*Bava Basra* 115b) opines that Anah was a woman. *Tosefos* adds that although it is written in the Torah "*hu* Anah," and *hu* is a pronoun used for a man, in this instance since Anah inherited land as a man does [according to Jewish law women do not inherit], the Torah uses a masculine pronoun by the name.

If we apply *Tosefos's* axiom, the grammar of this *pasuk* can now be comprehended. Hashem is now declaring that the daughters of Tzelaphchad should receive land in Eretz Yisrael. Since they will be inheriting land like a man, the masculine *lahem* is therefore appropriate. Similarly, we find in *parashas Masei* (36:6) when discussing the daughters of Tzelaphchad, the words *b'eineihem* [in their eyes] and *avihem* [their father] are written, both being masculine form. The same explanation applies there too.

(*Chanukas HaTorah; Gan Raveh*)

יִפְקֹד ה׳ אֱלֹקֵי הָרוּחֹת לְכָל בָּשָׂר אִישׁ עַל הָעֵדָה. אֲשֶׁר יֵצֵא לִפְנֵיהֶם ... (כ"ז:ט"ז,י"ז)

> May Hashem, G-d of the spirits of all flesh,
> appoint a man over the assembly,
> who shall go out before them... (27:16-17)

The Gemara (*Sanhedrin* 97a) predicts that the generation in which Mashiach will come will be one whose "face will be similar to the face of a dog!" One wonders to what this cryptic remark is referring.

Rav Yisrael Salanter explains as follows:

When a dog is walked by its master, it trots ahead and thus appears to be leading. In reality, however, it is the master who chooses the direction in which to go. When the dog comes to a fork in the road, it stops and waits for its master to direct it.

All throughout Jewish history, the Jewish nation had great leaders who voiced their opinions on all matters, based on what was correct according to the Torah. They were not concerned whether the populace liked what they heard. The aforementioned Gemara is predicting that in the epoch preceding the coming of Mashiach there will be weak leaders who will always ascertain beforehand that their words will be acceptable to the masses. They will merely echo the feelings of the masses. This is akin to the conduct of a dog. It is not a leader; it is a follower. The people are the real leaders. This is the intent of the Gemara in comparing the leaders, or "face," of the pre-Mashiach generation to the face of a dog.

This insight of Rav Yisrael Salanter inspires us to a new explanation of the above *pasuk*. Moshe requested that Hashem provide the Jewish nation with a leader that "will go out before them." The meaning of this phrase is that the leader should truly be a leader and not a follower. A leader who is concerned with public opinion and acts accordingly is not one who "goes out before them." He is in fact "going behind them." Hashem responded that Yehoshua, "a man of spirit," would be his successor. The Midrash (*Sifri* par.140) explains that to mean that he has the courage and independence to resist every other "spirit" [person]. If what the people want to do is not in accordance with Hashem's will, he will not be swayed by them. Yehoshua is the type of leader for whom Moshe asked.

> (*R' Moshe Mendel*, quoted by *Beis Yitzchak*. The explanation of Rav Yisrael Salanter is also quoted by Rav Elchonon Wasserman in *Ikvasa DiMeshicha*, par. 13)

Mattos

וַיְדַבֵּר מֹשֶׁה אֶל הָעָם לֵאמֹר הֵחָלְצוּ מֵאִתְּכֶם אֲנָשִׁים לַצָּבָא ... אֶלֶף לַמַּטֶּה אֶלֶף לַמַּטֶּה לְכֹל מַטּוֹת יִשְׂרָאֵל תִּשְׁלְחוּ לַצָּבָא. וַיִּמָּסְרוּ מֵאַלְפֵי יִשְׂרָאֵל אֶלֶף לַמַּטֶּה שְׁנֵים עָשָׂר אֶלֶף חֲלוּצֵי צָבָא. (ל"א:ג-ה)

> *Moshe spoke to the nation as follows: "People should arm themselves to fight a war... a thousand per tribe, **all the tribes** should send to the army." A thousand from every tribe **were handed over**; all together there were **twelve thousand soldiers**. (31:3-5)*

Rashi quotes a Midrash (Sifri, *Piskah* 157) that explains that the phrase "all the tribes" includes even the tribe of Levi. They too should send a thousand of its people to fight this war. Many commentaries have a difficulty with this Midrash. The Torah sums up and writes that there were twelve thousand soldiers all together. If the tribe of Levi is included in the supplying of soldiers there should be a total of thirteen thousand, since Ephraim and Menashe are counted as two tribes.

The Torah records that the twelve thousand soldiers "were handed over." The Midrash (ibid.) comments that this implies that these soldiers did not want to go willingly but had to be coerced. They knew that Moshe was destined to die following the battle with Midian, and were reluctant to go to war and thus hasten the death of their beloved leader. Therefore they had to be coerced to go fight.

After the sin of the *eigel hazahav* [golden calf], Moshe instructed the Levites to kill all the worshipers of the calf, regardless of who they may be. The Levites subdued their feelings of love, and obediently killed all the idol worshipers, including brothers, grandparents, and grandchildren (*Ki Sisa* 32:26-9; *VeZos HaBerachah* 33:9; *Yoma* 66b)! If so, we can conjecture that here too, despite their tremendous love for Moshe, they stifled that love and were willing to go to war, since that was Hashem's will. With this presumption we can answer the question of the commentaries. The Levites did join in the fighting. The *pasuk* that counts only twelve thousand soldiers is mentioning how many soldiers were "handed over." The soldiers of Levi were not handed over; they willingly went to obey Hashem's will, as difficult as it was emotionally for them!

(R' Avrohom Mordechai Alter — Gerer Rebbe,
quoted in *Likutei Yehudah*)

וַיֹּאמֶר ה' אֶל מֹשֶׁה לֵּאמֹר. שָׂא אֵת רֹאשׁ מַלְקוֹחַ הַשְּׁבִי בָּאָדָם וּבַבְּהֵמָה אַתָּה וְאֶלְעָזָר הַכֹּהֵן וְרָאשֵׁי אֲבוֹת הָעֵדָה. וְחָצִיתָ אֶת הַמַּלְקוֹחַ בֵּין תֹּפְשֵׂי הַמִּלְחָמָה הַיֹּצְאִים לַצָּבָא וּבֵין כָּל הָעֵדָה. וַהֲרֵמֹתָ מֶכֶס לַה' מֵאֵת אַנְשֵׁי הַמִּלְחָמָה הַיֹּצְאִים לַצָּבָא אֶחָד נֶפֶשׁ מֵחֲמֵשׁ הַמֵּאוֹת מִן הָאָדָם וּמִן הַבָּקָר וּמִן הַחֲמֹרִים וּמִן הַצֹּאן. מִמַּחֲצִיתָם תִּקָּחוּ וְנָתַתָּה לְאֶלְעָזָר הַכֹּהֵן תְּרוּמַת ה'. וּמִמַּחֲצִת בְּנֵי יִשְׂרָאֵל תִּקַּח אֶחָד אָחֻז מִן הַחֲמִשִּׁים מִן הָאָדָם מִן הַבָּקָר מִן הַחֲמֹרִים וּמִן הַצֹּאן מִכָּל הַבְּהֵמָה וְנָתַתָּה אֹתָם לַלְוִיִּם שֹׁמְרֵי מִשְׁמֶרֶת מִשְׁכַּן ה' ... וַתְּהִי הַמֶּחֱצָה חֵלֶק הַיֹּצְאִים בַּצָּבָא מִסְפַּר הַצֹּאן שְׁלֹשׁ מֵאוֹת אֶלֶף וּשְׁלֹשִׁים אֶלֶף וְשִׁבְעַת אֲלָפִים וַחֲמֵשׁ מֵאוֹת. וַיְהִי הַמֶּכֶס לַה' מִן הַצֹּאן שֵׁשׁ מֵאוֹת חָמֵשׁ וְשִׁבְעִים. וְהַבָּקָר שִׁשָּׁה וּשְׁלֹשִׁים אָלֶף וּמִכְסָם לַה' שְׁנַיִם וְשִׁבְעִים. וַחֲמֹרִים שְׁלֹשִׁים אֶלֶף וַחֲמֵשׁ מֵאוֹת וּמִכְסָם לַה' אֶחָד וְשִׁשִּׁים. וְנֶפֶשׁ אָדָם שִׁשָּׁה עָשָׂר אָלֶף וּמִכְסָם לַה' שְׁנַיִם וּשְׁלֹשִׁים

נָפֶשׁ. וַיִּתֵּן מֹשֶׁה אֶת מֶכֶס תְּרוּמַת ה' לְאֶלְעָזָר הַכֹּהֵן כַּאֲשֶׁר צִוָּה ה' אֶת מֹשֶׁה ... וַיִּקַּח מֹשֶׁה מִמַּחֲצִת בְּנֵי יִשְׂרָאֵל אֶת הָאָחֻז אֶחָד מִן הַחֲמִשִּׁים מִן הָאָדָם וּמִן הַבְּהֵמָה וַיִּתֵּן אֹתָם לַלְוִיִּם שֹׁמְרֵי מִשְׁמֶרֶת מִשְׁכַּן ה' ... (ל״א:כ״ה-ל, ל״ו-מ״א,מ״ז)

> Hashem spoke to Moshe, and said, "Take count of the booty seized, of what was captured of the men and animals, you together with Elazar the Kohen, and the leaders of the community. Divide the plunder equally, giving half to the soldiers and the other half to the rest of the Jews. From the soldiers levy a tax to Hashem consisting of one out of five hundred of the humans, cattle, donkeys, and sheep. Take this from their half and give it to Elazar the Kohen as a terumah [gift] to Hashem. From the half that is going to the rest of the Jews, take one part out of fifty of the humans, cattle, donkeys, sheep and all animals, and give it to the Levites who are entrusted with the Mishkan of Hashem... The soldiers received 337,500 sheep and gave 675 sheep for a tax; 36,000 cattle and gave 72 for a tax; 30,500 donkeys and gave 61 for a tax; 16,000 humans and gave 32 for a tax. Moshe gave the tax...as a terumah to Hashem... From the half that went to the rest of the Jews, Moshe took one out of fifty and gave them to the Levites... (31:25-30, 36-41,47)

The Jews captured a lot of booty from Midian when they vanquished it. Hashem instructed them that the booty should be split equally between the soldiers who had fought and the rest of the Jews. Then they were told to give a specific sum as a tax. The soldiers had to give one out of five hundred for Elazar the Kohen, and the rest of the Jews had to give one out of fifty to the Levites.

One can discern two differences between how the Torah describes the tax of the soldiers and the tax of the rest of the Jews. First, regarding the tax of the Jews, after listing the various animals, it is written "and all animals." This phrase does not appear regarding the tax of the soldiers. Incidentally, this phrase needs further clarification. Since the Torah already lists many animals, what is being added? Second, after listing the animals that the soldiers received, the Torah calculates how much of each type went for tax. This calculation is not made when mentioning the animals received by the rest of the Jews. Frankly, this calculation seems superfluous, since using simple arithmetic anyone can figure it out. But if for some reason the Torah found it necessary to calculate, why did it do it only by the tax of the soldiers?

These two differences can be explained with yet a third discrepancy. The Torah twice classifies the tax that the soldiers gave to Elazar the Kohen as a *terumah*. [See *pesukim* 29 and 41.] The tax of the Jews is never referred to as *terumah*. The Mishnah (*Terumos* 2:4) states that any present which is classified as a *terumah* must be of the same species from which it is taken. For example, if a person has a bushel of apples, which requires *terumah* to be taken, he cannot fulfill his obligation by giving a pear. This answers all our questions. The Torah wants to emphasize that when the soldiers gave their animals as a *terumah* they were careful to give sheep for sheep, donkeys for donkeys, etc. Therefore the Torah calculates the exact amount of each animal. However, when the rest of the Jews gave their tax they were permitted to give one type of animal as a compensation for another type. They did not necessarily give the exact fraction of that specific animal mentioned in the Torah. Likewise, the Torah adds the phrase "from all animals" regarding the tax of the Jews, to point out that the primary part of that tax was that collectively from all animals there should be the equivalent of that sum.

(*Binyan Shlomo*)

וַיָּבֹאוּ בְנֵי גָד וּבְנֵי רְאוּבֵן וַיֹּאמְרוּ אֶל מֹשֶׁה ...
הָאָרֶץ אֲשֶׁר הִכָּה ה' לִפְנֵי עֲדַת יִשְׂרָאֵל אֶרֶץ מִקְנֶה הִוא וְלַעֲבָדֶיךָ
מִקְנֶה. וַיֹּאמְרוּ אִם מָצָאנוּ חֵן בְּעֵינֶיךָ יֻתַּן אֶת הָאָרֶץ הַזֹּאת לַעֲבָדֶיךָ
לַאֲחֻזָּה אַל תַּעֲבִרֵנוּ אֶת הַיַּרְדֵּן. (ל"ב:ב-ה)

> *The tribes of Gad and Reuven came and said to Moshe ...*
> *"The land, which Hashem struck down before the Jewish*
> *nation, is suitable for cattle and your servants have cattle."*
> *"... If we find favor in your eyes, this land should be*
> *given as permanent property to your servants;*
> *do not bring us over the Jordan River" (32:2-5).*

The request of the people of Gad and Reuven to settle east of the Jordan River is detailed in *pasuk* 2 until *pasuk* 5. One would expect these few *pesukim* to constitute one paragraph. Surprisingly, before *pasuk* 5 there is a space in the Torah which indicates the beginning of a new paragraph! Furthermore, *pasuk* 5 begins with the words "and they said," which is an even stronger indication of a new paragraph. This appears quite puzzling. Why did the Torah make an interruption in the middle of the speech of the people of Gad and Reuven?

There is a mitzvah of *bikkurim*, to give the first fruits of each year's crop of the indigenous fruits of Eretz Yisrael [the *shivas haminim*] to a Kohen. The Gemara (*Yerushalmi, Bikkurim* 1:8) states that the inhabitants of the east bank of the Jordan River are exempt from this mitzvah despite the fact that the area is part of Eretz Yisrael. The source for this exemption is a clause in the mitzvah which says that only land which was **given** to the Jews requires *bikkurim* to be appropriated; land that was **taken** is exempt. Since the people of Gad and Reuven asked for the land on the east bank it is considered "taken" land and not "given."

In light of this, the following scene can be projected. The people of Gad and Reuven wanted to participate in the mitzvah of *bikkurim*. They were aware that if they would request their land outright it would disqualify them. Therefore they found a method to circumvent this problem. They merely presented the facts to Moshe without following up with their request. They told Moshe that the east bank has a lot of grazing area, and that they have a lot of cattle, and they stopped there! They hoped that Moshe on his own would offer them that land. To their dismay, Moshe did not suggest that they should remain where they were. Reluctantly, they then proceeded and outright requested the east bank.

The Torah faithfully records the event. Since the people of Gad and Reuven paused between the presentation of the facts and the actual request, the Torah also "writes a pause" in between, by creating a new paragraph. *Pesukim* 3-4 mention their presentation; *pasuk* 5 is their request. Likewise, since their request followed a pause the Torah starts again with the introductory phrase "and they said." *(Taamah D'Kra)*

וַיָּבֹאוּ בְנֵי גָד וּבְנֵי רְאוּבֵן וַיֹּאמְרוּ אֶל מֹשֶׁה וְאֶל אֶלְעָזָר הַכֹּהֵן וְאֶל נְשִׂיאֵי הָעֵדָה לֵאמֹר. עֲטָרוֹת וְדִיבֹן וְיַעְזֵר וְנִמְרָה... **הָאָרֶץ אֲשֶׁר הִכָּה ה' לִפְנֵי עֲדַת יִשְׂרָאֵל** אֶרֶץ מִקְנֶה הִוא וְלַעֲבָדֶיךָ מִקְנֶה. (ל״ב:ב-ד)

The children of Gad and Reuven came and said to Moshe and to Elazar the Kohen, and to the leaders of the community, saying, "Atarot, Divon, Yazer, Nimrah, [etc.] which are part of the land **that Hashem smote before the Assembly of Israel,** *is a land which is suitable for grazing, and your servants have cattle." (32:2-4)*

The Alshich asks two questions on this *pasuk*. First, why did the people of Gad and Reuven list all those cities? They merely should have said that they want the east bank to reside in. Second, why did they add, "that Hashem smote before the Assembly of Israel"? There seems to be no purpose in mentioning that fact.

Those cities that were mentioned by the people of Gad and Reuven originally belonged to the nation of Moav. Later on, Sichon captured them. The Jews took them from Sichon. The

Mattos / 253

Gemara states that Hashem orchestrated events that the land should reach the Jews via Sichon. Since Hashem prohibited the Jews from attacking Moav directly, it had to be captured only after it was in the possession of Sichon (*Gittin* 38a).

It is mentioned in the Gemara that the land of Moav was rocky and not fit for planting (*Sotah* 34b). It could only be used for grazing cattle. It follows logically that Hashem performed all this in order that the tribes, which had many cattle, should have a place to graze.

With all this information the questions of the Alshich can be answered. The people of Gad and Reuven meant the following: "The cities that we want to occupy are known to have once belonged to Moav. Why did Hashem direct events that Sichon should capture them? Only in order that the Jews should eventually possess it. What type of land is it? A land that is fit only for grazing. It must therefore be that Hashem wants those tribes with lots of cattle to reside there. Which tribes have a lot of cattle? Our tribes!"

(*Binyan Ariel*)

וַיִּגְּשׁוּ אֵלָיו וַיֹּאמְרוּ גִּדְרֹת צֹאן נִבְנֶה לְמִקְנֵנוּ פֹּה וְעָרִים לְטַפֵּנוּ. (ל"ב:ט"ז)

> They approached him and said, "We will build here enclosures for our sheep and cities for our children." (32:16)

The tribes of Reuven and Gad requested to settle on the east side of the Jordan River, and not in the west with the rest of the Jewish nation. They began their request by saying, "We will build here enclosures for our sheep and cities for our children." When Moshe expressed his consent to their entreaty, his words were, "Build cities for your children and enclosures for your sheep..." (32:24).

One is immediately struck by the fact that Moshe reversed the order, and mentioned the children before the sheep. The Midrash (*Tanchuma* par. 7), quoted by Rashi, notes this discrepancy and explains as follows. Whatever is dearer to a person comes to his mind first. The people of Gad and Reuven mentioned their livestock first, thus revealing that they were more concerned about their material wealth than they were about their children! Moshe purposely repeated their statement in reverse order to point out to them that their priorities were distorted. First and foremost of importance is one's family; only afterwards comes one's possessions. The Midrash then makes a disparaging remark concerning the people of Gad and Reuven for having warped priorities.

The Midrashim and classic commentators repeat over and over that the Jews of that generation were of a very lofty stature. In light of that, it is difficult to comprehend how such noble people could express greater concern for their sheep than for their children. Even a simple Jew cares more for his family than for his monetary possessions.

The Gemara relates a story about the great *tzaddik* Nachum Ish Gam Zu. He was blind, missing hands and feet, and had boils covering his body. He lived in a ramshackle house that was ready to collapse at any moment. Fearing for his safety, his disciples wanted to evacuate him, and afterwards remove his possessions. He instructed them to do the opposite. First clear out all the furniture, and then carry him out. He explained that he was confident that as long as he is in the house Hashem will protect him and would not allow the house to cave in. Sure enough, only after the students carried him out did the house collapse (*Taanis* 21a).

This narrative can assist us in understanding the mindset of the people of Gad and Reuven. Throughout the many years of their journeying in the dangerous Wilderness, Hashem protected them miraculously. They were so accustomed to this Divine protection that they were not so concerned about the safety of their children. They were more anxious about their physical possessions, which might not merit Divine protection [similar to the case of Nachum Ish Gam Zu]. Therefore they first planned on building fortifications for their livestock. Moshe, however, knew that this era of Divine protection was going to cease as soon as the Jews would enter Eretz Yisrael. Consequently, he instructed them to be more concerned with their children than with their livestock, and to first provide protection for them and only afterwards for their sheep. Despite this rationalization of their behavior, the Midrash felt that it was not befitting for such refined people to utter words which seem to manifest more concern for animals than one's own children, and therefore belittled them for this.

(*Kehilas Yitzchak*, in the name of *R' Yaakov Yosef*)

וַיִּגְּשׁוּ אֵלָיו וַיֹּאמְרוּ גִּדְרֹת צֹאן נִבְנֶה לְמִקְנֵנוּ פֹּה וְעָרִים לְטַפֵּנוּ. וַאֲנַחְנוּ נֵחָלֵץ חֻשִׁים לִפְנֵי בְּנֵי יִשְׂרָאֵל עַד אֲשֶׁר אִם הֲבִיאֹנֻם אֶל מְקוֹמָם **וְיָשַׁב טַפֵּנוּ בְּעָרֵי הַמִּבְצָר** מִפְּנֵי יֹשְׁבֵי הָאָרֶץ ... וַיֹּאמֶר אֲלֵיהֶם מֹשֶׁה אִם תַּעֲשׂוּן אֶת הַדָּבָר הַזֶּה ... בְּנוּ לָכֶם **עָרִים לְטַפְּכֶם** וּגְדֵרֹת לְצֹנַאֲכֶם וְהַיֹּצֵא מִפִּיכֶם תַּעֲשׂוּ. וַיֹּאמֶר בְּנֵי גָד וּבְנֵי רְאוּבֵן אֶל מֹשֶׁה לֵאמֹר **עֲבָדֶיךָ יַעֲשׂוּ כַּאֲשֶׁר אֲדֹנִי מְצַוֶּה** (ל״ב:ט״ז,כ,כ״ד,כ״ה)

> *The tribes of Reuven and Gad approached Moshe and said, "We will build enclosures for our flocks here, and cities for our children. We will then arm ourselves rapidly, and will be ready to go before the Jews, until we have brought them to their place.* ***Our children will dwell in fortified cities*** *because of the inhabitants of the land." ... Moshe said to them, "If you will do this... Build for yourselves* ***cities for your children*** *and enclosures for your sheep, and what you have expressed verbally you must fulfill." The tribes of Gad and Reuven said to Moshe, "Your servants will do* ***as my master instructs.****" (32:16,20,24,25)*

The tribes of Gad and Reuven requested permission to build cities for their children and enclosures for their sheep, and were granted their request by Moshe. They in turn responded, "Your servants will do as my master instructs." This seems odd, since it does not seem that Moshe did anything other than repeat their words and tell them that they should keep their word. They should have said, "We'll keep our word."

A careful reading will point out a difference. They mentioned that their children would reside in **fortified** cities. They placed their trust in man-made defenses. Moshe instructed them to build plain cities and trust in Hashem. They agreed to that and proclaimed that they will do as Moshe instructed them.

(*Gan Raveh,* in the name of *Yavin Shemuah*)

MASEI

אֵלֶּה מַסְעֵי בְנֵי יִשְׂרָאֵל אֲשֶׁר יָצְאוּ מֵאֶרֶץ מִצְרַיִם לְצִבְאֹתָם בְּיַד מֹשֶׁה וְאַהֲרֹן. (ל״ג:א)

These are the journeys of the children of Israel who went forth from the land of Egypt according to their legions, **under the leadership of Moshe and Aharon.** *(33:1)*

The Torah tells us that, "These are the travels of the Jewish people who went out of Egypt, led by Moshe and Aharon. Anyone who studies the Torah is well aware that Moshe and Aharon were the ones who led the Jews throughout their various journeys. Therefore it is superfluous for the Torah to mention this here.

The Gemara relates that when Aharon died the protective *ananei hakavod* [Clouds of Glory] departed, and the Canaanites attacked the Jews. The Jews were so taken aback and depressed by this that they began retracing their steps to Egypt. It was only after they had gone back eight steps that the tribe of Levi was able to forcefully halt the Jews and coerce them into continuing forward toward Eretz Yisrael (*Yerushalmi, Yoma* 1:1).

One sees from this Gemara that with these journeys the Jew made an additional journey than is recorded here. However, this was not authorized, and was surely not led by Moshe and Aharon. This explains our *pasuk*. The Torah is emphasizing that it will now list only those journeys that were led by Moshe and Aharon, and not the others.

(Ya'alas Chein)

וַיַּעַל אַהֲרֹן הַכֹּהֵן אֶל הֹר הָהָר עַל פִּי ה' וַיָּמָת שָׁם בִּשְׁנַת הָאַרְבָּעִים לְצֵאת בְּנֵי יִשְׂרָאֵל מֵאֶרֶץ מִצְרַיִם בַּחֹדֶשׁ הַחֲמִישִׁי בְּאֶחָד לַחֹדֶשׁ. (ל"ג:ל"ח)

Aharon the Kohen ascended Hor Mountain at Hashem's command, and he died there, in the fortieth year of the exodus of the Jews from Egypt, on the first day of the fifth month. (33:38)

The Torah lists all the stops that the Jews made in their travels through the desert. When it mentions the stay at the Hor Mountain, the Torah diverges from its mere listing and mentions the death of Aharon with accompanying details. It strikes one as odd that the Torah should interrupt its uniformly styled listing, with the mention and discussion of Aharon's death. Moreover, one of the facts mentioned here is that the Canaanites heard about Aharon's demise. This episode in its entirety is already discussed earlier, in *parashas Chukas* (21:1-3). Why was it necessary to repeat it here? Admittedly, the Gemara states that there is a message in the juxtaposing of these two events — that it was the death of Aharon and the subsequent departure of the *ananei hakavod* [Clouds of Glory] which prompted the Canaanites to attack the Jews. But why does the Torah digress from its narrative to teach us this here? This could have been taught in a different place.

The Gemara relates that after the Canaanites attacked the Jews, they became disheartened and began retracing their steps to Egypt. They succeeded in going back eight steps before the Levites fought with their fellow Jews and coerced them into continuing their journey to Eretz Yisrael (*Yerushalmi Yoma*, 1:1).

With this information we can resolve our questions. The Torah is listing here all the journeys of the Jews. Included in this list should be the eight journeys that they made going in the opposite direction. Out of deference to the Jews, the Torah did not want to mention them explicitly. Instead, it succinctly referred to them, by mentioning the demise of Aharon and the subsequent war with the Canaanites, which were the catalyst of those eight journeys.

(Taamah D'Kra)

... זֹאת הָאָרֶץ אֲשֶׁר תִּפֹּל לָכֶם בְּנַחֲלָה אֶרֶץ כְּנַעַן לִגְבֻלֹתֶיהָ. (ל״ד:ב)

> ...this is the land which will fall to you as hereditary property, the land of Canaan according to its borders. (34:2)

Before Moshe died, Hashem instructed him to outline to the Jews the precise boundaries of Eretz Yisrael that they will capture. The commentaries offer reasons as to the purpose of this.

In *parashas Mattos*, it is recorded that the tribes of Gad and Reuven expressed to Moshe their desire to remain and settle east of the Jordan River. Moshe consented, but stipulated that all able-bodied men of them must first assist the rest of the Jews in capturing Eretz Yisrael. Only after the land would be taken and divided would the men of Gad and Reuven be allowed to return home.

If so, there is a simple explanation for the detailing of the borders. The people of Gad and Reuven had to know which land had to be captured and divided in order to know when they could return home! They would have to remain and fight with the rest of the Jews, until they conquered all the land within the prescribed borders.

(Meshech Chochmah)

וְאֵלֶּה שְׁמוֹת הָאֲנָשִׁים לְמַטֵּה יְהוּדָה כָּלֵב בֶּן יְפֻנֶּה. וּלְמַטֵּה בְּנֵי שִׁמְעוֹן שְׁמוּאֵל בֶּן עַמִּיהוּד. לְמַטֵּה בִנְיָמִן אֱלִידָד בֶּן כִּסְלוֹן. וּלְמַטֵּה בְנֵי דָן נָשִׂיא בֻּקִּי בֶן יָגְלִי. (ל״ד:י״ט)

*These are the names of the men: for the tribe of Yehudah, Kaleiv son of Yefuneh. For the tribe of **the children of** Shimon, Shmuel, son of Ammihud. For the tribe of Binyamin, Elidad, son of Kislon. For the tribe of **the children of** Dan, the leader was Buki, son of Yagli. (34:19)*

Hashem appointed the *Nesiim* of each tribe to be the executors of the distribution of each tribe's land among its members. Their acts would be final and binding. Hashem then listed the names of all the tribes and their *Nesiim*. When mentioning almost every tribe Hashem says, "For the tribe of the children of so-and-so [Reuven, Shimon, etc.]…" There are two exceptions to this — Yehudah and Binyamin. Regarding them Hashem merely says, "For the tribe of so-and-so," and omits the words "the children of." Why is this so?

The Gemara states that the Beis HaMikdash was constructed partly on land of the tribe of Yehudah and partly on land of the tribe of Binyamin (*Yoma* 12a). All of the Jews used the services of the Beis HaMikdash. If so, the *Nesiim* of the tribes of Yehudah and Binyamin were not merely parochial *Nesiim*, but in a sense *Nesiim* of all the Jews. It is possible that this is the reason for the difference in wording used regarding the *Nesiim* of Binyamin and Yehudah. The words "the children of" imply that they looked after the needs of the people of their own tribes. This was not the case regarding the *Nesiim* of Yehudah and Binyamin, and therefore that phrase was omitted. Those *Nesiim* are referred to as "of the tribe of so-and-so," which implies that in their official capacity they served as the leaders of those specific tribes, but not that they attended solely to the needs of their own tribes.

(*Taamah D'Kra*)

Another possible explanation can be offered. The Gemara states that the primary function of the *Nesiim* was to apportion land in Eretz Yisrael even for young children who could not contest the decisions of the *Nesiim* (*Kiddushin* 42a). Each portion of land that was assigned to a specific child was his regardless of the quality of the land. There is another Gemara which explains that the factor which determined the quality of each parcel of land was its proximity to the Beis HaMikdash. The closer it was, the greater its value (*Bava Basra* 122a).

Based upon this, we can suggest as follows. By all *Nesiim* the phrase "of the children" is used to emphasize that despite the fact that there were many children in the tribe, the *Nasi* had the right to execute the apportioning of the land, although it would inevitably be detrimental to some. In contradistinction, the children of the tribes of Yehudah and Binyamin all lived relatively close to the Beis HaMikdash and would all be receiving choice land, since the Beis HaMikdash was in their territory. Therefore, it was not necessary to mention "the children" of those tribes.

(*R' Chaim Berlin* and *R' Y.M. Epstein*,
quoted by *Haamek Davar*)

אֵת שְׁלֹשׁ הֶעָרִים תִּתְּנוּ מֵעֵבֶר לַיַּרְדֵּן וְאֵת שְׁלֹשׁ הֶעָרִים תִּתְּנוּ בְּאֶרֶץ כְּנָעַן עָרֵי מִקְלָט תִּהְיֶינָה. (ל״ה:י״ד)

Three cities shall you designate on the other side of the Jordan River, and three cities shall you designate in Eretz Yisrael; they shall be cities of refuge. (35:14)

Hashem commanded the Jews to build six cities of refuge for people who killed unintentionally, in order to be protected from the wrath of the next of kin of those they had killed. Three cities were to be built east of the Jordan River for those residing there, and three on the west for those dwelling in Eretz Yisrael proper. The Gemara, quoted by Rashi, expresses amazement that the area to the east which was home to only two and a half tribes should have as many cities of refuge as

Eretz Yisrael which contained nine and a half tribes! It then explains this by proving from Tanach that murderers abounded in the east bank; therefore it was necessary to have many cities of refuge there (*Makkos* 9b).

Many [see Ramban and *Sifsei Chachamim*] ask an obvious question on the Gemara that Rashi quotes. Only a person who killed unintentionally was permitted to reside in a city of refuge. A willful murderer was tried and put to death. Why should the existence of many murderers necessitate having more cities of refuge, which were designated for unintentional killers?

The Mishnah (*Makkos* 9b) states that anyone who killed and was caught would automatically be sent to the cities of refuge. The *beis din* would then try that person and determine if the murder was committed deliberately or unwittingly. A deliberate murderer would be executed and an unintentional killer would be returned to the city of refuge. This Mishnah can illuminate the previously mentioned Gemara. Since all killers, even premeditated ones, would spend some time in the cities of refuge, it was necessary to have many cities of refuge in the east bank that was replete with murderers.

Another explanation can be offered based on an insight in human nature. If a person is careful and concerned not to do something, then it is unusual for him to do it even unintentionally. On the other hand, if a person is nonchalant about doing a certain act, the chances are a lot greater that he will slip and do it accidentally. In Eretz Yisrael where murder was abhorred, it was rare for even an unintentional killing to occur. The east bank was a different story. Since there were many murders committed there, people there had become desensitized to it and were more prone to committing accidental killings. Therefore, both sides of the Jordan needed the same amount of cities despite the fact that many more people lived in Eretz Yisrael.

(*Beis Av*)

וְהִצִּילוּ הָעֵדָה אֶת הָרֹצֵחַ מִיַּד גֹּאֵל הַדָּם וְהֵשִׁיבוּ אֹתוֹ הָעֵדָה אֶל
עִיר מִקְלָטוֹ אֲשֶׁר נָס שָׁמָּה וְיָשַׁב בָּהּ עַד מוֹת הַכֹּהֵן הַגָּדֹל
אֲשֶׁר מָשַׁח אֹתוֹ בְּשֶׁמֶן הַקֹּדֶשׁ. (ל״ה:כ״ה)

> *The Assembly shall rescue the killer from the hand*
> *of the avenger of the blood, and return him to his city of*
> *refuge where he had fled; he shall dwell in it until*
> *the death of the Kohen Gadol whom one had*
> *anointed with the sacred oil. (35:25)*

The Torah instructs us that if a person kills unintentionally then he must reside in a "city of refuge" until the Kohen Gadol dies. This impacted negatively on the Kohen Gadol since all these people would pray that the Kohen Gadol should die, in order to secure their release! What did the Kohen Gadol do wrong that he deserved this? The Gemara answers that he should have prayed that no such mishaps occur during his tenure (*Makkos* 11a).

The Gemara (ibid. 11b) proves from a *pasuk* that even if the Kohen Gadol was appointed after the killing but before the indictment, nevertheless the killer's release is dependent upon the death of that Kohen. What did this Kohen Gadol do wrong now? The Gemara answers, "He should have prayed to Hashem that the verdict should be that the killer is innocent!" This answer seems incomprehensible. If the *beis din* concluded that the man is guilty, it surely is so. Does then the Torah expect the Kohen Gadol to pray to Hashem that the verdict should be wrong and that *beis din* should mistakenly release a guilty person?!

There is a rule mentioned in Gemara that if a *beis din* declares unanimously that a person is guilty of a crime which deserves capital punishment, then that person is not put to death (*Sanhedrin* 17a). There must be at least one dissenting vote in *beis din* in order for a person to receive capital punishment. The Rambam (*Sanhedrin* 11:4) writes that this rule applies equally to a case involving a question of accidental murder, where the sentencing to *galus* is at stake.

Herein lies the solution to our problem. The Kohen Gadol should have prayed that all the judges should make the correct decision, which is that the man is guilty! If all the judges had said that the person is guilty then he would not have gone into *galus*! It is therefore partly the fault of the Kohen Gadol that the killer is in *galus*, and consequently the Kohen Gadol suffers for that.

(*Teshuvah MeAhavah*, 1:194, quoted by *Gan Ravah*)

Devarim

אֵלֶּה הַדְּבָרִים אֲשֶׁר דִּבֶּר מֹשֶׁה אֶל כָּל יִשְׂרָאֵל בְּעֵבֶר הַיַּרְדֵּן בַּמִּדְבָּר בָּעֲרָבָה מוֹל סוּף בֵּין פָּארָן וּבֵין תֹּפֶל וְלָבָן וַחֲצֵרֹת וְדִי זָהָב. (א:א)

These are the words that Moshe spoke to all Israel, on the other side of the Jordan, concerning the Wilderness, concerning the Aravah, opposite the Sea of Reeds, between Paran and Tophel, and Lavan, and Chazeros, and Di-zahav (1:1).

THE MIDRASH (*SIFRI*) INTERPRETS THE NAMES MENTIONED IN THIS *pasuk* as not being places where Moshe spoke to the Jews, but rather names that allude to various sins which the Jews did. Chazeros is the place where Korach challenged the legitimacy of Aharon's priesthood. Di-zahav is not even a name of a place! It means literally "enough gold," and refers to the sin of the "golden heifer," which was initiated by the abundance of gold which the Jews possessed.

There is a difficulty with this interpretation. Chronologically, the episode of the golden heifer preceded the episode of Korach. Yet in the *pasuk*, Chazeros, which corresponds to the story of Korach, precedes Di-zahav, which corresponds to the golden heifer incident.

When Hashem recited the first of the Ten Commandments to the Jews, He said, "I am your G-d" in singular form, seeming as though He was only addressing Moshe. The Midrash (*Shemos Rabbah* 43:5) states that Moshe took advantage of this ambiguity in his defense of the Jews. When the Jews worshiped the golden heifer and aroused Hashem's anger, Moshe pleaded on their behalf. His defense was that the Jews were never told not to worship idols — only he was instructed not to.

The Midrash (*Tanchuma*, *Korach* Chap.4) records that Korach's complaint against Moshe was that every Jew was equal to Moshe since they all equally heard on Mt. Sinai the commandment "I am your G-d."

In light of these two Midrashim the *pasuk* can be explained. Initially the sin of the golden heifer was forgiven due to Moshe's defense. But once the Jews themselves, led by Korach, disclaimed Moshe's statement, they became responsible for the sin. The Torah alludes to the sin of the golden heifer after the sin of Korach, since the blame for that sin only began after the incident of Korach. (*Chanukas HaTorah*)

ה' אֱלֹקֵי אֲבוֹתֵכֶם יֹסֵף עֲלֵיכֶם כָּכֶם אֶלֶף פְּעָמִים וִיבָרֵךְ אֶתְכֶם כַּאֲשֶׁר דִּבֶּר לָכֶם. (א:י"א)

May Hashem, the G-d of your forefathers, add to you a thousand times yourselves, and bless you as He has spoken of you. (1:11)

The Midrash (*Sifri*), quoted by Rashi, explains the *pasuk* as follows. Moshe blessed the Jews that they should increase one thousandfold. The Jews complained that Hashem had already promised them to increase an infinite amount. Moshe then explained that he was only adding his own personal blessing; Hashem shall bless them as He promised. The question is obvious: If Hashem had blessed the Jews with a more comprehensive blessing, of what need was there for a lesser blessing from Moshe?

The Midrash (*Bamidbar Rabbah* 21:1) states that the Jews are not capable of receiving Hashem's blessings if there is disunity among them. At this point in time there was considerable squabble between them (see *pasuk* 12). Therefore, since they would not be receiving Hashem's blessings, Moshe offered his own, albeit limited, blessing. Moshe then added that they should be privileged to have their unity restored and thus merit Hashem's much larger blessing.

This explanation could also shed light on the juxtaposition of this *pasuk* to the next. In the next *pasuk* Moshe complains, "How can I alone carry your contentiousness, your burdens, and your quarrels"? Moshe was urging the Jews to desist from their quarrels in order to be able to receive Hashem's blessings.

(*Binyan Ariel*)

ה' אֱלֹקֵי אֲבוֹתֵכֶם יֹסֵף עֲלֵיכֶם כָּכֶם אֶלֶף פְּעָמִים ... (א:י״א)

May Hashem, the G-d of your forefathers, add to you a thousand times yourselves...(1:11)

Why did Moshe pick the number "a thousand times" when blessing the Jews?

After the incident of the golden heifer, Hashem offered a proposition to Moshe. He would destroy the Jews and make him into a great nation. Likewise, after the episode of the *meraglim,* Hashem repeated the offer. The Gemara states that Hashem fulfills all that he promises, even if it was said conditionally (*Berachos* 7a). Therefore these offers would be fulfilled even though the Jews were not decimated.

The Midrash (*Tosefta, Sotah* 4:1) writes that Hashem's acts of kindness are five hundred times those of his strict justice. If so, Hashem blessed Moshe twice that he would be five hundred times as large as the Jewish nation that He is considering to destroy. This blessing, of being a thousand times as great as the Jews, Moshe passed on to the Jews themselves!

The Midrash (*Sifri*) quoted by Rashi writes that Moshe told the Jews that he is giving them now his own blessing. In light of the above, this can be explained to mean that Moshe gave them the blessing destined for himself.

(*Panim Yafos*)

You shall not provoke them... (2:5)   אַל תִּתְגָּרוּ בָם ... (ב:ה)

There is a noticeable difference between the command given to Moshe concerning the nation of Moav to that of Eisav. When warning the Jews not to provoke a war against the descendants of Eisav the plural term is used [**tisgaru**], as though Hashem would be addressing all the Jews. Yet when the warning against starting a war against Moav is said, the word used is singular [**tisgar**], implying that only Moshe is being instructed. What is the reason for this change?

The Gemara states a tradition that the descendants of Eisav will only be conquered by the descendants of Yosef (*Bava Basra* 123b). Moshe was aware of this, and thus would not wage war against Eisav, since he was not a descendant of Yosef. Therefore he was not personally cautioned against it. Only the Jewish nation as a whole, which includes descendants of Yosef, was warned. But the admonition against provoking war against Moav was directed to Moshe, since he too might want to do it.

(*Meshech Chochmah*)

אֹכֶל בַּכֶּסֶף תַּשְׁבִּרֵנִי וְאָכַלְתִּי וּמַיִם בַּכֶּסֶף תִּתֶּן לִי וְשָׁתִיתִי ... (ב:כ"ח)

*You will **sell** food to me for money and I shall eat; and you will **give** me water for money, and I shall drink... (2:28)*

One notices a discrepancy in the *pasuk*. Concerning the food it says that it should be sold, yet concerning the water it says that it will be given. Furthermore, concerning the water, it says that it will be given for money, which is essentially buying. If so, why is the verb "giving" used?

The Rambam (*Gezeilah* 6:13) teaches that a river whose waters flow into springs is public property. If so, the Jews did not actually have to purchase the water from the children of Sichon. They promised to pay them anyway; but it is more appropriately referred to by the Torah as a "giving" of money rather than a sale.

(*R' Yitzchak Zev Soloveitchik zt"l*, quoted by *Shai LeTorah*)

יָאִיר בֶּן מְנַשֶּׁה **לָקַח** אֶת כָּל חֶבֶל אַרְגֹּב ... וּלְמָכִיר **נָתַתִּי** אֶת הַגִּלְעָד. (ג:י"ד,ט"ו)

*Yair son of Menashe **took** the entire region of Argov...*
*To Machir **I gave** the Gilead (3:14,15)*

Why does the *pasuk* state that Yair **took** his land, and that Moshe **gave** the land to Machir?

Moshe made a stipulation with the tribe of Menashe that they would only receive land in Eretz Yisrael if they would cross the Jordan with the rest of the Jews and capture Eretz Yisrael (see *Bamidbar* 32:29). The Gemara records that Yair was killed in the beginning of the war for Eretz Yisrael, and did not live to conquer it (*Bava Basra* 121b). Therefore, he could not receive it from Moshe. However he did automatically acquire possession of a piece of land by dying in the battle for it (see *Sanhedrin* 72a). This is more appropriately referred to as Yair taking the land on his own, and not receiving it from Moshe as did the rest of the Jews.

(*Tzafnas Pane'ach*)

VA'ESCHANAN

וָאֶתְחַנַּן אֶל ה׳ **בָּעֵת הַהִוא** לֵאמֹר. (ג:כ״ג)

I implored Hashem **at that time** saying. (3:23)

WHY DID MOSHE MENTION THAT HE PLEADED TO HASHEM AT **that time**? What was special about that time that he thought he might then have been permitted to bring the Jews into Eretz Yisrael?

Originally, Moshe and Aharon together were informed that they would not be privileged to lead the Jews into Eretz Yisrael. Moshe thought it was possible that only together they were not allowed to enter Eretz Yisrael, but now that Aharon was no longer living perhaps he alone would be permitted. Furthermore, Moshe was told that he would not bring in "this congregation" to Eretz Yisrael, i.e. the generation that left Egypt. But perhaps now after forty years, that the old generation was dead, he would be allowed to lead the new generation into Eretz Yisrael. (*Tiferes Yehonasan*)

וָאֶתְחַנַּן אֶל ה׳ **בָּעֵת הַהִוא** לֵאמֹר. (ג:כ״ג)

I implored Hashem at that time saying. (3:23)

The Midrash (*Devarim Rabbah* 11:10) states that Moshe prayed five hundred and fifteen prayers to be allowed to enter

Eretz Yisrael, as indicated by the *gematria* of *va'eschanan*, which is 515. There is an additional way to calculate that this is the number of times Moshe prayed.

The Midrash (*Sifri*), quoted by Rashi, states that Moshe only thought of beseeching Hashem to let him enter Eretz Yisrael after the conquest of Sichon. Although Hashem had sworn that Moshe would not enter Eretz Yisrael, Moshe then thought that it was possible that Hashem had nullified his vow. When was Sichon conquered? From a Torah perspective the real conquest occurred when Hashem "handed over" the protective angel of Sichon to Moshe (see *Rashi* 2:31). From that moment Sichon was doomed. Moshe was informed of Sichon's fate on the fifteenth of Av, the day the people stopped dying in the Wilderness (see *Devarim*, 2:31; *Bava Basra* 121a). If so, Moshe began beseeching on the fifteenth of Av.

Let us calculate how many times Moshe would have prayed from the fifteenth of Av until the day he died, the seventh of Adar. In that period of time there are two hundred days. Since Moshe's prayers were the same as ours (see *Berachos* 32a; *Devarim Rabbah* ibid.), he would have prayed three times a day, for a total of six hundred prayers. However, since a person is prohibited from asking private requests from Hashem on Shabbos, one deducts the twenty-eight *Shabbosim* that occur in that period of time. This leaves us with 172 days, times three prayers a day, for a total of 516 prayers. However, since Hashem only spoke to Moshe during the daytime (see *Rashi*, *Shemos* 12:2), He must have told him about the downfall of Sichon during the day. If so, on the fifteenth of Av Moshe only prayed two prayers – *Shacharis* and *Minchah* – on his own behalf. Thus we have a total of 515 prayers!

(*Pnei Yehoshua, Berachos* 32a)

... וַיֹּאמֶר ה' אֵלַי רַב לָךְ אַל תּוֹסֶף דַּבֵּר אֵלַי עוֹד בַּדָּבָר הַזֶּה. (ג:כ"ו)

> ...Hashem said to me, "It is too much for you! Do not continue to speak to Me further about this matter." (3:26)

The Gemara states that the angels "gave presents to Moshe" when he went up on Mt. Sinai (*Shabbos* 89a). Earlier sources explain that this refers to his being informed that if he would twice mention the word "please" (נָא) in his prayer then it would be answered.

When Moshe prayed for his sister Miriam (*Bamidbar* 12:13) he said "please" twice and his prayer was answered. Here too Moshe started praying "to please be allowed to go over the Jordan River." Moshe intended to continue this request with the inclusion of another "please." But Hashem cut him off and said "do not speak to me further," i.e. do not say "please" again.

(Chanukas HaTorah)

... וַיֹּאמֶר ה' אֵלַי רַב לָךְ אַל תּוֹסֶף דַּבֵּר אֵלַי עוֹד בַּדָּבָר הַזֶּה. (ג:כ"ו)

> ...Hashem said to me, "It is too much for you! Do not continue to speak to Me further about this matter." (3:26)

The Midrash (*Tanchuma* par. 4) informs us that Moshe pleaded to Hashem that he receive the same treatment that the Torah accords a Jewish slave. If a slave tells his master after his term is up that he loves him and wishes to stay with him, then he remains with his master as a slave. So too, said Moshe, he loves Hashem and wants to remain longer in this world as a slave to Hashem. The Midrash then says that Hashem merely replied as is written in the *pasuk*, "Do not continue to speak to Me further etc." It seems that Moshe had a justified claim; how did Hashem's reply counter it?

The Gemara states that a slave only remains with his master if he twice proclaims his intent to remain (*Kiddushin* 22a). Based upon this, Hashem's retort is understood. Hashem told Moshe not to repeat his request of remaining a slave, thus not qualifying to remain alive as a "slave"!

(*Chanukas HaTorah*)

... וַיֹּאמֶר ה' אֵלַי רַב לָךְ אַל תּוֹסֶף דַּבֵּר אֵלַי עוֹד בַּדָּבָר הַזֶּה. (ג:כ"ו)

> ...Hashem said to me, "It is too much for you! Do not continue to speak to Me further about this matter." (3:26)

Rambam (*Yesodei HaTorah* 10:4) writes that if a prophet portends a calamity and it does not occur, it does not refute the validity of the prophet, since Hashem is merciful and possibly rescinded His decree. But if there was a prophecy forecasting something good, and it did not occur, then it proves that the prophet was a fraud, since Hashem will never retract a beneficial prophecy.

Therefore, although Moshe was informed of the decree against his entering Eretz Yisrael, he nevertheless pleaded his own cause, since it was possible that Hashem would relent. Hashem responded to him and said, "Do not continue to speak to Me further about this matter." It seems that Hashem did not explain to him why this decree was unique and would always stand.

It can be suggested that two *pesukim* later Hashem did allude to the explanation. Hashem instructed Moshe to encourage Yehoshua because he was the one destined to lead the Jews into Eretz Yisrael. Thus although the decree was detrimental to Moshe it was beneficial for Yehoshua, and therefore Hashem would not recant!

(*R' Yitzchak Zev Soloveitchik zt"l*)

כִּי אָנֹכִי מֵת בָּאָרֶץ הַזֹּאת אֵינֶנִּי עֹבֵר אֶת הַיַּרְדֵּן וְאַתֶּם עֹבְרִים וִירִשְׁתֶּם אֶת הָאָרֶץ הַטּוֹבָה הַזֹּאת. הִשָּׁמְרוּ לָכֶם פֶּן תִּשְׁכְּחוּ אֶת בְּרִית ה' אֱלֹקֵיכֶם אֲשֶׁר כָּרַת עִמָּכֶם וַעֲשִׂיתֶם לָכֶם פֶּסֶל תְּמוּנַת כֹּל אֲשֶׁר צִוְּךָ ה' אֱלֹקֶיךָ. (ד:כ"ב,כ"ג)

> For I will die in this land; I am not crossing the Jordan – but you are crossing and you shall possess this good Land. Beware for yourselves lest you forget the covenant of Hashem, your G-d, that He has sealed with you, and you make yourselves a carved image, a likeness of anything, as Hashem, your G-d, has commanded you. (4:22,23)

The *pesukim* imply that Moshe was only warning them against idolatry because he was not entering Eretz Yisrael with them. Why is one dependent upon the other?

The Gemara relates that in the past there had been a *Yetzer Hara*, Evil Inclination, to worship idols. When this urge became too overwhelming, Ezra prayed to Hashem and it was removed. The Gemara then states that Moshe did not offer that prayer since he knew that he did not have the merit of being in Eretz Yisrael and thus his prayer for this would not be effective (*Arachin* 32b).

It follows that if Moshe had entered Eretz Yisrael he would not have had to warn the Jews against idolatry, since he would have abolished it with his prayers!

The Midrash (*Devarim Rabbah, Devarim* 11:8) writes that Moshe requested one thing from Hashem before he died: to open the heavens before the Jews, that they see that there is only one G-d. In light of the above, this request is better understood. Now that he definitely would not enter Eretz Yisrael, Moshe was concerned that the Jews might go astray after idol worship, and therefore made this request. Had he entered with them this request would not have been necessary.

(Maaseh Roke'ach)

EIKEV

וְהֵסִיר ה׳ מִמְּךָ כָּל חֹלִי וְכָל מַדְוֵי מִצְרַיִם הָרָעִים אֲשֶׁר יָדַעְתָּ
לֹא יְשִׂימָם בָּךְ וּנְתָנָם בְּכָל שֹׂנְאֶיךָ. (ז:ט״ו)

*Hashem will remove from you every illness; and all the bad maladies of Egypt that you knew – He will not **put** them upon you, but will **give** them upon all your foes. (7:15)*

THE *PASUK* STATES THAT HASHEM WON'T **PUT** THE DISEASE UPON the Jews, but will **give** them to the enemies of the Jews. Why does the Torah change verbs, from "put" to "give"?

The Gemara distinguishes between the words "give" and "put" written in the Torah. The word "put" connotes even a minute amount; the word "give" refers to a substantial sum (*Menachos* 59b).

The *pasuk* is telling us that not a drop of pain shall befall the Jews, while a substantial amount of sickness shall befall the enemies of the Jews! (*Maharil Diskin*)

שִׂמְלָתְךָ לֹא בָלְתָה מֵעָלֶיךָ וְרַגְלְךָ לֹא בָצֵקָה זֶה אַרְבָּעִים שָׁנָה. (ח:ד)

Your garment did not wear out upon you and your feet did not swell, these forty years. (8:4)

A similar *pasuk* is found in *Ki Savo* (29:4), but with two noticeable differences. Here it is written "garment," and there it is written "garments"; here it mentions the feet of the Jews, there it mentions the shoe ["your shoe did not rot"]. How can these differences be explained?

The Gemara states that one who is *menudah*, excommunicated, is prohibited to wear shoes (*Moed Kattan* 15b). The Jews were legally considered excommunicated the years they spent in the Wilderness (see ibid. *Tosefos*). The *pasuk* in this *parashah* does not mention their shoes, but rather their feet, since they did not wear shoes in the Wilderness.

It can be suggested that the *pasuk* in *Ki Savo* is discussing the tribe of Levi. The tribe of Levi was unique in that, unlike the rest of the Jewish nation, it was not excommunicated (see *Chagigah* 6b, and ibid. *Rashi*), and thus were permitted to wear shoes. Therefore shoes are mentioned there.

The Ra'avad (commentary on *Sifra, Tzav*) posits that the Levites wore communal garments while they performed the services of the Mishkan. The word "garments" is written regarding the Levites to reflect the two types of garments worn by the Levites — personal ones and communal ones. However the word "shoe" written by the Levites is in the singular. The Gemara teaches that it is forbidden to wear shoes in the area of the Mishkan (*Berachos* 62b). Thus the Levites did not wear shoes when they performed the services. Therefore, unlike the garments, the Levites owned only one type of shoes — personal ones. (*Tzafnas Pane'ach*)

הַמּוֹלִיכְךָ בַּמִּדְבָּר הַגָּדֹל וְהַנּוֹרָא נָחָשׁ שָׂרָף וְעַקְרָב וְצִמָּאוֹן אֲשֶׁר אֵין מָיִם הַמּוֹצִיא לְךָ מַיִם מִצּוּר הַחַלָּמִישׁ. (ח:ט"ו)

Who leads you through the great and awesome Wilderness – of snake, fiery serpent, and scorpion, and thirst where there was no water – Who brings forth water for you from the rock of flint (8:15)

The *pasuk* begins by relating that the Wilderness contained two dangers — poisonous creatures, and no water. Yet it only concludes with a solution for the problem of thirst — that Hashem brought water from a rock. Why is no mention made of how the Jews were saved from the other threats?

The Gemara informs us that there are poisonous snakes whose effectiveness upon biting a person are dependent upon the actions of the bitten person. If the person drinks water before the snake that bit him does, then the snake will die. If, however, the snake drinks water first, the person will die (*Yerushalmi, Berachos* 5:1).

In light of this, the *pasuk* can be interpreted as follows. Hashem saved the Jews from the poisonous snakes by not placing any water in the Wilderness. Thus if a Jew was bitten by a snake the snake would not be able to reach the water before the Jew. Then Hashem miraculously created water that was only available for the Jews to drink. If a Jew was bitten, he would drink the water and live.

(*Gan Raveh*, in the name of *Minchah Belulah*)

וָאֵפֶן וָאֵרֵד מִן הָהָר וְהָהָר בֹּעֵר בָּאֵשׁ וּשְׁנֵי **לוּחֹת הַבְּרִית** עַל שְׁתֵּי יָדָי. וָאֵרֶא וְהִנֵּה חֲטָאתֶם לַה׳ אֱלֹקֵיכֶם עֲשִׂיתֶם לָכֶם עֵגֶל מַסֵּכָה סַרְתֶּם מַהֵר מִן הַדֶּרֶךְ אֲשֶׁר צִוָּה ה׳ אֶתְכֶם. וָאֶתְפֹּשׂ בִּשְׁנֵי **הַלֻּחֹת** וָאַשְׁלִכֵם מֵעַל שְׁתֵּי יָדָי וָאֲשַׁבְּרֵם לְעֵינֵיכֶם. (ט׳:ט״ו-י״ז)

> *So I turned and descended from the mountain as the mountain was burning in fire, and the two **Tablets of the Covenant** were in my two hands. Then I saw and behold! you had sinned to Hashem, your G-d; you made yourselves a molten calf; you strayed quickly from the way that Hashem commanded you. I grasped the two **Tablets** and threw them from my two hands, and I smashed them before your eyes. (9:15-17)*

One notes a discrepancy between the two *pesukim*. The first time it is written "the two Tablets of the Covenant," but the

Eikev / 279

second time it merely says the "two Tablets." What explanation can be given?

The Midrash (*Tanchuma, Ki Sisa* Chap. 26) informs us that when Moshe saw the golden heifer which the Jews made, the writing on the Tablets disappeared, and the Tablets became heavy, and he threw them down.

This Midrash elucidates the choice of words of the *pesukim*. The first *pasuk* describes Moshe before seeing the golden heifer, thus calling the Ten Commandments "Tablets of the Covenant." But the last *pasuk* describes the Tablets immediately after Moshe's seeing the golden heifer, and the disappearance of the letters, thus only warranting being called merely Tablets.

(*Gan Raveh*, in the name of *Bikkurei Aviv*)

וְעָשִׂיתָ לְךָ אֲרוֹן עֵץ... (י:א)

*...and **you shall make** a wooden Ark for yourself. (10:1)*

Here it is written that Moshe was instructed to personally make the Ark (וְעָשִׂיתָ). Earlier, in *Terumah* (25:10), it is written that "they" (וְעָשׂוּ), i.e. the Jewish people, should make the Ark. The Gemara notes this discrepancy, and explains that a lesson is being taught by this. When the Jews were observant of the laws of the Torah, then it was considered as if they were the ones who constructed the Mishkan. But if they were not, then it was considered as though Moshe alone built it (*Yoma* 3b).

Ramban (beginning of *Vayakhel*) is of the opinion that Moshe was instructed to build the Mishkan before the sin of the golden heifer, but he only relayed the message to the Jews afterwards. This view enhances the above-mentioned Gemara. The incident in *Terumah* occurred before the sin of the golden heifer, when the Jews were still fully observant of the Torah; thus the plural *v'asu* is used. The command in this *parashah* was said after the sin; therefore the singular *v'asisa* is used. (*Techeiles Mordechai*)

וְהָיָה אִם שָׁמֹעַ תִּשְׁמְעוּ אֶל מִצְוֹתַי אֲשֶׁר אָנֹכִי מְצַוֶּה אֶתְכֶם הַיּוֹם לְאַהֲבָה אֶת ה' אֱלֹקֵיכֶם וּלְעָבְדוֹ בְּכָל לְבַבְכֶם וּבְכָל נַפְשְׁכֶם. (י"א:י"ג)

> *It will be that if you hearken to My commandments that I command you today, to love Hashem, your G-d, and to serve Him with all your heart and with all your soul. (11:13)*

In the *krias Shema* there is twice mentioned an admonition to love Hashem with "all one's heart and soul." The Midrash (*Sifra*), quoted by Rashi, explains that the first *parashah* is directed toward the individual, and the second *parashah* is speaking to the community as a whole.

There is however a noticeable difference between the admonitions written. In the first *parashah* of *krias Shema* it is written that one should love Hashem with "all his heart, soul, and money." The second *parashah* only mentions heart and soul, but omits money. Why?

The Gemara (*Berachos* 61b) explains that although the Torah requires a person to love Hashem "with all his soul [i.e. give up his life for Hashem]," it still is necessary to instruct the Jews to give up one's money for the service of Hashem. There exists a possibility of a person who values his money more than his life, and he would not know that he is required to sacrifice even his money if it would not be specified.

Although there might exist some individuals who value money more than their lives, it is unlikely that there should exist such a community. Therefore only in the first *parashah*, which is directed toward the individual, is this warning written. The community as a whole does not have to be instructed in this matter.

(*Biurei Rav Yisrael Isserlin*)

RE'EH

אֶת הַבְּרָכָה אֲשֶׁר תִּשְׁמְעוּ אֶל מִצְוֹת ה' אֱלֹקֵיכֶם אֲשֶׁר אָנֹכִי מְצַוֶּה אֶתְכֶם הַיּוֹם. וְהַקְּלָלָה אִם לֹא תִשְׁמְעוּ אֶל מִצְוֹת ה' אֱלֹקֵיכֶם וְסַרְתֶּם מִן הַדֶּרֶךְ אֲשֶׁר אָנֹכִי מְצַוֶּה אֶתְכֶם הַיּוֹם לָלֶכֶת אַחֲרֵי אֱלֹקִים אֲחֵרִים אֲשֶׁר לֹא יְדַעְתֶּם. (י"א:כ"ז,כ"ח)

> *The blessing: that you hearken to the commandments of Hashem, your G-d, that I command you today. And the curse: if you do not hearken to the commandments of Hashem, your G-d, and you stray from the path that I command you today, to follow gods of others, that you did not know. (11:27,28)*

THE GEMARA STATES THAT HASHEM REWARDS A PERSON FOR merely intending to do a mitzvah, but does not punish one for intending to sin — with one exception. Idol worship is punishable for the mere intent (*Kiddushin* 40a).

This engenders a novel explanation of the *pesukim*. Hashem says that He will bless the Jews for "listening" to His laws. This means that even if they listen, i.e. intend to perform the mitzvos, but ultimately are not able to perform them, they will still be blessed. But the curse for "not listening" will only befall them even if they only *intend* to "follow gods of others," i.e. worship idols. Only that sin warrants punishment for mere intent.

(*Tiferes Yehonasan*)

כִּי אַתֶּם עֹבְרִים אֶת הַיַּרְדֵּן לָבֹא לָרֶשֶׁת אֶת הָאָרֶץ אֲשֶׁר ה'
אֱלֹקֵיכֶם נֹתֵן לָכֶם וִירִשְׁתֶּם אֹתָהּ וִישַׁבְתֶּם בָּהּ. (י"א:ל"א)

For you are crossing the Jordan to come and possess the Land that Hashem, your G-d, gives you; you shall possess it and you shall settle in it. (11:31)

The Midrash (*Sifri*), quoted by Rashi, interprets the *pasuk* as meaning that the miraculous crossing of the Jordan River that will occur in the future will be an omen that they will indeed eventually capture the Land of Israel. One wonders why this miracle will serve as an indication of their future success.

The Gemara relates that Rebbi Pinchas ben Yair once traveled to attempt to ransom someone from captivity. When he reached the Ginai River he called out, "Split your waters for me in order that I can cross through them!" To which the river replied, "I definitely do the will of my Creator by continuing to flow and not parting. You, on the other hand, might not be successful in your endeavor, and will thus not have accomplished the will of your Creator" (*Chullin* 7a). The river did not want to part its waters only because it was not sure of the future. Had it been certain that Rebbi Pinchas would accomplish what he set out to do, then it might have split.

This can be applied here. Only if the Jews would definitely "do the will of their Creator" and enter Eretz Yisrael would the Jordan River split for them. Thus the splitting of the river is a sign that the Jews will conquer Eretz Yisrael.

(*Chasam Sofer* on Torah)

כִּי יַרְחִיב ה' אֱלֹקֶיךָ אֶת גְּבֻלְךָ כַּאֲשֶׁר דִּבֶּר לָךְ וְאָמַרְתָּ אֹכְלָה בָשָׂר
כִּי תְאַוֶּה נַפְשְׁךָ לֶאֱכֹל בָּשָׂר בְּכָל אַוַּת נַפְשְׁךָ תֹּאכַל בָּשָׂר. (י"ב:כ)

> When Hashem, your G-d, will broaden your boundary as He spoke to you, and you say, "I would eat meat," for you will have a desire to eat meat, to your heart's entire desire may you eat meat. (12:20)

The Midrash (*Tosefta, Arachin* 4:10) explains that "broaden your boundary" refers to someone becoming wealthier, and the amount alluded to is one hundred *manah*. One wonders how the Midrash arrived at that sum.

The Mishnah (*Pe'ah* 8:8) states that someone who is in possession of two *manah* is prohibited from collecting charity. The reason for this is that two *manah* is the minimal amount one needs for himself and his wife to live on for one year (see *Mordechai, Bava Basra* Chap.1). It follows then that for one person a *manah* suffices for a year. Since a person is assumed to live for seventy years (see *Psalms* 90:10), it follows that a person needs a minimum of seventy *manah* for his lifetime.

The *pasuk* writes that "Hashem will broaden your boundary as He spoke to you." The Midrash (*Sifri*) explains this to mean that the Jews will now have conquered three nations in addition to the original seven. If so, one can infer that a "broadening of boundary" indicates from seven to ten. Likewise, one can posit that from seventy to one hundred may also be called a "broadening of boundary". Thus the Gemara refers to one hundred *manah* as being a "broadening of the boundary" compared to a minimal amount of seventy *manah* that one needs to subsist on.

(*R' Meir Yechiel of Ostrovtze, quoted by Talelei Oros*)

כָּל צִפּוֹר טְהֹרָה תֹּאכֵלוּ. וְזֶה אֲשֶׁר לֹא תֹאכְלוּ מֵהֶם הַנֶּשֶׁר וְהַפֶּרֶס וְהָעָזְנִיָּה. (י"ד:י"א,י"ב)

Every clean bird you may eat. This is what you shall not eat from among them: the nesher, the peres, the ozniah. (14:11,12)

The Torah permits consuming some birds and prohibits others. The permitted ones are called "pure" birds and the forbidden ones are called "defiled." The Torah writes that one may eat "the pure birds," and **from among them** there are those that one may not eat, such as the *nesher*, etc. This language is awkward since it implies that the *nesher*, etc., are pure birds. The problem is compounded by the fact that the Torah uses the word **tzipor** which is only used in conjunction with a pure bird.

Tosefos (*Niddah* 50b) posits that a bird without kosher characteristics is prohibited to be eaten even if it emerges from an egg that was laid by a kosher bird. We may suggest that the Torah is alluding to this halachah. The Torah is teaching that even from among the pure birds one should not eat a bird that was born with similar characteristics to the nesher, etc. — i.e. if it does not have the kosher indications.   (*Meshech Chochmah*)

וְשָׂמַחְתָּ לִפְנֵי ה' אֱלֹקֶיךָ... וְהַגֵּר וְהַיָּתוֹם וְהָאַלְמָנָה אֲשֶׁר בְּקִרְבֶּךָ... (ט"ז:י"א)

You shall rejoice before Hashem... the proselyte, the orphan, and the widow who are among you... (16:11)

Here, when discussing the Yom Tov of Shavuos, the Torah writes that the convert, orphan, and widow are "among you." Yet in *pasuk* 14 regarding the Yom Tov of Succos, they are referred to as being "in your gates [cities]." Why did the Torah change its description?

During Shavuos, which concludes the season of the cutting of the crops, these people are out in the fields gathering the gifts to the poor which the Torah provides for them to take [*leket, shich'chah, pe'ah*]. But the Torah calls Succos the holiday celebrating "the ingathering of the crops." At that time, the crops have already been collected and are no longer in the field. Therefore these people are not in the fields but rather "in your gates."

(*Meshech Chochmah*)

שָׁלוֹשׁ פְּעָמִים בַּשָּׁנָה יֵרָאֶה כָל זְכוּרְךָ אֶת פְּנֵי ה׳ אֱלֹקֶיךָ בַּמָּקוֹם אֲשֶׁר יִבְחָר ... (ט״ז:ט״ז)

Three times a year all your males should appear before Hashem, your G-d, in the place that He will choose... (16:16)

The Gemara relates a story concerning Rebbi Yehudah ben Beseira from which it is evident that he did not perform the mitzvah of *oleh regel* — traveling to Yerushalayim for Yom Tov (*Pesachim* 3b). *Tosefos* (ibid.) explains that Rebbi Yehudah did not own land in Eretz Yisrael and thus was exempt from that mitzvah (see *Pesachim* 8b). It is puzzling why Rebbi Yehudah would not have been an owner of a parcel of land; every Jew owned land which had been inherited from his ancestors.

In *Yechezkel* (37:10) it is reported that the prophet Yechezkel resurrected some people from dry bones which he found in the desert. The Gemara reveals that these people were members of the tribe of Ephraim who miscalculated and left Egypt prematurely, and were murdered in the desert. The Gemara further relates that Rebbi Yehudah ben Beseira once declared that he was a descendant of these people (*Sanhedrin* 92b).

The Gemara (*Bava Basra* 117a) states that the land of Eretz Yisrael was distributed among those Jews who entered Eretz Yisrael after the exodus from Egypt. If so, those children of Ephraim who never reached Eretz Yisrael did not receive a portion of land. Thus Rebbi Yehudah ben Beseira who was their descendant did not own land in Eretz Yisrael.

(*Peninim MeShulchan HaGra*)

SHOFTIM

צֶדֶק צֶדֶק תִּרְדֹּף לְמַעַן תִּחְיֶה וְיָרַשְׁתָּ אֶת הָאָרֶץ
אֲשֶׁר ה' אֱלֹקֶיךָ נֹתֵן לָךְ. (ט"ז:כ)

*Righteousness, righteousness shall you pursue,
so that you will live and possess the Land that
Hashem, your G-d, gives you. (16:20)*

THE MIDRASH (*SIFRI*), QUOTED BY RASHI, EXPLAINS THE PHRASE "pursue righteousness" as meaning that the Jewish people should appoint righteous judges. One may ask: Why are the rewards of "living" and "possessing the Land" specifically given for that act?

The Mishnah (*Avos* 5:11) writes that death comes to the world due to delay of justice and perversion of justice; exile comes because of idol worship.

The Gemara (*Sanhedrin* 7b) states that the appointment of an unqualified judge is tantamount to idol worship. If so, having unrighteous judges causes two punishments to befall. First, death comes to the world. Also, the Jews will be exiled, since exile is the punishment for idol worship.

It is logical to assume that the appointment of righteous judges warrants the opposite of the aforementioned punishments. Thus the *pasuk* declares that the reward shall be "living" and "possessing the Land."

(*Binyan Ariel*)

כִּי יִמָּצֵא בְקִרְבְּךָ בְּאַחַד שְׁעָרֶיךָ אֲשֶׁר ה' אֱלֹקֶיךָ נֹתֵן לָךְ אִישׁ אוֹ אִשָּׁה אֲשֶׁר יַעֲשֶׂה אֶת הָרַע בְּעֵינֵי ה' אֱלֹקֶיךָ לַעֲבֹר בְּרִיתוֹ. וַיֵּלֶךְ וַיַּעֲבֹד אֱלֹקִים אֲחֵרִים וַיִּשְׁתַּחוּ לָהֶם וְלַשֶּׁמֶשׁ אוֹ לַיָּרֵחַ אוֹ לְכָל צְבָא הַשָּׁמַיִם אֲשֶׁר לֹא צִוִּיתִי. וְהֻגַּד לְךָ וְשָׁמָעְתָּ וְדָרַשְׁתָּ הֵיטֵב וְהִנֵּה אֱמֶת נָכוֹן הַדָּבָר נֶעֶשְׂתָה הַתּוֹעֵבָה הַזֹּאת **בְּיִשְׂרָאֵל**. וְהוֹצֵאתָ אֶת הָאִישׁ הַהוּא אוֹ אֶת הָאִשָּׁה הַהִוא אֲשֶׁר עָשׂוּ אֶת הַדָּבָר הָרַע הַזֶּה אֶל שְׁעָרֶיךָ אֶת הָאִישׁ אוֹ אֶת הָאִשָּׁה וּסְקַלְתָּם בָּאֲבָנִים וָמֵתוּ. (י"ז:ב-ה)

*If there will be found among you in one of your cities, which Hashem, your G-d, gives you, a man or woman who commits what is evil in the eyes of Hashem, your G-d, to violate His covenant, and he will go and serve gods of others and prostrate himself to them, or to the sun or the moon, or to any host of heaven, which I have not commanded, and it will be told to you, and you will hear; then you shall investigate well, and behold! it is true, the testimony is correct — this abomination was done in **Israel** — then you shall remove that man or that woman who did this evil thing to your cities — the man or the woman — and you shall pelt them with stones, so that they will die. (17:2-5)*

The Gemara (*Sanhedrin* 71b) states that if a Gentile commits a sin which warrants capital punishment and then converts to Judaism, he is put to death only if the form of punishment is the same for Jew and Gentile alike. Therefore, if a Gentile murders and then converts he is still put to death, since both a Jew and a Gentile receive death by the sword for murder. But if a Gentile worships an idol and then converts he is not put to death, since as a Gentile he would have received death by the sword, but as a Jew he would have been stoned.

There is a category of idol worship which is known as *ir hanidachas*. That is, if most of the inhabitants of a city worship idols special laws apply to the entire city. One of them is that the inhabitants are killed by sword, and not stoned. Therefore, in such an instance, since the punishment remains the same, the Gentile would be put to death even if he converts.

In order for a city to qualify as an *ir hanidachas* there must be an actual majority of inhabitants who sinned. One can suggest that even a Gentile who resides in the city [that is, a *ger toshav* whom the Torah permits to reside among Jews] is included in the count. Since he also will eventually be killed for his sin — even if he converts — it is appropriate to include him.

The words of the *pesukim* are now better appreciated. Concerning the death of an individual idol worshiper by stoning, the Torah writes, "this abomination was done in **Israel**." Only a Jew gets stoned. But by the laws of *ir hanidachas*, it is written (earlier, 13:15) "this abomination was done **in your midst**." Even if the residents are not all Jews, as long as the majority of inhabitants sinned, the city is declared an *ir hanidachas*.

(*Ohr Same'ach, Avodah Zarah* 4:2; see also *Toras Chaim*)

עַל פִּי שְׁנַיִם עֵדִים אוֹ שְׁלֹשָׁה עֵדִים יוּמַת הַמֵּת לֹא יוּמַת
עַל פִּי עֵד אֶחָד. (י"ז:ו)

By the testimony of two witnesses or three witnesses shall the condemned person be put to death; he shall not be put to death by the testimony of a single witness. (17:6)

In this pasuk, the word for two is **shenayim**. Later (19:15), when mentioning the necessity of two witnesses with regard to money matters, the word used is **shenei**. Why did the Torah use different words?

The Midrash (*Midrash Rabbah, Masei* 23:9) understands that the word **shenayim** has a unique connotation. It implies that the two items being mentioned should be exactly the same.

The Gemara differentiates between the laws of capital punishment and civil law. Witnesses to a case of capital punishment are only eligible if they both saw the incident together from the exact same spot. Testimony pertaining to money matters is acceptable even if one witness was at one location and the other elsewhere (*Makkos* 6b).

Here the *pasuk* is discussing capital punishment. Since the witnesses must be located in the exact same location at the time of the murder, the word **shenayim** is used. Regarding money matters, the word **shenei** is written since they can be located at different sites.

(*R' Eliezer Silver*, quoted by *MiShulchan Gavoha*)

וְכִי יִהְיֶה אִישׁ שֹׂנֵא לְרֵעֵהוּ וְאָרַב לוֹ וְקָם עָלָיו וְהִכָּהוּ נֶפֶשׁ וָמֵת וְנָס אֶל אַחַת הֶעָרִים הָאֵל. וְשָׁלְחוּ זִקְנֵי עִירוֹ וְלָקְחוּ אֹתוֹ מִשָּׁם וְנָתְנוּ אֹתוֹ בְּיַד גֹּאֵל הַדָּם וָמֵת. לֹא תָחוֹס עֵינְךָ עָלָיו וּבִעַרְתָּ דַם הַנָּקִי מִיִּשְׂרָאֵל וְטוֹב לָךְ. לֹא תַסִּיג גְּבוּל רֵעֲךָ ... (י"ט:י"א-י"ד)

> *But if there will be a man who hates his fellow, and ambushes him. and rises up against him, and strikes him mortally, and he dies, and he flees to one of the cities – then the elders of his city shall send and take him from there and place him in the hand of the redeemer of blood, and he shall die. Your eye shall not pity him; you shall remove the innocent blood from Israel and it shall be good for you. You shall not move a boundary of your fellow... (19:11-14)*

Although superficially it appears that the prohibition of moving the boundary of a Jew is not related to the previous *pesukim*, the Baal HaTurim explains that it is. One might assume that it is permitted to take for oneself the property of someone who received capital punishment. Therefore, after mentioning capital punishment, the Torah admonishes us not to "move the boundary" of any Jew, including an executed murderer.

This explanation can be carried a step further. The *Ohr Zaruah* (quoted by *Hagahos Ashri, Bava Kamma* Chap. 4) posits that if the heirs of a murdered person take possession of belongings of the murderer they are permitted to keep that which they took. This only applies to portable items, not to land (*Responsa* of *Rashba* 2 *siman* 229). The *pasuk* is going a step further. Even merely pushing back the border is also prohibited.

(*Meshech Chochmah*)

וְלֹא תָחוֹס עֵינֶךָ נֶפֶשׁ בְּנֶפֶשׁ עַיִן בְּעַיִן שֵׁן בְּשֵׁן יָד בְּיָד רֶגֶל בְּרָגֶל. (י"ט:כ"א)

Your eye shall not pity; life for life, eye for eye, tooth for tooth, hand for hand, foot for foot. (19: 21)

Earlier the Torah (*Shemos* 21:21:24, *Vayikra* 24:20) states the same punishment mentioned here — "an eye for an eye, etc.," but the wording is slightly different. There it says "עַיִן תַּחַת עַיִן," whereas here it is written "עַיִן בְּעַיִן." What is the reason for this change?

From a careful reading of other places in the Torah, one can detect a pattern. The word תַחַת is used when the first item no longer exists and the second one comes to replace it {see *Bereishis* 4:25, 36:36, *Psalms* 45:17). The letter ב is used when the first item still exists (see *Vayikra* 27:10).

The Gemara (*Makkos* 5b) states the laws of *eidim zomemim* (false witnesses) only apply if the punishment was never carried out. Thus the *pesukim* are very consistent. The earlier *pesukim* discuss cases where a person was actually maimed, and is missing an eye, etc. Therefore the punishment is coming to compensate for something missing. Thus the word תַחַת is written. But here, with regard to *eidim zomemim*, an eye was never removed! The witnesses intended that it be taken out, but it never reached fruition. Therefore the letter ב is employed, since the eye still exists.

(*Sha'ar bas Rabim*, in the name of *R' Bentzion Tzizling*)

כִּי תָצוּר אֶל עִיר יָמִים רַבִּים לְהִלָּחֵם עָלֶיהָ לְתָפְשָׂהּ לֹא תַשְׁחִית אֶת עֵצָהּ לִנְדֹּחַ עָלָיו גַּרְזֶן כִּי מִמֶּנּוּ תֹאכֵל וְאֹתוֹ לֹא תִכְרֹת ... רַק עֵץ אֲשֶׁר תֵּדַע כִּי לֹא עֵץ מַאֲכָל הוּא אֹתוֹ תַשְׁחִית וְכָרָתָּ ... (כ:י"ט-כ)

> When you besiege a city for many days to wage war against it in order to seize it, do not destroy its trees by swinging an axe against them, for from it you will eat, and you shall not cut it down ... Only a tree that you know is not a fruit tree, it you may destroy and cut down... (20:19-20)

The Rambam (*Tumas Meis* 9:12) opines that according to the Torah in matters pertaining to a halachah which is of Torah origin, one could be lenient when in doubt. It is the Sages who declared that when in doubt in matters of Torah law, one is required to be stringent.

This *pasuk* seems to contradict the Rambam. The pasuk emphasizes that one can only cut down a tree **when one knows** that it is not a fruit-bearing tree. According to the Rambam even if one is unsure, one should be allowed to act leniently and cut down the tree.

It may be inferred from the words of the Rambam (*Melachim* 6:9), that he understood that this *pasuk* is discussing a tree that was once fruit bearing but has aged. If so, the problem is resolved. Since there was, at one point, certainly a prohibition on cutting down this tree, one must now be sure that the situation has definitely changed, and that it is in a state of permissibility. One is permitted to be lenient only with regard to matters that were never known to have been prohibited.

(*Divrei Shaul*)

Ki Seitzei

וְרָאִיתָ בַּשִּׁבְיָה אֵשֶׁת יְפַת תֹּאַר וְחָשַׁקְתָּ בָהּ וְלָקַחְתָּ לְךָ לְאִשָּׁה. (כ"א:י"א)

You will see among its captivity a woman who is beautiful of form, and you will desire her; you may take her to yourself for a wife. (21:11)

THE GEMARA, QUOTED BY RASHI, STATES THAT "THE *YEFAS TO'AR* is permitted **only** as a deterrent to the Evil Inclination" [i.e. the Torah permits the soldier to marry the woman since otherwise he will live with her in sin] (*Kiddushin* 21b). Many comment that the word "only" seems superfluous.

The Gemara states that even a husband who has an abusive wife should nevertheless be content with his lot, since his wife provides two important services: She raises his children in the Torah way of life, and she prevents him from having evil thoughts (*Yevamos* 63a).

The Midrash (*Tanchuma*), quoted by Rashi, writes that from the juxtaposition of the various topics of this week's *parashah* it can be derived that if one marries a *yefas to'ar* the child born to them will be a *ben sorer umoreh*, a rebellious child who is put to death for his evil actions. If so, a wife who is a *yefas to'ar* does not provide the usual two benefits. She does not raise her husband's children properly, she **only** prevents him from sinning. That is what the Gemara is alluding to by the word "only."

(Chanukas HaTorah)

> כִּי תִהְיֶיןָ לְאִישׁ שְׁתֵּי נָשִׁים הָאַחַת אֲהוּבָה וְהָאַחַת שְׂנוּאָה וְיָלְדוּ לוֹ בָנִים הָאֲהוּבָה וְהַשְּׂנוּאָה וְהָיָה הַבֵּן הַבְּכֹר לַשְּׂנִיאָה. וְהָיָה בְּיוֹם הַנְחִילוֹ אֶת בָּנָיו אֵת אֲשֶׁר יִהְיֶה לוֹ לֹא יוּכַל לְבַכֵּר אֶת בֶּן הָאֲהוּבָה עַל פְּנֵי בֶן הַשְּׂנוּאָה הַבְּכֹר. כִּי אֶת הַבְּכֹר בֶּן הַשְּׂנוּאָה יַכִּיר לָתֶת לוֹ פִּי שְׁנַיִם בְּכֹל אֲשֶׁר יִמָּצֵא לוֹ כִּי הוּא רֵאשִׁית אֹנוֹ לוֹ מִשְׁפַּט הַבְּכֹרָה. (כ"א:ט"ו-י"ז)

> *If a man will have two wives, one beloved and one hated, and they bear him sons, the beloved one and the hated one, and the firstborn son is the hated one's; then it shall be, that on the day that he causes his sons to inherit whatever will be his, he cannot give the right of the firstborn to the son of the beloved one ahead of the son of the hated one, the firstborn. Rather, he must recognize the firstborn, the son of the hated one, to give him the double portion in all that is found with him; because he was conceived first, to him is the right of the firstborn. (21:15-17)*

It once happened that a man divorced his wife shortly after their marriage, and soon after remarried. Seven months into his second marriage, his wife gave birth prematurely. Not long after, his first wife gave birth to a full-term baby. There arose a dispute between the family of the divorcee and the divorcer as to who is considered the rightful firstborn heir to eventually collect the double portion of the inheritance. When the matter reached the Vilna Gaon he declared that the Torah, with an accompanying solution, alludes to this case. He explained:

There are several difficulties with the above *pesukim*: a) At first it is written that the one whom he loves and the one whom he hates will give birth, implying from the order that the loved one gave birth first. Yet immediately following this it is written, "and the firstborn was born to the hated one." b) The Torah writes that it is prohibited to choose the child of the loved one over the child of the hated one to inherit the double portion. Isn't this self-understood? He is not the firstborn! c) Why does the Torah use the word "hated"? The

Torah prohibits hatred. d) Unlike other places, the Torah writes a reason for the law ["because he was conceived first"].

To answer all of the above it can be suggested that the Torah is discussing a scenario similar to the one which actually occurred. The "hated wife" refers to the woman who was divorced, and the "loved one" is the one whom he married afterwards. The husband wants to give the double portion to the child of the second wife based on the claim that since that baby was **born** first, he is the rightful firstborn. Therefore the Torah instructs us that the son of the divorcee receives the double portion. Since this may seem surprising, the Torah explains that since he was **conceived** first he is the rightful firstborn.[9]

(Kol Eliyahu)

כִּי יִהְיֶה לְאִישׁ בֵּן סוֹרֵר וּמוֹרֶה אֵינֶנּוּ שֹׁמֵעַ בְּקוֹל אָבִיו וּבְקוֹל אִמּוֹ וְיִסְּרוּ אֹתוֹ וְלֹא יִשְׁמַע אֲלֵיהֶם ... וּרְגָמֻהוּ כָל אַנְשֵׁי עִירוֹ בָאֲבָנִים וָמֵת... (כ"א:י"ח,כ"א)

> *If a man will have a wayward and rebellious son, who does not hearken to the voice of his father and the voice of his mother, and they discipline him, but he does not hearken to them... all the men of the city shall pelt him with stones and he shall die... (21:18,21)*

The Gemara explains that the *ben sorer umoreh* is not now deserving of death, but rather is put to death in anticipation of what he will commit in the future. In all probability he will eventually resort to armed robbery to pay for his lavish eating habits, and will even murder for it. He is killed now for that inevitable murder (*Sanhedrin* 72a).

---

9. EDITOR'S NOTE: This *dvar Torah* has elicited much comment since its appearance in print, since according to *halachah* the right of firstborn is determined by birth and not by conception. A number of variant readings of this *dvar Torah* have been offered, in order to have it conform to the *halachah*.

There is a difficulty with that explanation. Within the Torah there are four categories of capital punishment, referred to as: stoning, burning, sword, and choking. A murderer receives death by the sword. If so, the *ben sorer umoreh*, who is punished now for the eventual murder that he will commit, should be put to death by sword as is every murderer. Why is he stoned?

This leads us to offer a novel explanation of the above Gemara. The *ben sorer umoreh* is not being stoned now for the murder that he will later commit. Rather he is being stoned now for sins that he will eventually commit which warrant stoning, e.g. desecration of Shabbos, cursing one's parents. Because of these sins the *ben sorer umoreh* would not be put to death now, only upon the actual commission of sin. However, since the Torah anticipates that the *ben sorer umoreh* will then go on and commit murder, in order to prevent innocent blood from being spilled, the Torah instructs us to stone him now before that scene is played out.

(*Maharil Diskin*)

וְעָנְשׁוּ אֹתוֹ מֵאָה כֶסֶף וְנָתְנוּ לַאֲבִי הַנַּעֲרָה... (כ״ב:י״ט)

And they shall fine him one hundred silver [shekels] and give them to the father of the girl ... (22:19)

In the mentioning the laws of a wanton accusation of a husband against his wife, several times the word *naarah* is spelled in an unusual manner – without a *hei* at the end. Only here is it spelled with the *hei*. Why is this so? The Baal HaTurim explains that the reason the Torah changed the spelling earlier is to indicate that because she acted in the manner of a *naar*, a foolish person, therefore her husband suspected her of wrongdoing and falsely accused her.

If so, in this *pasuk*, after her innocence has been proven, it is only appropriate that no derogatory reference is made, and that *naarah* is spelled in full.

(*Sifsei Kohen*)

לֹא יָבֹא עַמּוֹנִי וּמוֹאָבִי בִּקְהַל ה' ... עַל דְּבַר אֲשֶׁר לֹא קִדְּמוּ
אֶתְכֶם בַּלֶּחֶם וּבַמַּיִם בַּדֶּרֶךְ בְּצֵאתְכֶם מִמִּצְרָיִם ... (כ"ג:ד,ה)

An Ammonite or Moavite shall not enter the congregation of Hashem... because of the fact that they did not greet you with bread and water on the road when you were leaving Egypt... (23:4,5)

The Midrash (*Sifri*), quoted by Rashi, interprets this *pasuk* as meaning that Moav is not allowed to intermarry with the Jewish people because they caused the Jews to sin with their daughters. There seems to be no indication of this interpretation in the *pasuk*. How did the Midrash derive this?

The Gemara states that there are many benefits to eating bread in the morning. Among them are that one is content with one's spouse, and therefore will not be inclined toward immoral behavior (*Bava Metzia* 107b).

Thus if the people of Moav would have offered bread to the Jews they would not have acted immorally and would not have sinned with the daughters of Moav. The Torah's mentioning of the lack of offering of bread therefore alludes to the sin with the daughters of Moav. (*Gan Raveh*)

לֹא יָבֹא עַמּוֹנִי וּמוֹאָבִי בִּקְהַל ה' ... עַל דְּבַר אֲשֶׁר לֹא קִדְּמוּ
אֶתְכֶם בַּלֶּחֶם וּבַמַּיִם בַּדֶּרֶךְ בְּצֵאתְכֶם מִמִּצְרַיִם וַאֲשֶׁר שָׂכַר עָלֶיךָ
אֶת בִּלְעָם בֶּן בְּעוֹר מִפְּתוֹר אֲרַם נַהֲרַיִם לְקַלְלֶךָּ. (כ"ג:ד,ה)

An Ammonite or Moabite shall not enter the congregation of Hashem... because of the fact that they did not greet you with bread and water on the road when you were leaving Egypt, and because he hired against you Balaam son of Beor, of Pesor, Aram Naharaim, to curse you (23:4,5)

Two questions can be raised about this *pasuk*. First, why does the Torah specify that Bilaam was hired? Even if his services had been obtained without a fee it would have been deplorable. Second, in Jewish law there is an axiom that one cannot be an agent to commit a sin. If an agent commits a crime, he is held responsible and not the sender. If so, Ammon should not be blamed for that which Bilaam did.

The Gemara states that although punishing one for hiring false witnesses falls outside the jurisdiction of *beis din*, nevertheless Hashem will punish him (*Bava Kamma* 55b). This implies that in all cases Hashem will punish the sender of an agent to sin. Therefore, here too, Hashem punished Ammon and did not let them intermarry with the Jewish people.

Tosefos (ibid. 56a) qualifies the above Gemara, and writes that Hashem only punishes one for **hiring** an agent to commit a crime, but not for merely requesting him. This answers the second question. It was only because Bilaam was hired that Ammon was responsible for Bilaam's actions; therefore the Torah makes note of it.

(*Kehillas Yitzchak*, in the name of *R' Shmuel Yevnin*)

KI SAVO

וְלָקַחְתָּ מֵרֵאשִׁית כָּל פְּרִי הָאֲדָמָה אֲשֶׁר תָּבִיא מֵאַרְצְךָ
אֲשֶׁר ה׳ אֱלֹקֶיךָ נֹתֵן לָךְ וְשַׂמְתָּ בַטֶּנֶא... (כ״ו:ב)

You shall take of the first of every fruit of the ground that you bring in from your Land that Hashem, your G-d, gives you, and you shall put it in a basket... (26:2)

ACCORDING TO THE TORAH EVEN THE MINUTEST AMOUNT OF FRUIT may be brought as *bikkurim*. However, the Sages decreed a minimum of one sixtieth be brought (*Rambam, Bikkurim* 2:17). Can we find an allusion to this in the Torah?

The Gemara (*Kesubos* 111b) writes, "There is no tree in Eretz Yisrael which does not produce at least an amount which is carried by two donkeys." Elsewhere (*Bava Metzia* 80a) it is written that a donkey carries at least an amount of 15 *se'ah*. If so, every tree produces at least 30 *se'ah*.

It is logical to assume that the Torah is discussing the minimal amount of trees from which it is required to separate *bikkurim*. According to the Mishnah (*Bikkurim* 1:11) *bikkurim* must be separated even from a lone tree. If so, the Torah is discussing a single tree which produces 30 *se'ah*. How much should one separate from that tree? The Torah writes that one should place the *bikkurim* in a basket. How much does a basket contain? Half of a *se'ah* (see *Bartenura, Keilim* 12:3). Thus one sixtieth of the fruits of that lone tree will be brought as *bikkurim*!

(*MiShulchan Gavoha*, in the name of *R' Menachem Kupishker*)

וְעָנִיתָ וְאָמַרְתָּ לִפְנֵי ה' אֱלֹקֶיךָ אֲרַמִּי אֹבֵד אָבִי ... (כ"ו:ה)

> Then you shall **call out** and say before Hashem, your G-d,
> "An Aramean tried to destroy my forefather" ... (26:5)

According to Rashi's interpretation of the *pasuk*, the Torah instructs the person who brings *bikkurim* to the Beis HaMikdash to declare aloud that an Aramean attempted to annihilate his ancestor, yet despite that he is alive today to bring the first of his fruits to the Beis HaMikdash.

The Gemara (*Berachos* 24b) states that if someone prays loudly he is considered a "person of little faith." The logic behind this statement is that if one prays loudly it appears as though he thinks that Hashem does not hear him otherwise. This statement seems to contradict the instruction written here: "Then you shall call out...before Hashem."

It can be suggested that based upon the reason for the prohibition of praying loudly, it follows that if someone makes a statement from which it is clearly evident that he believes that Hashem can read one's thoughts, then that statement can even be said aloud.

Rashi explains that the words "An Aramean tried to destroy my forefather" refer to Lavan and Yaakov. When Lavan was chasing Yaakov, he intended to murder him. Although Lavan never said so explicitly, Hashem, Who knows everyone's thoughts, informs us that this was Lavan's intention.

If so, it is not improper for the bearer of *bikkurim* to say his declaration out loud, since his very words imply that Hashem reads thoughts.

(Chanukas HaTorah)

וַיְבִאֵנוּ אֶל הַמָּקוֹם הַזֶּה וַיִּתֶּן לָנוּ אֶת הָאָרֶץ הַזֹּאת ... (כ"ו:ט)

*He brought us to this place,
and He gave us this Land... (26:9)*

The bearer of *bikkurim* declares in front of Hashem that "He brought us to this place, and He gave us this Land." Rashi explains that "this place" refers to the Beis HaMikdash and "this Land" refers to the Land of Israel. The commentators wonder why the words are not in chronological order. First the Jews received Eretz Yisrael, and only afterwards they arrived at the location of the future Beis HaMikdash.

There is an ancient Midrash (see *Yonason ben Uziel, Shemos* 19:4) which states that on the night following the slaughter of the *pesach*-offering in Egypt, the Jews were miraculously transported to the site of the future Beis HaMikdash and ate their *pesach*-offering there. When they finished they were returned to Egypt.

This is alluded to by the *pasuk*. The Jews were first in the location of the Beis HaMikdash, and only afterwards received and entered Eretz Yisrael.

(*Yalkut HaUrim*, in the name of *Eitz HaChaim*)

אָרוּר הָאִישׁ אֲשֶׁר יַעֲשֶׂה פֶסֶל וּמַסֵּכָה... (כ"ז:ט"ו)

*Accursed is the man who will make a graven
or molten image...(27:15)*

In the list of curses, all the acts that bring upon their doers a curse are mentioned in present tense [e.g. "Accursed is the one who **moves** the boundary of his fellow"]. This case is the one exception as it is expressed in future tense ["Accursed is the man who **will make** a graven or molten image"]. Why is this so?

The Gemara infers that idol worship is the one sin for which one is punished for mere intent (*Kiddushin* 40a). If so, one who even thinks of making an idol in the future deserves to be cursed. Therefore the words are written in future tense, implying that the *pasuk* is discussing one who thought about making it in the future.

(*MiShulchan Gavoha*, in the name of *R' Nachum Mindes*)

וְהָיָה אִם לֹא תִשְׁמַע בְּקוֹל ה' אֱלֹקֶיךָ לִשְׁמֹר לַעֲשׂוֹת אֶת כָּל מִצְוֹתָיו וְחֻקֹּתָיו אֲשֶׁר אָנֹכִי מְצַוְּךָ הַיּוֹם וּבָאוּ עָלֶיךָ כָּל הַקְּלָלוֹת הָאֵלֶּה וְהִשִּׂיגוּךָ. (כ"ח:ט"ו)

But it will be that if you do not hearken to the voice of Hashem, your G-d, to observe, to perform all His commandments and all His decrees that I command you today, then all these curses will come upon you and overtake you. (28:15)

These curses are written in two places in the Torah — here and in *parashas Bechukosai*. There is a noticeable difference between the two. Here they are written in singular form, as though addressing the individual, and earlier it is written in plural form. Why the change in wording?

The first time the curses were told to them was before their arrival at Arvos Moav. Prior to that there was no concept of *arvus*, responsibility of one Jew toward another. Therefore the curses were said in plural, implying that they apply to all individual Jews. The curses in this week's *parashah* were said after their arrival in Arvos Moav and their acceptance of responsibility for each other's sins. Thus they were all collectively considered as one person. Therefore they were spoken to in singular form.

(*MiShulchan Gavoha*, in the name of *R' Yehoshua Heller*)

כְּרָמִים תִּטַּע וְעָבָדְתָּ וְיַיִן לֹא תִשְׁתֶּה וְלֹא תֶאֱגֹר כִּי תֹאכְלֶנּוּ הַתֹּלָעַת. זֵיתִים יִהְיוּ לְךָ בְּכָל גְּבוּלֶךָ וְשֶׁמֶן לֹא תָסוּךְ כִּי יִשַּׁל זֵיתֶךָ. (כ"ח:ל"ט-מ)

You will plant vineyards and work them, but you will not drink wine, and you will not gather in, for the worm will eat it. You will have olives throughout your boundaries, but you will not anoint with oil, for your olives will drop. (28:39-40)

One notices a discrepancy between the two curses. Concerning the lack of oil, it is written that there will be olives, but no oil will be produced. But concerning the lack of wine, it does not mention that there will be grapes. Why did the Torah change the curse?

The Gemara states that eating olives causes one to forget what one has learned. But if one subsequently drinks olive oil it will restore that which was forgotten (*Horayos* 13b). This illuminates the above *pesukim*. At first it is written that the Jews will work hard planting vineyards, but they will not see results from their labor. They will have neither wine nor grapes. Then it says that they will have olives without olive oil. Under the circumstance the olives themselves are harmful since there is no olive oil to undo the detrimental affects of the eating of the olives. Having olives is a curse, having grapes is a blessing.

(*Kehillas Yitzchak*, in the name of *R' Yehoshua of Nishvitz*)

NITZAVIM

אַתֶּם נִצָּבִים הַיּוֹם כֻּלְּכֶם לִפְנֵי ה' אֱלֹקֵיכֶם...
מֵחֹטֵב עֵצֶיךָ עַד שֹׁאֵב מֵימֶיךָ. (כ"ט:ט,י)

*You are standing today, all of you, before Hashem,
your G-d... from the hewer of your wood to
the drawer of your water. (29:9,10)*

THE GEMARA EXPLAINS THAT THE WATER-DRAWERS AND WOOD-cutters mentioned in the *pasuk* refer to the Giveonites who converted in the times of Moshe and were assigned those duties (*Yevamos* 79a).

One wonders: How could there have been proselytes during Moshe's era? The halachah is that three steps are essential to conversion: circumcision, immersion in a *mikveh*, and acceptance of mitzvos (see *Yevamos* 46a). While the Jews were in the Wilderness they did not perform circumcisions, since due to climactic conditions the incision would not heal properly and it could have led to the death of a child (see *Yevamos* 72a). If so, conversion could not have been done.

The Gemara explains that there is a logical basis for exempting one from performing a mitzvah in a life-threatening situation: It is better that he live and perform many mitzvos than die performing only one (*Yoma* 85b). This logic only applies to someone who is Jewish. Thus a Gentile may place himself in a possible life-threatening situation in order to convert. Therefore there were Gentiles who converted during the time the Jews were in the Wilderness.

(*Panim Yafos*)

פֶּן יֵשׁ בָּכֶם אִישׁ אוֹ אִשָּׁה אוֹ מִשְׁפָּחָה אוֹ שֵׁבֶט אֲשֶׁר לְבָבוֹ פֹנֶה הַיּוֹם מֵעִם ה' אֱלֹקֵינוּ לָלֶכֶת לַעֲבֹד אֶת אֱלֹקֵי הַגּוֹיִם הָהֵם ... וּמָחָה ה' אֶת שְׁמוֹ מִתַּחַת הַשָּׁמָיִם. וְהִבְדִּילוֹ ה' לְרָעָה מִכֹּל שִׁבְטֵי יִשְׂרָאֵל ... (כ"ט:י"ז,י"ט-כ)

> *Perhaps there is among you a man or a woman, or a family or a tribe, whose heart turns away today from being with Hashem, our G-d, to go and serve the gods of those nations ... and Hashem will erase his name from under the heavens. Hashem will set him aside for evil from among all the tribes of Israel... (29:17,19-20)*

The Torah declares that Hashem will eradicate one who worships idols. The Torah then adds that it will "set him aside for evil from among all the tribes of Israel." This second curse seems superfluous: If the person is eradicated, there is nothing more that is possible to do to him.

The Gemara states that there is an ancient tradition that no tribe of Israel will ever be annihilated. If so, the *pasuk* can be explained as follows. If a person worships idols he will be annihilated. But if a whole tribe worships idols [see *pasuk* 17, "...or a tribe"], then although it will not be annihilated, it will nevertheless be "set aside for evil from among all the tribes" (*Bava Basra* 116a).

(*Maharam Galanti*, quoted by *Yosef Lekach*)

פֶּן יֵשׁ בָּכֶם אִישׁ אוֹ אִשָּׁה אוֹ מִשְׁפָּחָה אוֹ שֵׁבֶט אֲשֶׁר לְבָבוֹ פֹנֶה הַיּוֹם מֵעִם ה' אֱלֹקֵינוּ לָלֶכֶת לַעֲבֹד אֶת אֱלֹקֵי הַגּוֹיִם הָהֵם... וְהָיָה בְשָׁמְעוֹ אֶת דִּבְרֵי הָאָלָה הַזֹּאת וְהִתְבָּרֵךְ בִּלְבָבוֹ לֵאמֹר שָׁלוֹם יִהְיֶה לִּי ... לֹא יֹאבֶה ה' סְלֹחַ לוֹ... (כ"ט:י"ז-י"ט)

> Perhaps there is among you a man or a woman, or a family or a tribe, whose heart turns away today from being with Hashem, our G-d, to go and serve the gods of those nations ... And it will be that when he hears the words of this curse he will bless himself in his heart saying, "Peace will be with me..." Hashem will not be willing to forgive him ... (29:17-19)

One finds it difficult to understand how a person could be so complacent in the face of a curse of Hashem. A possible explanation could be that there is an axiom that Hashem only punishes Jews for actual sins but not for thoughts (*Kiddushin*, 40a). Therefore, this person assumes that he will not be punished for merely believing in other gods. But he is mistaken. There is an exception to that rule. Idolatry is the one sin that one transgresses even by mere thought (ibid.). Therefore Hashem will not forgive him and will punish him.

(R' Dovid Oppenheim, quoted by *Talelei Oros*)

וְהָיָה כִי יָבֹאוּ עָלֶיךָ כָּל הַדְּבָרִים הָאֵלֶּה **הַבְּרָכָה וְהַקְּלָלָה** אֲשֶׁר נָתַתִּי לְפָנֶיךָ וְשַׁבְתָּ עַד ה' אֱלֹקֶיךָ ... (ל:א,ב)

> It will be that when all these things come upon you — **the blessing and the curse** that I have presented before you... and you will return unto Hashem, your G-d... (30:1,2)

If distressing events occur to a person they cause him to do soul-searching and to repent. Not so in good times. If so, why does the Torah mention that when the "blessing" will befall them they will return to Hashem?

It can be suggested that the meaning of the *pasuk* is that when blessing will befall others, i.e. the Gentiles, and at the same time curses will befall the Jews, then the Jews will be motivated to repent. If there will be curses all over the world then the Jews will not see it as a curse but rather as a chance occurrence. Only if the Gentiles have it good while the Jews are suffering will the Jews see the hand of G-d and repent.

(*Ohel Yaakov*)

וְשַׁבְתָּ עַד ה' אֱלֹקֶיךָ ... בְּכָל לְבָבְךָ וּבְכָל נַפְשֶׁךָ. (ל:ב)

You will return unto Hashem, your G-d ...
with all your heart and all your soul (30:2)

The *pasuk* declares that people will repent and serve Hashem with "all their heart and soul." At other places in the Torah, the ideal service of Hashem is described as being with "all your heart, soul, and money" (see *Va'eschanan* 6:5). Why is "money" omitted here?

According to the commentaries, this prediction will occur in the era preceding the coming of the Mashiach. The Gemara states that in the epoch of the arrival of the Mashiach people will be impoverished (*Sanhedrin* 97a). Since people will not have money then, the Torah does not mention that people will serve Hashem with their money!

(*Sha'ar Bas Rabim*)

כִּי הַמִּצְוָה הַזֹּאת אֲשֶׁר אָנֹכִי מְצַוְּךָ הַיּוֹם לֹא נִפְלֵאת הִוא מִמְּךָ וְלֹא רְחֹקָה הִוא. לֹא בַשָּׁמַיִם הִוא ... וְלֹא מֵעֵבֶר לַיָּם הִוא ... (ל:י"א-י"ג)

> For this commandment that I command you today ...
> it is not hidden from you and it is not distant. It is not
> in heaven ... Nor is it across the sea ... (30:11-13)

Why did the Torah elaborate and emphasize that it is not impossible to observe the laws of the Torah?

The Gemara quotes an opinion that if one hands his wife a divorce with an impossible stipulation such as that she must "go up to heaven" or cross the ocean by foot, then the stipulation is not valid (*Gittin* 84a). Hashem stipulated to the Jews that if they observed the mitzvos then they would be rewarded, but if they did otherwise they would be cursed. If this would be an impossible task, the stipulation would not stand. Therefore the Torah emphasizes that it is easy to observe Hashem's laws and thus the conditions stand.

(Kosnos Ohr, quoted by Talelei Oros)

VAYELECH

וַיִּקְרָא מֹשֶׁה לִיהוֹשֻׁעַ וַיֹּאמֶר אֵלָיו לְעֵינֵי כָל יִשְׂרָאֵל חֲזַק וֶאֱמָץ ... (ל״א:ז)

Moshe summoned Joshua and said to him before the eyes of all Israel, "Be strong and courageous..." (31:7)

THE SIMPLE EXPLANATION OF THE *PASUK* IS THAT IN FRONT OF ALL the Jews Hashem instructed Yehoshua to be strong and courageous. However in a light vein an alternate explanation can be offered. A king is obligated to retain the respect of the people. He is prohibited from acting in public in a manner which is beneath his dignity (*Kesubos* 17a). Only in private may he humble himself before others (see *Makkos* 24a). Thus Hashem is instructing him that "before the eyes of all Israel, i.e. in public, be strong and courageous." (*Meshech Chochmah*)

הַקְהֵל אֶת הָעָם הָאֲנָשִׁים וְהַנָּשִׁים וְהַטַּף וְגֵרְךָ אֲשֶׁר בִּשְׁעָרֶיךָ... (ל״א:י״ב)

Gather together the people — the men, the women, and the small children, and your proselyte who is in your gates ... (31:12)

Why does the Torah specify that even the proselyte is required to participate in the mitzvah of *Hakhel*? Why would one think otherwise?

A person who does not own land in Eretz Yisrael is exempt from the mitzvah of *aliyah laregel* (*Pesachim* 8b). A proselyte cannot own land in Eretz Yisrael since the land was distributed to the original conquerors of Eretz Yisrael, and always reverts back to them. Thus a proselyte is exempt from journeying to Yerushalayim and performing the mitzvah of *aliyah laregel*. Therefore, the Torah informs us that nevertheless the proselyte must travel to Yerushalayim at the end of Succos and participate in the mitzvah of *Hakhel*.

This explanation also has a basis in the words of the *pasuk*. The phrase "in your gates" which is found several times in the Torah refers to outside of Yerushalayim (see *Rambam*, *Maaser Sheini* 2:5). Thus the *pasuk* can be interpreted as follows: The proselyte who is outside of Yerushalayim ["in your gates"] every Yom Tov, i.e. is exempt from being *oleh regel*, must nevertheless travel to Yerushalayim to participate in *Hakhel*.

(*Maharil Diskin*)

הַקְהֵל אֶת הָעָם הָאֲנָשִׁים וְהַנָּשִׁים וְהַטַּף ... (ל"א:י"ב)

Gather together the people — the men, the women, and the small children... (31:12)

The Gemara relates that the students of Rebbi Yehoshua once went to visit him on Yom Tov. Upon being asked to recite words of Torah that they had heard from others, they at first declined. Only after being pressed, they responded that they had learned that the reason the Torah requires the bringing of infants to participate in *Hakhel* is in order to reward those who bring them. Upon hearing this he exclaimed, "You possessed such a precious jewel, and you wanted me not to have it (*Chagigah* 3a)!"

This episode can better be understood in light of what is recorded in a different Gemara (*Yerushalmi*, *Yevamos* 1:6). The Gemara relates that the mother of Rebbi Yehoshua would bring him to *shul* when he was a baby in order that his ears should hear words of Torah. Therefore Rebbi Yehoshua felt it was most appropriate that he should have heard this explanation of the mitzvah of *Hakhel*.

(*Meshech Chochmah*)

הַקְהֵל אֶת הָעָם הָאֲנָשִׁים וְהַנָּשִׁים וְהַטַּף ... לְמַעַן יִשְׁמְעוּ וּלְמַעַן יִלְמְדוּ וְיָרְאוּ אֶת ה' אֱלֹקֵיכֶם וְשָׁמְרוּ לַעֲשׂוֹת אֶת כָּל דִּבְרֵי הַתּוֹרָה הַזֹּאת. וּבְנֵיהֶם אֲשֶׁר לֹא יָדְעוּ יִשְׁמְעוּ וְלָמְדוּ לְיִרְאָה אֶת ה' אֱלֹקֵיכֶם ... (ל"א:י"ב-י"ג)

> *Gather together the people — the men, the women, and the small children...so that they will hear and so that they will learn, and they shall fear Hashem, your G-d, and be careful to perform all the words of this Torah. And their children who do not know — they shall hear and they shall learn to fear Hashem your G-d... (31:12-13)*

One notes a discrepancy between the adults and children as to what is expected of them. The adults are expected to "fear Hashem" and "perform all the words of this Torah." The children are only expected to fear Hashem. Why is this so?

The words "fear Hashem" refer to refraining from doing prohibited acts [*mitzvos lo sa'aseh*]. The words "perform all mitzvos" refer to the performance of the *mitzvos aseh*. It is a requirement that children be prevented from sinning (*Yevamos* 114a). Therefore it is written that they should "fear Hashem." But they are exempt from performing the positive mitzvos (*Nazir* 29a). Therefore it is not mentioned in conjunction with them that they should be careful to perform the mitzvos.

(*Meshech Chochmah*)

Vayelech / 311

הַקְהֵל אֶת הָעָם הָאֲנָשִׁים וְהַנָּשִׁים וְהַטַּף ... (ל"א:י"ב)

Gather together the people — the men, the women, and the small children... (31:12)

The Gemara (*Chagigah* 3a), quoted by Rashi, asks, "It is understandable why the men and women participate in the mitzvah of *Hakhel*, but why do the children come?" Answers the Gemara, "In order to reward those who bring them!" It seems superficially that there is no tangible purpose to this mitzvah. One finds it hard to accept this.

The Mishnah states that Hashem issued many mitzvos to the Jews in order to provide them with much reward (*Makkos* 23b). Rashi explains that this refers to rational mitzvos that the Jews would anyway heed even without being so instructed by Hashem.

This idea can be applied here. The intent of the Gemara's question is, that if the men and women both go up to Yerushalayim, then surely they will anyway take their children with them; why did Hashem have to command the Jews to do that? To this question the Gemara responds, that this way they will be rewarded for that act.

(*Yalkut HaUrim*, in the name of *Tzintzenes HaMan*)

כִּי אָנֹכִי יָדַעְתִּי אֶת מֶרְיְךָ וְאֶת עָרְפְּךָ הַקָּשֶׁה הֵן בְּעוֹדֶנִּי חַי עִמָּכֶם הַיּוֹם מַמְרִים הֱיִתֶם עִם ה' וְאַף כִּי אַחֲרֵי מוֹתִי. (ל"א:כ"ז)

For I know your rebelliousness and your stiff neck; behold! while I am still alive with you today you have been rebels against Hashem — and surely after my death. (31:27)

The Gemara relates that there were people in the neighborhood of Rav Zeira who were evildoers in his lifetime but repented after his demise. When asked to explain their behavior they responded, "As long as Rav Zeira was alive we were assured of peace due to his righteousness. Now that he is dead we are afraid to live sinful lives since there is no one in whose merit we will be protected from harm" (*Sanhedrin* 37a). If so, it is difficult to understand why Moshe was sure that the Jews would surely be sinners after his demise.

The Gemara relates that the Jews misunderstood which day Moshe intended to return from Mt. Sinai. *Satan* showed the Jews the image of the bier of Moshe being carried, and they believed that he had died. They then proceeded to commit the terrible sin of the *eigel hazahav* (*Shabbos* 89a). Based upon this, the *pasuk* can be explained as follows. Moshe told them: Even when I was alive and you only thought that I had died you sinned; for sure after I will be definitely dead you will sin!"

(*Yalkut HaUrim*, in the name of *Minchas Yehudah*)

HA'AZINU

הַאֲזִינוּ הַשָּׁמַיִם וַאֲדַבֵּרָה וְתִשְׁמַע הָאָרֶץ אִמְרֵי פִי. (ל"ב:א)

> *"Listen, O heavens, and I will speak, and may the earth hear the words of my mouth." (32:1)*

IN THE SONG THAT MOSHE SANG, HE TURNED TO THE HEAVEN DIRECTLY and told it to listen, but to the earth he spoke indirectly. Why? The Gemara (*Sanhedrin* 23a) relates that the honorable people of Yerushalayim would not sign on a document unless they knew who was signing alongside them. Based upon this it can be suggested that Moshe was addressing the heaven the whole time, and told the heaven to listen to him and be a witness, and then he added to the heaven that it should know that the earth will be the other witness.

(*Yalkut HaUrim*, in the name of *R' Yitzchak Halpern*)

הַאֲזִינוּ הַשָּׁמַיִם וַאֲדַבֵּרָה וְתִשְׁמַע הָאָרֶץ אִמְרֵי פִי. (ל"ב:א)

> *"Listen, O heavens, and I will speak, and may the earth hear the words of my mouth." (32:1)*

Rashi explains that Hashem took the heaven and earth as witnesses to testify that he warned the Jews. One wonders why it is necessary to have witnesses against the Jews if they sin. Can not Hashem Himself be the witness and judge against them?

The prophet Yeshayahu declares (1:2), "Listen, heaven, and pay attention, earth, **I have raised children** and have uplifted them, and they have sinned against me." In these words lie the answer to the above question. Yeshayahu is saying in the Name of Hashem that the heaven and earth should testify. And then the reason is given. Since Hashem is the father of the Jews, Hashem is disqualified from testifying as are all fathers. More so, the Jews have sinned against Hashem, and thus Hashem is the litigant against the Jews, and surely cannot testify.

(*Tiferes HaGershuni*, quoted by *Talelei Oros*)

כִּי חֵלֶק ה' עַמּוֹ יַעֲקֹב חֶבֶל נַחֲלָתוֹ. (ל״ב:ט)

For Hashem's portion is His people; Jacob is the measure of His inheritance. (32:9)

The Midrash (*Tanna D'Vei Eliyahu* Chap. 1) lists all the attributes of Hashem, and one of them is that He is content with His lot. This perplexed Rav Chaim of Volozhin. Since the whole world belongs to Hashem, to what does "His lot" refer?

His mentor, the Vilna Gaon, explained, "The Torah refers to the Jews as being 'the lot' of Hashem. The intent of the Midrash is that Hashem is always satisfied with the Jewish people no matter on what level they are, and He will never forsake them."

(*Chafetz Chaim* on Torah)

...וְהוֹשֵׁעַ בִּן נוּן (ל״ב:מ״ד)   ...*and Hoshea son of Nun. (32:44)*

Moshe changed the name of Hoshea son of Nun to Yehoshua before the episode of the *meraglim*. If so, why here is he referred to as Hoshea?

Ha'azinu / 315

Hashem changed the name of Avraham's wife from Sarai to Sarah. This occurred one year before Yitzchak was born. Sarah was then 89 years old. Sarah lived for 127 years. Thus her name change was for 38 years.

The Gemara relates that the letter *yud* which was taken from Sarah's name complained to Hashem. Hashem therefore had the *yud* added to Yehoshua's name. This change took place in the second year of the Exodus from Egypt (*Sanhedrin* 107a). At this point in time, when Moshe was addressing the Jews, it was 38 years from the Exodus (see *Rashi, Devarim* 2:17).

If so, the present manner of writing the name can be understood. Since the adding of the *yud* to Yehoshua's name was meant to rectify its being taken away from Sarah, it only had to remain in place for the length of time it was missing. Thus the name only had to be changed for 38 years. Now that the 38 years were up, the name reverted back to the original.

(*Chanukas HaTorah*)

וּמֻת בָּהָר אֲשֶׁר אַתָּה עֹלֶה שָׁמָּה וְהֵאָסֵף אֶל עַמֶּיךָ כַּאֲשֶׁר מֵת אַהֲרֹן אָחִיךָ בְּהֹר הָהָר וַיֵּאָסֶף אֶל עַמָּיו. (ל״ב:נ)

And die on the mountain where you will ascend, and be gathered to your people, as Aaron your brother died on Mt. Hor, and was gathered to his people. (32:50)

Earlier, in *parashas Pinchas* (*Bamidbar* 27:13), Moshe is told by Hashem, "And you will be gathered to your people as Aharon your brother **was gathered**." Here Moshe is told that he will be gathered as Aharon his brother **died**. Why is there a change of language?

In *parashas Pinchas*, Moshe was instructed to appoint Yehoshua as his successor. He was also told that Yehoshua would consult Eliezer the son of Aharon just as Moshe consulted Aharon. This indicates that Eliezer was on the same level as Aharon.

Subsequently Eliezer once resolved a halachic question in front of Moshe (*Bamidbar* 31:21-24). The Gemara considers this disrespectful, and notes that Eliezer was punished by not being privileged to ultimately have Yehoshua consult him (*Eruvin* 63a). In other words, ultimately Eliezer did not attain his father's level.

The Gemara states that the word "died" is used in regard to someone who did not leave over a son on his level (*Bava Basra* 116a). If so, the discrepancy can very well be explained. In *parashas Pinchas*, when Eliezer was still on Aharon's level the word "died" is not used. Only here, after Eliezer was no longer on his father's level, is the word "died" used.

(*Meshech Chochmah*)

וּמֵת בָּהָר אֲשֶׁר אַתָּה עֹלֶה שָׁמָּה ... עַל אֲשֶׁר מְעַלְתֶּם בִּי ...
עַל אֲשֶׁר לֹא קִדַּשְׁתֶּם אוֹתִי ... (ל"ב:נ-נ"א)

And die on the mountain where you will ascend ...
because you trespassed against Me ...
because you did not sanctify Me ... (32:50-51)

In *Pirkei Avos* (3:1) it is written that one should be aware that after one dies he will have to undergo a "judgment" and an "accounting" before Hashem. The Vilna Gaon explains that the judgment is for the actual sin committed, and the accounting is for the mitzvah that one could have done instead of the sin.

This explains this *pasuk*. Hashem told Moshe that he did two wrongs. The first is that he transgressed against Hashem by not listening to Him. The second is that if he would have listened it would have been a constructive act, since it would have sanctified Hashem's Name by showing that even inanimate objects that are not rewarded listen to Hashem, so surely we should (see Rashi, *Bamidbar* 20:12).

(*Meshech Chochmah*)

Vezos HaBerachah

וּלְלֵוִי אָמַר תֻּמֶּיךָ וְאוּרֶיךָ לְאִישׁ חֲסִידֶךָ ... (ל״ג:ח)

Of Levi he said, "Your Tumim and Your Urim befit Your devout one ... (33:8)

In the entire Torah we find the phrase "*Urim* and *Tumim*." This is the only time it mentions first the *Tumim* and then the *Urim*. Why?

The Gemara explains how the *Urim VeTumim* worked. First the letters would light up [*urim*]. Then the Kohen, through the Divine spirit, would grasp the meaning of the letters [*tumim*] (*Yoma* 73b). This explains the process experienced by the Kohen. But in relation to Hashem, it worked reversely. First Hashem knew the message that He wanted to transmit, and then He would send it. Thus with regard to Hashem it is appropriate to describe it as *Tumim* and then *Urim*, as is done here.

This is what Rashi meant when he explains the word *Tumechu* that Moshe was addressing the Divine Presence.

(*R' Chaim of Volozhin*, quoted by *Devash VeChalav*)

וּלְגָד אָמַר ... וְטָרַף זְרוֹעַ אַף קָדְקֹד. (ל"ג:כ)

Of Gad he said ... tearing off arm and even head. (33:20)

Rashi explains that those who were killed by the people of Gad were recognizable, since they would have their heads cut off simultaneously with their arms.

The Gemara tells us that one who speaks between donning his arm-*tefillin* and his head-*tefillin* is considered a sinner, and is thus disqualified from going to battle (*Menachos* 36a). It can be suggested that since Gad was perfect in this respect, he merited to strike such a blow, to point this out to them.

In *Bereishis* (49:19) it is written about Gad that every soldier who goes out to fight will return at the end of the battle. They were privileged to this since they were so careful not to transgress even a seemingly minor sin.

(*Peninim MiShulchan HaGra*)

וּלְגָד אָמַר בָּרוּךְ מַרְחִיב גָּד ...
וַיַּרְא רֵאשִׁית לוֹ כִּי שָׁם חֶלְקַת מְחֹקֵק סָפוּן ... (ל"ג:כ-כ"א)

Of Gad he said, "Blessed is He Who broadens Gad ... he chose the first portion for himself, for that is where the lawgiver's plot is hidden..." (33:20-21)

Rashi quotes a Midrash (*Sifri*) that explains that the "broadening of Gad" refers to the land of Gad that was unusually broad on its eastern border. Also, Rashi explains that "the lawgiver's plot is hidden" refers to the burial plot of Moshe, about which the Torah writes that to this day no one knows the precise location of his burial place.

Several questions can be raised about this *pasuk*. First, why was Gad privileged to have a larger portion than others? Second, why is mention made here of Moshe's burial place being hidden?

Third, it seems from the wording of the *pasuk* that Gad received his large portion because Moshe was buried in his land. Why are these two things connected?

The Gemara states that it is prohibited to graze sheep in a cemetery (*Megillah* 29a). A different Gemara relates that it is possible that Moshe's grave is anywhere on Har Nevo (*Sotah* 14a). If so, because of this uncertainty, one would be prohibited to graze anywhere on Har Nevo. Thus, because of this, Gad was being deprived of precious grazing land. This was especially hard on Gad since the reason they chose to be on the other side of the Jordan River was because of the extensive grazing land.

Based on this, the questions can now be answered. Gad received a larger portion of land since part of his land could not be used for grazing because Moshe was buried there. Therefore, mention is made of the lack of knowledge of the whereabouts of Moshe's burial place since that is the reason for the broadening of Gad's land.

(R' David Oppenheim, quoted by *Rosh David* [Chida])

וַיָּמָת שָׁם מֹשֶׁה עֶבֶד ה' בְּאֶרֶץ מוֹאָב עַל פִּי ה'. (ל"ד:ה)

So Moshe, servant of Hashem, died there, in the land of Moav, by the mouth of Hashem. (34:5)

The Gemara relates that Moshe's body did not decay. This phenomenon can better be understood in light of the fact that the Gemara states that Hashem personally took Moshe's soul and not the Angel of Death (*Bava Basra* 17a). Another Gemara states that decay of a dead body is caused by a drop of *marah* which is injected into the person by the Angel of Death (*Avodah Zarah* 20b).

(*Torah Temimah*)

וַיִּקְבֹּר אֹתוֹ בַגַּי בְּאֶרֶץ מוֹאָב מוּל בֵּית פְּעוֹר ... (ל״ד:ו)

He buried him in the depression, in the land of Moav, opposite Beis-peor ... (34:6)

It is difficult to understand why Moshe was buried near the idol of Beis-peor. The Gemara says that a *tzaddik* should not be buried near a *rasha* (*Sanhedrin* 47a); if so, surely not in proximity to an idol.

The Gemara (*Pesachim* 54a), quoted by Rashi, says that Moshe's gravesite was prepared from the time of Creation. If so, it is now understood. One should not bury anyone next to something evil, but here the evil came later (see *Avodah Zarah* 44b for a similar *halachah*).

(*Maayanah Shel Torah*, in the name of *Shnei HaMe'oros*)

... וְלֹא יָדַע אִישׁ אֶת קְבֻרָתוֹ עַד הַיּוֹם הַזֶּה. (ל״ד:ו)

... and no one knows his burial place to this day. (34:6)

The Midrash (*Sifri*) states that there is an opinion that Moshe himself did not know where he was to be buried. The language implies that this is a singular opinion and is not accepted by everyone. We also find a dispute as to who buried Moshe. One opinion is that he buried himself (*Sifri, Nasso* 32); the other opinion is that Hashem buried Moshe (*Sotah* 9b).

It can be suggested that the two disputes are related. The view that holds that Moshe himself did not know where he was buried holds that Hashem buried him, whereas the other view holds that since Moshe was aware of his burial spot he buried himself.

(*R' Yitzchak Zev Soloveitchik*, quoted by *Shai LaTorah* [revised])

לעילוי נשמות
בלומה בת משה הכהן
מרדכי בן צבי
חנוך בן משה
שלמה שמעון בן חיים
רבקה בת מאיר

by:

Mr. and Mrs. Joel Gold
Mr. and Mrs. Evan Genack
Mr. And Mrs. Chanoch Gold

In memory of

'Nana' – Ethel Wolinsky
Loving grandmother, great-grandmother,
great-great-grandmother

Dedicated by the
**Gindoff, Davidson, Samuelson,
Weinreb, and Wiener families**

In memory of
Allan H. Rozner ע"ה
ר' אברהם חיים אשר בן ר' אליהו אליעזר מנחם ע"ה

We are sorry that he is unable to see our family grow and flourish
though his memory shall always remain imbedded
in our hearts and in our minds.
He was a true oved Hashem, who always displayed
his total bitachon and emunah in Hashem,
up until his neshamah was taken from this world.
May this sefer glorify his name, and may we his children and
grandchildren be zoche to follow in the righteous path
which he laid forth for us.

Michael and Lauren Zuckerman
Chava Rena

לעי"נ
אבי: ר' בן-ציון הלוי לופיאנסקי
הסבא וסבתא שלי: ר' אהרן דוד וחיה יענטא לופיאנסקי
ובניהם: **איטא (ובני משפחתה), חנה, מיכאל,**
פייבוש (ובני משפחתו), הי"ד
הסבא וסבתא שלי: ר' שרגא פיוועל ולאה ברלינער
ובניהם: **אהרן, בריינדל, יעקב הירש,**
פנחס, חיים יצחק, שמואל, אברהם יחזקאל,
חנהביילא, יוכבד, הי"ד

ומצד אשתי:
הסבא וסבתא: **הרב דוד ומלכה רחל קוליק**
הסבא וסבתא: ר' **יחיאל מיכל וחיה ריבנער**
הדוד: **הרב אברהם קוליק**

ת.נ.צ.ב.ה.
הוצנח ע"י המחבר

This volume is part of
THE ARTSCROLL SERIES®
an ongoing project of
translations, commentaries and expositions
on Scripture, Mishnah, Talmud, Halachah,
liturgy, history, the classic Rabbinic writings,
biographies and thought.

For a brochure of current publications
visit your local Hebrew bookseller
or contact the publisher:

Mesorah Publications, ltd

4401 Second Avenue
Brooklyn, New York 11232
(718) 921-9000
www.artscroll.com